Sigrid Beck, Remus Gergel
Contrasting English and German Grammar

Sigrid Beck, Remus Gergel

Contrasting English and German Grammar

An Introduction to Syntax and Semantics

De Gruyter Mouton

ISBN 978-3-11-030005-5
e-ISBN 978-3-11-034619-0

Library of Congress Cataloging-in-Publication Data
A CIP catalog record for this book has been applied for at the Library of Congress.

Bibliographic information published by the Deutsche Nationalbibliothek

The Deutsche Nationalbibliothek lists this publication in the Deutsche Nationalbibliografie; detailed bibliographic data are available in the Internet at http://dnb.dnb.de.

© 2014 Walter de Gruyter GmbH, Berlin/Boston

Cover image: Igor Sokolov/iStock/Thinkstock
Printing: CPI books GmbH, Leck
♾ Printed on acid-free paper

Printed in Germany

www.degruyter.com

Preface

In this book, we offer an introduction to the linguistic analysis of language structure and meaning. It is important to us to develop these two aspects of linguistic analysis in tandem, because we believe that syntax and semantics should always go hand in hand. We try to keep technicalities to a bare minimum and concentrate on the application to data. The book is intended for an audience with no particular formal background, whose motivation for studying linguistics is empirical rather than theoretical. Our hope is that the material covered in the book will interest students in syntactic and semantic analysis by convincing them that it is impossible to understand language, even fairly simple and obvious facts about a language, without it. We wrote the book in the hope that it would help other lecturers to accomplish this.

The material covered in this book was developed over the years for the purpose of teaching undergraduate syntax and semantics classes in the US, Germany and Austria. The language under investigation is predominantly English. Students entering our classes did not necessarily have a prior interest in linguistics, nor any particular preparation.

We want to convince students that linguistic analysis is interesting, and worth the effort of understanding it, by showing them all the facts that can be explained with it but not without it. The book thus has a clear focus on discussing interesting data. We chose the simplest forms of syntactic and semantic analysis that would allow us to do this. The syntax is an unpretentious version of Government & Binding theory (Chomsky 1981, Haegeman 1994, Haegeman and Guéron 1999). The semantics is a set theoretic system of compositional interpretation. We sacrifice theoretical elegance and sophistication in the interest of simplicity. Our framework should be a good conceptual preparation for a more intense and advanced study of syntax and semantics.

There are numerous excellent introductions to syntax, as well as to semantics. But there is no basic level textbook that introduces them both together. We want to provide such a textbook. We think that the purpose of syntactic analysis is better understood by seeing how it is the input to semantic interpretation. Conversely, compositional semantic analysis is impossible without a specification of the input structures. We present the two as intertwined. The selection of phenomena discussed in this book is partly guided by the consideration that they have to be interesting both in terms of syntactic and semantic analysis.

We use contrast between languages as a central fact motivating syntactic and semantic analysis. Our experience is that it helps students to understand the purpose of detailed linguistic analysis when they see that things could very well be different. Sometimes our contrastive perspective is broad, but we in particular compare English to German. This is because we taught this material mostly in English departments in German speaking parts of the world, where this contrast is particularly relevant. Lecturers not especially interested in the contrast between English and German may skip those sections, or skip some of them, or replace German with a language that suits their needs better.

Our goal is to end up with a consistent theory of structure and meaning covering a set of core phenomena in the English language (as well as German and occasionally other languages). In order to implement such a framework, we practically always draw from sources in the literature, and hardly ever propose something new. Almost invariably, alternative analyses to the one we implement are available. We do not wish to get bogged down in a controversial literature discussion on the way to developing and explaining a workable analysis. Therefore, references to the literature and a short review of the discussion in the literature are delegated to their own short section at the end of each chapter. This should enable readers who want to pursue a topic further to orient themselves, while not disrupting our explanation of the issue at hand.

The overall structure of the book is as follows. Its first part is an introduction to syntax and semantics. A system of syntactic analysis (phrase structure, X' schema and movement rules) is developed and combined with a compositional semantics (a set of interpretive rules that take syntactic structures as their input and map them to their meanings). The object language is English, but we do highlight points of crosslinguistic variation and how the theory can capture them. The second part of the book investigates in more depth a bunch of phenomena interesting in terms of the syntax-semantics interface: quantifiers, scope, polarity, ellipsis, focus, tense and aspect. English is contrasted explicitly with German, which differs in interesting ways in these areas. The contrast emphasizes the need for theoretical analysis since we can't understand the differences without it.

There are several ways the material can be mapped to courses. We have in the past taught the first part as one course, taught 2-3 hours per week for one semester. The second part was taught in various versions as a second such course in a subsequent semester (mostly not all of the second part in one semester). However, the material we cover should be adaptable to different situations.

It has taken us a long time to write this book. Over the years, our teachers, colleagues and students have supported us. The book could not have been written without their help. A special thank you to Angelika Kratzer and Kyle Johnson, whose lecture notes on semantics and syntax, respectively, provided the starting point of the enterprise.

We dedicate this book to Thilo Götz and Conceição Cunha.

Tübingen and Graz, March 2014

Contents

Preface   v

Part I – Structure and Meaning:
An Introduction to Syntax and Semantics

Chapter I-1
Introduction to the field: Syntax and semantics   3
1.   The scientific study of language   3
2.   Goals and models in syntax and semantics   8
2.1.   Syntax   8
2.2.   Semantics   11
3.   About this book   14
4.   The structure of Part I   15
5.   Selected references   16

Chapter I-2
Categories, phrases and phrase structure rules   18
1.   Grammar makes reference to syntactic categories   18
1.1.   Categories   18
1.2.   Major lexical categories in English   19
1.3.   Crosslinguistic variation in the properties of categories   20
2.   Phrases   22
2.1.   Noun phrases   22
2.2.   First steps towards a formal model: phrase structure rules   24
2.3.   Other phrases   27
3.   Phrase Structure Grammar and phrase structures   30
3.1.   Phrase Structure Grammar   30
3.2.   Phrase structure trees and constituency   31
3.3.   Structural ambiguities   33
4.   Selected references   36

Chapter I-3
A systematic way of constructing phrases   38
1.   NPs revisited: more internal structure   38
1.1.   Intermediate levels: N'   39
1.2.   Complements vs. adjuncts   41
1.3.   The new set of phrase structure rules   45
2.   Evidence for intermediate projections within verb phrases   46

2.1.	First evidence for V'	46
2.2.	Complements and adjuncts again	47
3.	Generalizing from nouns and verbs: the X' schema	49
3.1.	Adjectives and prepositions	49
3.2.	The four players: heads, complements, adjuncts, and specifiers	52
4.	A loose end: subcategorization	53
5.	Universal and variable aspects of syntactic structure	56
6.	Selected references	59

Chapter I-4
Clause structure and movement — 61

1.	Clausal structure	61
1.1.	Finding the head of the clause	61
1.2.	Excursus: Mood selection in Romance and Balkan languages	65
2.	Head movement	67
2.1.	V-to-I movement and affix hopping	67
2.2.	I-to-C movement	71
2.3.	Differences in head movement: The case of French	74
2.4.	An intermediate summary and a note on the model of grammar	75
3.	Wh-movement	77
3.1.	Basic wh-questions	78
3.2.	Wh-phrases	80
3.3.	Embedded wh-questions	81
3.4.	Complex wh-questions: an analysis and corroborating evidence from German	82
4.	Selected references	87

Chapter I-5
Goals and methods in semantics — 89

1.	What we have to account for	89
1.1.	Elements of reasoning: contradiction and consequence	89
1.2.	Several meanings: ambiguity	93
1.3.	Method: compositionality	94
1.4.	Semantic and pragmatic meaning	95
2.	Tutorial on sets	96
2.1.	Sets and elements	96
2.2.	Relations between sets	97
2.3.	Operations on sets	98
3.	Selected references	100

Chapter I-6
Composing sentence meanings – first steps 102
1. Sentence meanings - some distinctions and a first composition rule 102
2. Meanings of parts of sentences: first steps 104
2.1. Referential NPs 105
2.2. Predicates 107
3. Selected references 110

Chapter I-7
Extending the theory 111
1. Step by step composition – some trivial steps 111
2. Modifiers 115
2.1. Intersective modifiers 115
2.2. Adjuncts with non-intersective meanings 117
3. Relations 118
3.1. Transitive verbs 118
3.2. Transfer to prepositions 120
3.3. Three-place relations 120
3.4. Interpretability 121
4. Selected references 122

Chapter I-8
NP Semantics 123
1. Definites: referential NPs with presuppositions 123
2. Quantifiers 130
2.1. Quantifiers: non-referential NPs 130
2.2. No simpler meaning is possible for quantified NPs 133
3. Scope ambiguity ambiguity 135
3.1. Interpreting negation 135
3.2. Negation and quantifiers 139
4. Selected references 142

Appendix
Syntactic and semantic rules from Part I 144
1. Syntax 144
1.1. PS rules 144
1.2. The generalized X' schema 145
1.3. Transformations 145
2. Rules of composition 146

Part II – Extending the Theory and Applying it to Crosslinguistic Differences

Chapter II-1
Introduction and roadmap to the second part   151
1.   Aims and background   151
2.   The topics ahead   152
2.1.   Clause structure - English vs. German   152
2.2.   Quantifiers and scope   153
2.3.   Negation and polarity   154
2.4.   Focus   155
2.5.   Ellipsis   156
2.6.   Tense and aspect   157

Chapter II-2
Clause structure - English and German   159
1.   Review of English clause structure   159
2.   German clause structure   169
3.   Selected references   181

Chapter II-3
Quantifiers and scope   183
1.   Interpreting referential vs. quantified noun phrases   183
1.1.   Referential NPs   183
1.2.   Quantifiers: non-referential NPs   185
1.3.   Paraphrases   191
2.   Ambiguities   191
2.1.   Ambiguities between quantified subject NPs and elements in the I domain   191
2.2.   Digression: Pronouns, variables   199
2.3.   Ambiguities between quantified objects and elements in the I-domain   202
2.4.   Subject-object ambiguities   206
2.5.   Inverse linking   207
3.   Comparison with the German scope facts   209
3.1.   The middle field   209
3.1.1.   Negation   209
3.1.2   Two quantifiers   211
3.2.   The prefield   213
3.2.1.   Negation   213
3.2.2.   Two quantifiers   214
3.2.3.   Inverse linking   217
4.   Selected references   218

Chapter II-4
Negation and polarity 221
1. Negative and positive polarity items 221
1.1. Negative polarity items 221
1.2. Downward entailing contexts 224
1.3. Positive polarity items 228
2. Scope in the distribution of some vs. any 229
3. Selected references 233

Chapter II-5
Focus 235
1. What is focus? 235
1.1. Focus can make a difference in discourse appropriateness 236
1.1.1. Questions and answers 236
1.1.2. Contrast 236
1.2. Focus can make a truth conditional difference 237
1.2.1. Focus sensitive adverbs 237
1.2.2. Focus can disambiguate ellipsis 237
2. Focus introduces alternatives 238
2.1. Alternatives: The idea 238
2.2. Deriving focus alternatives 240
2.3. Applying focus alternatives 243
2.3.1. Only *revisited* 243
2.3.2. Contrast 244
2.3.3. Question/answer congruence 245
2.3.4. Implicatures 246
3. Some remarks on focus across languages 247
3.1. Topicalization vs. prefield 248
3.2. Focus in the middle field 249
4. Further readings 251

Chapter II-6
Ellipsis 253
1. What is ellipsis? 253
2. Structural identity at LF 255
2.1. Why LF? 255
2.2. A note on other kinds of ellipsis and crosslinguistic variation 257
3. Focus in ellipsis 259
3.1. The contrast condition 259
3.2. Pseudogapping 261
4. Antecedent Contained Deletion (ACD) 262
4.1. The phenomenon 262

4.2.	The analysis and some consequences	264
5.	Selected References	268

Chapter II-7
Tense and Aspect — 269

1.	What are tense and aspect?	269
1.1.	Tense	269
1.2.	Aspect	271
2.	Compositional semantics for tense and aspect	272
2.1.	Tenses are time pronouns	272
2.2.	The LF-structure for tense and aspect	273
2.3.	Composition rules for tense and aspect	275
2.4.	Temporal intensions and extensions	278
3.	The perfect	279
4.	Some tense and aspect contrasts crosslinguistically	282
4.1.	On German tense and aspect	282
4.2.	The bigger picture	287
5.	Selected references	290

Chapter II-8
Conclusions — 292

1.	What we have done	292
2.	Where to go from here	294
2.1.	For the linguist	294
2.2.	Related fields	296

References — 297
Index — 312

Part I

Structure and Meaning:
An Introduction to Syntax and Semantics

Chapter I-1
Introduction to the field: Syntax and semantics

> *No matter what you do, somebody always imputes meaning into your books.*
> (Dr. Seuss)

We give a short introduction to the field of linguistics in section 1. We explain what linguists mean by a grammar. In section 2 we introduce the components of the grammar that we investigate in this book: syntax and semantics, the study of sentence structure and sentence meaning. Sections 3 and 4 give a short preview of the book and its first part, respectively. Further readings are suggested in section 5.

1. The scientific study of language

Linguists study language and languages, like biologists study life and living organisms, and chemists study the structure and behavior of matter. The scientific study of language develops a formal or mathematical model of language. This model mirrors the properties of language in those respects that are under investigation. This is parallel to the way the natural sciences work. Chemistry, for example, has developed a model of substances that associates them with molecular structures. The chemical structure for sugar is given in Figure 1:

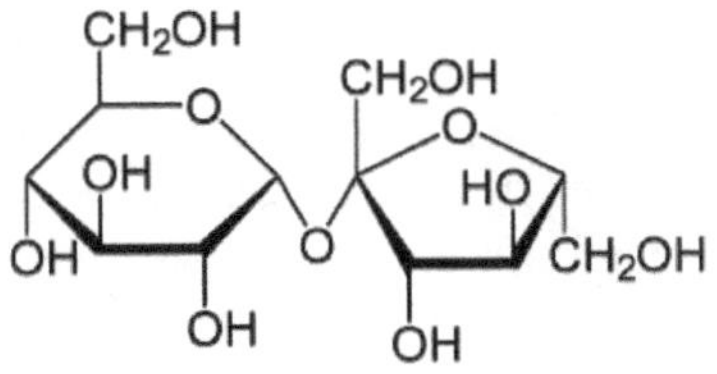

Fig. 1. Structure of sucrose also known as *sugar* [1]

---

[1] Available at http://en.wikipedia.org/wiki/Sucrose.

This formula is not related in a very obvious way to how you normally encounter sugar: it's white grainy stuff, it tastes sweet, you put it in your tea, you buy it by the kilogram and it is relatively inexpensive. Why do chemists associate it with the above formula? Because it allows them to explain the properties and behavior of sugar: that it dissolves in water, how it can be produced or reduced and so on. The formula does have something to do with your everyday experience of sugar (you wouldn't put it in your tea if it didn't dissolve), but it is pretty abstract. And it is at most very indirectly related to how sugar is sold and how much it costs.

Similarly, linguists associate the sentence in (1) with the structure in (2):

(1)   *Has Mary eaten chocolate?*

(2)

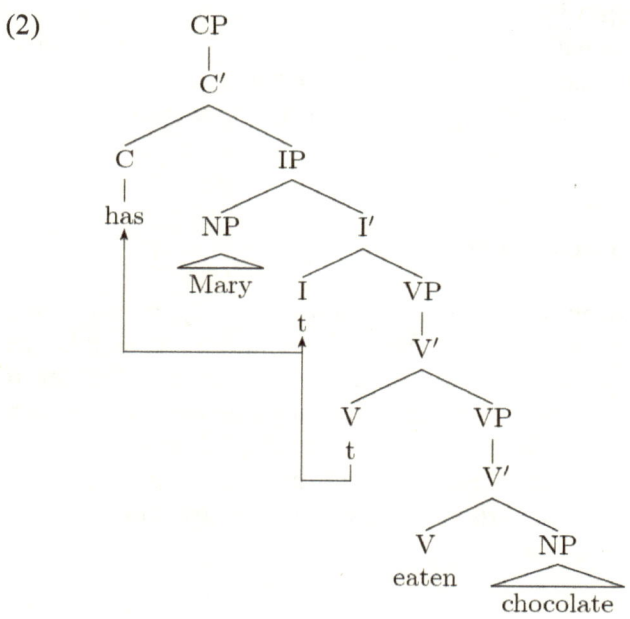

Here, also, the relation between your everyday experience of such a sentence and the model developed in the scientific study of the phenomenon is rather abstract. You would normally hear such a sentence as a sequence of sound waves. It would be produced by someone interested in communication, and it might convey emotion (outrage, perhaps). The representation in (2) has something to do with your everyday experience (it is related to a sequence of sound waves by representing a sequence of words). But it is at most very indirectly related to the communicative needs and emotional states of someone who utters (1).

Why do linguists associate the sentence with the structural representation? Because it allows us to explain the properties and behavior of the sentence and the elements contained in it. Linguistics, like other sciences, aims to provide models that make falsifiable predictions. For example, the fact that the question expressed in (1) cannot be expressed as in (3) follows from the representation in (2). The model also helps us to understand why English today cannot form the question in (4), although it once could, and has to use (5) instead; why (6) is word salad; and so on.

(3) *Eaten Mary has chocolate?*
(4) *Ate Mary chocolate?*
(5) *Did Mary eat chocolate?*
(6) *Has Mary likes the linguist who been to Samoa?*

Like the chemists' formal model of substances, the linguists' formal model of linguistic expressions allows us to explain the properties and behavior of the area under investigation. In our case, this is basically what you know when you know a language. For example, what is the knowledge that you possess which makes you accept (1) and (5), but reject (3), (4) and (6)? How do you know what (1) means? Relatedly, how was the knowledge of someone who accepted structures like (4) different from yours? Why were structures like (6) never accepted in the history of English or (as far as we know) in any other language? What information allows a child learning a language to acquire this kind of knowledge?

In short, linguists model knowledge of language. This textbook is an introduction to the scientific study of language in the sense of developing a formal model of knowledge of language.

This way of studying language scientifically is something many people encounter late in life or not at all. Most people are more familiar with the study of language as it is pursued in traditional grammars. Typically, in such a grammar you are told in a language that you have already mastered about a different language that you have probably not mastered. To stick with our example, you might consult a German grammar book about how to phrase questions that are answered by "yes" or "no." You might find the example in (7) as an illustration together with the information that it means the same as English (1).

(7) *Hat Maria Schokolade gegessen?*

This is certainly helpful for the traveller and the language student. But notice how it does not model knowledge of language. It transfers your knowledge of English by way of analogy to another language. It presupposes a large part of what the linguist still wants to explain. For example: What is a question? How do (1) and (7) come to express a question? Moreover, there is an interesting difference between (1) and (7): in (7), the verbal participle *gegessen* 'eaten' follows the object *Schokolade* 'chocolate', while it's the other way around in (1). Further examples would reveal a parallel effect. What is the systematic source of this difference? How is the knowledge that a German speaker posseses different from the knowledge that an English speaker has to produce this effect? Native speakers have this knowledge. But they are not aware of it: a native speaker's knowledge of the rules of language is subconscious. Linguistics brings this subconscious knowledge to light. (As a possible analogy, consider bats, which know how to use their sonar system instinctively from an early age on, but in all likelihood without having conscious insight into the interesting physical facts that they actually put to use.)

Another notion of grammar people commonly have is as a book that tells them how to speak properly. For example, you might have been taught a rule, "Don't end your sentence with a preposition!" This rule would rule out sentences like (8):

(8)   *Who did you talk to?*

Again, this is very different from what we do here. We model knowledge of language. This means that the linguist describes what linguistic knowledge is based on what speakers actually do. The model does not tell speakers what they should do. This difference is the distinction between descriptive and prescriptive linguistics. There may be a place for prescribing certain things about language use (for example, there may be contexts in which it is useful to encourage people to use a lingua franca instead of some other language or variety in order for everyone to be able to participate in the communication). But from a scientific point of view, such phenomena are of a more sociological interest. They are certainly not what we are interested in here. (To come back to our earlier analogy, imagine a biologist investigating how the sonar system of bats works and then telling them how to use it differently. That would very likely be a misguided thing for the biologist to do. This does not mean that there cannot be, subjectively, more or less 'elegant' or 'attractive' ways of flying. But scientifically, it is worth differentiating what somebody may find more or less 'elegant' or prescriptively appropriate and the actual facts.) Since native speakers of English systematically produce and accept sentences like (8), our model of their linguistic knowledge will include them.

Our notion of **grammar** is this:

> **Grammar**
> A grammar is a model of native speakers' knowledge of language.

As a fairly intuitive illustration of the purpose of the linguist's endeavor, think of computer programmers who write programs enabling computers to process language input (the area of natural language processing). Programmers cannot presuppose that any knowledge of language is already given. Instead, this is what the program has to implement. The information contained in such a program is (part of) the knowledge we want to model. This is what linguists call a grammar. You will see in the chapters to come that many phenomena can be explained in very simple terms when we have a formal model of the language, and not at all when we don't. A grammar in the linguist's sense allows us to understand in what ways languages differ from each other, and in what ways they are all the same; what has to be acquired to learn a language; and so on.

A final issue we address in this introduction is the empirical basis for defining the grammar. We want to model knowledge of language. How do we access this knowledge? Notice that this is an interesting and challenging question because our linguistic knowledge is subconscious. We cannot just sit down and write down what we know. Imagine asking a native speaker of English "How do you form yes/no-questions in your language?". Would that native speaker spontaneously answer "You move the first auxiliary verb of the main clause past the subject."? Probably not – even though this actually describes her knowledge fairly well. Knowledge of language has to be accessed more indirectly. How? There is no easy answer to this question. It seems that it is just as nontrivial for linguistics to gather good data as it is for any other empirical science.

In linguistics, it is not useful to simply consider every utterance ever made as part of the language to be described. People make mistakes (this issue is traditionally discussed under the key words competence versus performance). Also, there are varieties or dialects that we don't simply want to lump together. Modern linguistics considers various data sources in order to find out what is and isn't part of the language under investigation.

Native speakers' judgements on acceptability, appropriateness, and truth reveal their knowledge of language. In simple cases it may be enough to collect a few judgements (for example to establish that (1) is an acceptable English sentence: everyone would clearly agree). Often, the data are less clear. More sophisticated methods to collect data include judgements elicited, e.g., by a questionnaire study, controlled use of corpora, psycholinguistic experiments using reading or reaction times and many more. Methodologically, linguistics has made significant progress (and learned a lot from psychology) in recent years.

The good news for us is that many of the phenomena discussed in this textbook are empirically so clear that advanced methods are unnecessary. Where they are not, we will point this out.

2. Goals and models in syntax and semantics

A grammar in the linguistic sense has several components because your knowledge of language encompasses various aspects of language: its sound structure, the ways in which it can build new words, how it builds sentences, and the way it is interpreted. We are concerned here with the last two components: sentence structure and meaning, i.e., **syntax** and **semantics**.

2.1. Syntax

The task of syntax is to characterize the well-formed sentences of a language. Clearly, the ability to produce and recognize grammatical sentences is part of the knowledge that a speaker of the language has. Therefore, a grammar as understood by the linguist must capture this aspect of knowledge of language. Concentrating on English, the goal of syntax is to define a system of rules that describes all and only the well-formed sentences of English.

> **Syntax**
> The syntax component of the grammar defines a system of rules that describes the well-formed sentences of English.

Let us dwell on this characterization for a moment. Why do we say 'system of rules' above? There are many ways in which one could try to describe all and only the well-formed sentences of English. A very simple way to do so, it seems, would be to list them.

It turns out that a list is a very bad model of syntactic knowledge, for two reasons: (i) people know about novel sentences, and (ii) people know about infinitely many sentences. Let us look at these two facts in turn.

Like all science, syntax begins with a description of the basic parts or 'atoms' that go into the model. The atoms or basic building blocks of sentences are words; we construct complex expressions (sentences) by assembling strings of words in the appropriate ways. A well-known experiment in psycholinguistics introduced a new "word", wug. (The word was made up by psychologists, Jean Berko Gleason's group, who designed the original experiment in Boston.) Children were confronted with the word and the picture in (9) below.

(9)   *This is a wug.*

Fig. 2. Picture of a wug (Berko 1958: 154)[2]

The children had obviously not encountered a wug before. However, they learnt the word instantly and what is more: they correctly formed its plural in contexts such as (10).

(10)   *Now there are two of them. There are two_.*

The item they added to the sequence in (10) was the plural *wugs* with the correct voiced plural ending that the rules of English require for the phonological context in the word *wug*. That means that the children know the relevant morphological and phonological rules. Similar observations hold for syntax. Without having encountered a wug before, speakers of English have clear acceptability judgements about sentences such as the following:

(11)   a.   *Sandy doesn't like wugs.*

---

[2] Cf. the publication: Berko, Jean Gleason. 1958. "The Child's Learning of English Morphology." *Word* 14: 150–77

b. *Wugs decorated her homework.*
c. * *Sandy wug draw a picture.*
d. * *I saw wug new car.*

That is, while the sentences in (11a-b) comply with the rules of English grammar, those in (11c-d) do not. (A note on how we present the linguistic data: Our examples are presented in italics. This is to indicate that they are the object of investigation, not the text of the textbook. Acceptable examples look as in (11a,b). Unacceptable examples are marked with the asterisk * as in (11c,d). The * indicates that the example is rejected by native speakers and should be predicted as not part of the language.)

We can see in (11) that certain words can only be found in certain places in the sentence. That means we need to establish the combinatorial properties of words. You have probably figured out that *wug* is a noun, and that it can occur in those places in the sentence in which nouns can go. This demonstrates what we mean by a rule system: you know rules about the combinatory properties of nouns. This allows you to make judgements about sentences that you have never encountered before, with words that you have never heard before. The rules we develop in the next chapters predict that (11a,b) are acceptable and that (11c,d) are unacceptable. Those rules, moreover, associate sentence (1) above with the structure in (2). They predict that (1) and (5) are acceptable while (3) and (4) are unacceptable. And so on for a lot of further relevant facts about English.

Let us turn to the second point mentioned above: the fact that speakers have knowledge of infinitely many sentences of English. This can be illustrated with the following argument. Assume that there were only a limited number of possible sentences in English after all. Then we may also find, e.g., the putatively longest declarative sentence among them. Let's call this sentence L. But there is a simple way to show that there is always a longer sentence: a sentence into which L is embedded, for example *Lisa knows that L*, and then *Bart doubts that Lisa knows that L*, and so on. So the assumption that there was only a limited number of sentences with L as its longest representative must have been wrong. The principle which language applies, namely of taking recourse to the same rules of structure-building time and again to construct ever-larger structures, is called **recursion**. The rules that have the ability of producing an infinite number of sentences must be recursive.

Our reasoning that the syntax component of the grammar must be a rule system has also illustrated another point in the characterization above that you might have wondered about: we said that syntax characterizes sentences. It might seem surprising that we zoom in on sentences. But notice that automatically we also need to think about sentence parts, and embedding one sentence inside another, when we formulate the rules of syntax. The characterization is thus more comprehensive than it seems.

2.2. Semantics

The task of semantics is to associate each sentence of a language with its intuitive interpretation. We have just made the point that there are infinitely many possible sentences in a language. It follows that semantics also needs a rule system, not a list, to capture the association of each sentence with its meaning. But before we can begin to model this system, we need to know what meanings are. What is the interpretation of a sentence? Semanticists argue that we know the meaning of a sentence if we can judge when the sentence would be true and when it would be false. For example, you know the meaning of (12) if you know in which situations, or under which conditions, (12) would be true. Semantics characterizes the meanings of sentences in terms of their truth conditions.

(12)   *Some poems exist in both Esperanto and Russian.*

> **Semantics**
> The semantics component of the grammar defines a system of rules that associates each well-formed sentence of English with its truth conditions.

Let us dwell a little on this characterization as well. You should not be surprised that it talks about sentences only: we saw earlier that in order to model sentences, we also need to model their components and their embedding contexts. This applies to semantics as well as syntax. And we have immediately convinced ourselves that a rule system is needed. So what is most surprising in the characterization of the task of semantics is probably the notion of sentence meaning going into it. Why are truth and falsity the central meaning concepts in semantics?
Most people are puzzled that this is our fundamental notion of sentence meaning. This is not the aspect of meaning that we tend to think about when we normally think about meaning. Clearly there are other aspects to

our linguistic knowledge of meaning, for example: an utterance can be informative, contradictory, insulting, poetic?

Our suggestion is that truth conditions are the first step and the foundation on the basis of which other aspects of meaning arise. We do not deny that there are notions of meaning that go beyond truth conditions (and other subfields of linguistics investigate them). But we believe that we can only understand those other notions properly after we have grasped the literal meaning - the truth conditions.

We explain our position below by making two points: (i) intuitions about truth and falsity are at the heart of native speakers' knowledge of meaning; and (ii) other intuitions about meaning are based on them.

Consider the following poem by Emily Dickinson:

> *TO pile like Thunder to its close,*
> *Then crumble grand away,*
> *While everything created hid—*
> *This would be Poetry:*
> *Or Love,—the two coeval came—*
> *We both and neither prove,*
> *Experience either, and consume—*
> *For none see God and live.*

We experience difficulty when we try to interpret this text. While some thought and possibly a dictionary will probably get you through the first five lines, you stumble when you read line 6: *we both and neither prove*. Let's examine this line. There should be a noun following *both* and *neither* which is not spelled out in this poem. Also, the word order is unusual. Let's get rid of these superficial problems and consider (13) as a spelled out version of line 6:

(13)   *We prove both poetry and love,*
       and we prove neither poetry nor love.

(13) is contradictory. A simpler example that is contradictory in the same way is (14).

(14)   *I annoyed both Robin and Laura,*
       and I annoyed neither Robin nor Laura.

If you utter (14), you contradict yourself because the two subsentences in (14) couldn't both be true at the same time. The same is true of line 6 and our reconstruction of it in (13). The fact that the sentence is contradictory puzzles you. You begin to think that something different or something more must be meant than what is actually said. If somebody uttered the simpler sentence in (14), for example, you could wonder whether the speaker perhaps intends to convey that some emotional upheaval occurred, but those affected were ambivalent about it. As a fan of Emily Dickinson's poetry, you will try to come up with similarly indirect ways of understanding line 6 in the context of the poem.

But here is what is important for us: All your interpretive efforts start from the basic fact that line 6 is contradictory, and this in turn means that the two claims contained in it couldn't both be true at the same time. Your knowledge of when each subsentence would be true is the foundation of your interpretation.

This is our first point: intuitions about truth conditions are at the heart of speakers' interpretive abilities. Emily Dickinson's poem is helpful in our discussion because it brings to light interpretive processes that are normally subconscious. Our semantic abilities, like our syntactic knowledge, are not something we are aware of.

The poem is also helpful in the illustration of our second point; other meaning related intuitions are based on intuitions about truth conditions. This has become clear already with the intuition that a sentence may be contradictory: it is contradictory if everything that is claimed could not be true at the same time. Here are some further thoughts you might have in conncetion with our discussion of the poem: Contradictions are problematic because they are not informative. The language in the poem is poetic in that meaning is conveyed indirectly (for example, by way of reinterpreting the contradictory line 6). We will not pursue this further. Our point has been made.

We address one final point in the above characterization of the task of semantics: the notion of rule system that is relevant for semantics. The semantic rules we will introduce you to in the chapters to come will work very closely together with the syntactic rules. You can see in our simple example (14) that the meaning of the overall sentence arises from the words contained in the sentence and the way those words are put together structurally. That is, sentence meaning arises from the **composition** of word meanings according to syntactic structure. In the example, the use of *both* in the first subsentence, *neither* in the second, and their combination with

14 *Introduction to the field: Syntax and semantics*

and lead to the contradiction. If you replace *and* with *or* as in (15), there is no longer a contradiction. And if you arrange the same words differently in the structure as in (16), there is no longer a contradiction either.

(15)   *I annoyed both Robin and Laura,*
       or I annoyed neither Robin nor Laura.

(16)   *Both Robin and I annoyed Laura,*
       and neither Laura nor I annoyed Robin.

The tight connection between syntax and semantics is why we present a combined introduction to syntax and semantics in this textbook.

3. About this book

The book has two parts. Part I provides an introduction to syntax and semantics. It is designed to make the two areas connect and to equip us to study phenomena at the syntax/semantics interface. Part II continues with this plot. It explores particular phenomena that are interesting in terms of the syntax/semantics interface.

The language under investigation in Part I is English. However, we believe that what is interesting about English or any one language is often more easily grasped by considering how things could be different. We point out some contrasts between English and other languages in Part I, and we explain how they impact linguistic theory. Part II explores a series of phenomena contrastively by comparing English to German. We also offer comments on other languages.

Our goal is to provide an idea of what a model of native speakers' knowledge of sentence structure and interpretation should look like. We mean this in a very practical sense: We come out of Part I with a system of syntactic and semantic rules in place that is such a model (for part of the English language). We intend to equip students to perform their own analyses, to apply the rule system, to test it and to extend it.

We want to make modern syntactic and semantic theory accessible to students with no particular background in linguistics. We have therefore kept the theory and the rules we use as simple as possible. The model is a formal model in the sense that it is clear what a technical formalization would look like, and in that it is well-defined enough so that its predictions are clear. We have kept theoretical sophistication and technical formalization to the absolute minimum necessary for that purpose. We provide references to the relevant literature at the end of each chapter to make up for shortcomings that arise from this strategy. The book should enable students to move on to an in-depth study of theories of syntax and theories of semantics.

4. The structure of Part I

Just like the textbook, Part I is divided into two parts. We first develop the syntactic analysis in Chapters I-2 to I-4. We approach the question how to interpret the syntactic structures in a consonant way in Chapters I-5 to I-8. The syntactic part consists, more specifically, of an introduction to phrase structure grammar, to the X'-schema, and to syntactic movement. The semantics chapters establish the principle of compositionality. They introduce a set of semantic rules for the interpretation of very simple sentences, and move on to the semantics of definite and quantified noun phrases. Here is an overview of Part I:

Chapter 2: Categories, phrases and phrase structure rules
Chapter 3: A systematic way of constructing phrases
Chapter 4: Clause structure and movement
Chapter 5: Goals and methods in semantics
Chapter 6: Composing sentence meanings – first steps
Chapter 7: Extending the theory
Chapter 8: NP semantics

At the end of each chapter, we offer a summary of the main points in the basics box, followed by a section on relevant literature. We begin straight away.

☞ THE BASICS BOX: *Syntax and semantics*
- ✓ A grammar is a model of native speakers' knowledge of language.
- ✓ The syntax component of the grammar models knowledge of what is and is not an acceptable sentence in a language. It consists of a recursive rule system.

> ✓ The semantics component models the association of each sentence with its truth conditional meaning. It is a system of rules that builds on syntax.

5. Selected references

In the literature sections, we provide references to classical papers, textbooks, and overview articles as they relate to the topics discussed in the chapter. We include references to works on specific topics as much as we are able to. We will not, of course, be able to be exhaustive. Next, in line with the general character of this chapter, we offer some general references.

If you are interested in a general introduction to linguistics, you may consult, for instance, Dechaine et al.'s (2012) *Linguistics for Dummies*, Fromkin et al. (2013) or O'Grady et al. (1997). A readable introduction to the cognitive issues involved in grammar is Yang's (2006) *The Infinite Gift*, tailored for the general public. It embeds the wug test, but also many original ideas. The classic reading on the wug test is Berko (1958). Also written for non-specialists is Pinker's (1994) *The Language Instinct*.

If you are interested in the philosophical background of scientific inquiry, a classical reference is Popper (1959 – available also in subsequent editions or in the earlier orginal German editions). A key criterion for scientific investigation according to this work is falsifiability. For critical discussions of empirical methods in modern syntax and semantics, see, e.g., Schütze (1996), Featherston (2009), and Bott et al. (2011), together with the references cited there (Featherston and Bott et al. especially have the character of recent overviews; they offer broad perspectives of the field today).

The work of Noam Chomsky is generally seen as the beginning of modern formal syntax (cf. Chomsky [1957] 2002). It introduces important concepts such as recursion and the basic toolkit of phrase structure. It is interesting to note that the work has also had an impact on related fields like formal language theory in computer science. The syntactic framework this book concretely relies on stems from *Govenerment and Binding Theory* (GB; cf. Chomsky 1981, 1986). We only use a fraction of the technicalities here, basically the structure building mechanisms that are needed for interpretation. The GB framework developed into different directions especially in the wake of Chomsky (1995), a strand of research referred to as minimalism. Other alternative syntax theories include Lexical-Functional

Grammar (LFG, Kaplan and Bresnan 1982), Generalized Phrase Structure Grammar (GPSPG, Gazdar et al. 1985), and Head-Driven Phrase Structure Grammar (HPSG, Pollard and Sag 1994). This textbook does not offer a survey of syntactic theories. If you are interested in comparing syntactic frameworks, see Kim and Sells (2008) or Müller (2013) for recent discussion. Our own goal is to provide a working model of the interface between form and meaning.

The notion of truth-conditional semantics pursued here is essentially based on Alfred Tarski's theory of truth (Tarski 1935). Gottlob Frege is credited with the principle of compositionality (cf. Szabó 2013 for recent discussion) and Richard Montague's work has been particularly influential on the modern tradition of formal semantics (Montague 1970 and much subsequent work; cf. Dowty, Wall and Peters 1981 for an advanced introduction). As Dowty (1979) points out, Montague's concern has not been restricted to natural languages, but also included artificial ones. What we cover here is more constrained. In the chapters to follow we will be interested in the basic interpretive mechanisms of natural languages like English, German, and others.

If you are interested in a more comprehensive discussion of the Emily Dickinson poem, see Bauer et al. (2010).

Chapter I-2
Categories, phrases and phrase structure rules

By relieving the brain of all unnecessary work, a good notation sets it free to concentrate on more advanced problems.
(Alfred North Whitehead: *An Introduction to Mathematics*)

This chapter begins the task we have defined for the syntax component of the grammar. We introduce categories for words in section 1. Phrases and phrasal categories are discussed in section 2. Syntactic rules and syntactic representations are introduced in section 3. The last section provides pointers towards further readings.

1. Grammar makes reference to syntactic categories

1.1. Categories

Remember our goal: to define a set of rules that characterizes the set of well-formed sentences of English. Sentences are strings of words, so we basically need to predict where each word can occur in a sentence. Let us start with (1), an arbitrary example of a well-formed sentence:

(1) *The woman left with the new chain saw.*

Here is a very silly way of pursuing our goal, which will help us figure out some properties of a more successful strategy:

Non-rules of grammar
Rule1: Put *the* in the first or in the fifth position of a sentence.
Rule2: Put *woman* in the second position of a sentence.
...

A first, obvious problem is that this kind of rule is not general enough. It is not a special property of the word *woman* that it can occur in certain positions in the sentence. Other words (e.g. *boy, carpenter, customer,...*) occur in exactly the same positions. A second problem is that this kind of rule will never make the right predictions: for any n, *the* can occur as the nth word in a sentence; for instance:

(2) *Yesterday, the woman left with the new chain saw.*
Yesterday morning, the woman left with the new chain saw.
In the afternoon, the woman left with the new chain saw.
...

But this does not characterize the distribution of *the* accurately, because other strings in which *the* occurs in second (third etc.) position are not acceptable.

(3) **Yesterday the, Bill left with the new chain saw.*
**Tall woman the left with the new chain saw.*
...

Its distribution will be characterized accurately with reference to other categories. In particular: *the* occurs before a noun in English. What we can see, then, is that more appropriate syntactic rules make use of category information. When we model syntactic phenomena, we never talk about words, but always talk about categories.

1.2. Major lexical categories in English

Categories are sets of words that behave alike with respect to rules of the grammar. The major lexical categories of English are the ones given below, followed by the abbreviation commonly used and some linguistic criteria for deciding whether a word belongs to that category:

- **noun** (N): it typically has singular and plural forms; it can occur after a determiner such as *the* or a sequence consisting of a determiner and an adjective, as in *the expensive table*; instead of a determiner, we can also have a possessor, such as *Hillary's (expensive) table*;
- **verb** (V): it can show past/present forms and a third person singular *-s*; it can occur after auxiliaries like *will* as in *the linguist will dance*, or after subjects, as in *the linguist danced*;

- **adjective** (A): it typically forms adverbs by adding the suffix *-ly* and it may have comparative and superlative forms (e.g. *tall, taller, tallest*); it can occur between the determiner *the* and a noun;
- **preposition** (P): it can occur between a verb and a determiner (e.g. *the*), as in *talk to the linguist, play with the children*.

In general, we can use two types of diagnostics for identifying categories: **morphological** and **distributional** properties. Both derivational morphology (forming new words, e.g. *-ly*) and inflectional morphology (different forms of the same word, e.g. third person singular *-s*) makes reference to category. We won't be concerned with derivational morphology here, but we come back to inflection in Chapter I-4. Distribution, that is, where in the sentence a word can occur, is what syntax is about. More criteria than the ones above could be mentioned, but those will be enough to get us started.

In addition to the four major lexical categories, we will encounter the following categories: determiner (Det), as mentioned above (this includes articles (e.g. *the, a, this, those*) as well as quantifiers (*some, no, most*)); modal auxiliary (*must, can, should*), and adverbs (Adv). We refrain from putting a definitive label on the modals for now (we will come back to them in Chapter I-4).

How do speakers know what category a word has? This is part of our lexical knowledge. All words are listed in the mental **lexicon**. The lexical entry of a word contains (at least) information on: phonetics and phonology (pronunciation of a word), semantics (its meaning), and category (as well as information on special properties of the word, e.g. irregular tenses or irregular plurals in English).

1.3. Crosslinguistic variation in the properties of categories

There are significant differences between languages with respect to the morphological and syntactic properties of categories. We can begin to raise our awareness of this fact by means of an exercise:

🕐 **Exercise**. *Categories across languages*
a. If you speak a language different from English, collect an overview (e.g. by using your intuitions), of how categories inflect: which kinds of words show up in different forms, and which forms? Then compare it with English. Zoom in on the category that shows most differences in terms of the

richness of the inflectional paradigm and write down a paradigm of word forms for that category. Follow-up question: Are there connections arising from your comparison with the distribution of the category? Compare differences in morphological paradigms to the places in the sentence in which the category can occur.
b. If you don't speak a language different from English, you can still perform a similar task: collect a set of data in English. Then use a professional grammatical description of another language or ask speakers of that language to collect an overview of a parallel data set in the other language. Design a precise and careful questionnaire before eliciting data. ☐

Let us further follow the path of the exercise above. Languages may diverge not only in how much inflectional morphology they display, but also with respect to whether or not they show endings on certain categories. While all languages have categories, the rules affecting them can be very different. The fact that English does not show inflection on certain words does not mean that we cannot find such patterns in other languages.

Italian is one of the languages that has inflections on adjectives for grammatical gender:

(4) a. *bell**a***   *casa*
         nice.FEM   house.FEM
         'nice house'
     b. *bell**o***   *giardino*
         nice.MASC   garden.MASC
         'nice garden'

The Italian nouns and the adjective above have grammatical gender: feminine vs. masculine. The adjective must show this by the appropriate ending. In English, the adjective *nice* shows no corresponding inflection.

Let us just mention one more contrastive example here from another category that we may not expect to inflect from the perspective of English. Austrian and Bavarian varieties of German can show inflection also on words like 'if/when':

(5) *Wann**st** noch einmal sagst,*   *dass die Mama a Tratschn is,*
     if.2nd.sg still once   say.2.SG   that the mum   a gossip   is
     kannst   dir   gleich   *an Krankenschein   besorgen.*
     can.2.SG. you.DAT immediately a medical certificate   get

'If you say once more that mother is a gossip, then you can get yourself a medical certificate right away.'
(Viennese from the series *Mundl*, http://www.mundl.net/sprueche/)

We return to the category of words like 'if' in Chapter I-4. For now the point is that words invariant in one language may inflect in other languages or varieties.

Finally, even the existence of a category in a given language can sometimes be controversial. When it comes to adjectives in Navajo, an Athabaskan language spoken in the Southwestern United States, grammatical descriptions note that there is no dedicated class corresponding to English adjectives. There are, instead, verbs which express the same properties expressed by adjectives in English. An example is the verbal stem *-neez* '(be) tall/long' (example from Bogal-Albritten (2010)):

(6) *ni-ø-ø-neez*
     ABS-3S-CLASS-long
     'S/he/it is long or tall (in an absolute sense).'

To sum up, categories may vary from language to language. Moreover, there is also variation in how they can be identified in terms of their morphological and syntactic properties. Identifying categories is a language specific task.

2. Phrases

2.1. Noun phrases

Let us get back to our task: the syntax of English. We have seen that categories identify classes of words that are treated alike by the grammar. The same is true of certain sequences of words. We can find classes of word sequences that all behave alike in terms of their syntactic properties. Such sequences are called phrases. We consider noun phrases first. Take the string *the woman*. It can occur immediately before a verb (i.e. as a subject), immediately after a verb (object), immediately after a preposition (object of the preposition), and immediately preceding the genitive *'s*:

(7) a. *The woman left.*

b. *I met the woman.*
c. *I talked to the woman.*
d. *The woman's friend left.*

The sequence *the woman* consists of Det and N. All such sequences can occur in these positions, no matter which lexical items they contain:

(8) a. *I met that man.*
b. *That man left.*
c. *I talked to that man.*
d. *That man's friend left.*

(9) a. *I saw this boy.*
b. *I talked to a cat.*
c. *A carpenter's life is tough.*

We call Det N sequences noun phrases, NPs for short. Phrases are categories that include lexical categories. For instance, an NP includes an N. NPs are treated as units with respect to certain syntactic rules. One such rule is preposing, or **topicalization**. Topicalization can affect a phrase like the NP *the woman*, but not subparts of the phrase.

(10) a. *The woman, I met.*
b. * *The, I met woman.*
c. * *Woman, I met the.*

Consider the string *the woman listened angrily*. We know now that each word belongs to a category. We can annotate them with subscripts:

(11)   *The$_{Det}$ woman$_N$ listened$_V$ angrily$_{Adv}$*

We also know that *the woman* is treated as a unit with respect to certain grammatical regularities like topicalization, and in this sense it "belongs together." We indicate the closer relationship of *the* and *woman* by bracketing the two words together and labeling the bracket with the category label NP (for noun phrase):

(12)   [$_{NP}$ *The$_{Det}$ woman$_N$*] *listened$_V$ angrily$_{Adv}$*

24   *Categories, phrases and phrase structure rules*

What we have done, in effect, with introducing noun phrases, is to give this string a structure. We claim that *the woman* belongs together more closely than, say, *woman listened.* Thus, there is evidence that a sentence is not an unstructured string of words, but that it has an internal structure. All sorts of grammatical rules make reference to that structure.

2.2. First steps towards a formal model: phrase structure rules

We say that sequences consisting of a determiner and a noun form an NP, or alternatively, that an NP can consist of Det+N. We state this with what is called a **phrase structure rule** or rewrite rule as in (13):

(13)   NP → Det N

This may be read as: an NP can consist of a determiner followed by a noun (alternatively: NP can be expanded to Det N, NP can be rewritten as Det N).

This is not the only possible form an NP can have. An NP can contain more material. The strings in (14) all have the same distribution (except partly for genitive *'s*, which is somewhat more restricted); cf. their placement in sentences in (15) below.

(14)   a.   *the angry woman*
        b.   *the angry woman with the red bag*
        c.   *this man's best friend*

(15)   a.   *The angry woman left.*
        b.   *I met the angry woman.*
        c.   *I talked to the angry woman.*
        d.   *The angry woman with the red bag left.*
        e.   *I met the angry woman with the red bag.*
        f.   *I talked to the angry woman with the red bag.*

The NPs in question can all undergo topicalization, but only when all the material that belongs to the phrase is kept together. (Topicalization in English is often a little odd out of context. To make (16a) acceptable, imagine a situation in which there is a second woman with different properties, and we are wondering if you met the two women. Given all this, (16b) is still quite unacceptable.)

(16) a. *The angry woman with the red bag, I met.*
b. **The angry woman with, I met the red bag.*
c. *The angry woman with the red bag, I talked to.*
d. **The angry, I talked to woman with the red bag.*
e. *This man's best friend, I met.*
f. **This man's, I met best friend.*

Two further criteria for deciding whether a group of words forms a unit (i.e. a phrase) are **coordination** and **pronominalization**. Phrases of the same kind can be coordinated, but not any random substrings of phrases. Coordination is illustrated in (17):

(17) a. *the angry woman and a big sheepdog*
b. **the angry and a big sheepdog*
c. **the and a big sheepdog*

(We should note that coordination can be tricky to use as a criterion in general because its interaction with other grammatical processes sometimes makes it look as if non-phrases could be coordinated too; but this does not affect the point (17) makes.). Phrases can be pronominalized, but again, not all random parts of phrases. Pronominalization is shown in (18):

(18) a. *I met her.*
b. **I met the her.*
c. **I met the angry her.*

⊕ **Exercise**. The English cleft construction has also been brought forward as an argument for identifying phrases. In the example below, the NP *the woman* occurs between *was* and the relative pronoun *who*, but random subparts of the NP cannot occur there:

(E1) a. *It was the woman who listened angrily.*
b. **It was the who woman listened angrily.*
c. **It was woman who the listened angrily.*

Use this construction to argue that the sequences in (14) are also NPs. ☐

26   *Categories, phrases and phrase structure rules*

Generally, we have two types of evidence for deciding whether a sequence of words is a phrase of a certain kind. One type is distributional evidence (the positions in the sentence that such sequences can occur in) and the other type comes from grammatical processes that such sequences can undergo.

Distributional evidence tells us that strings consisting of Det+A+N, Det A+N+P+Det+A+N, Det+N's+A+N (as in (14)) are also NPs. All these different NPs have the same distribution. Not only is it irrelevant what lexical material they contain, it is also irrelevant what their internal structure is. We can only capture this by introducing the level of the phrase into the grammar. Hence, sentences are not just strings of words or strings of lexical categories. They have a hierarchical structure.

Our phrase structure rules will have to be amended to generate these NPs also. Adjectives can be added as in (19). Placing such a category in parentheses means that it is optional.

(19)   a.   NP → (Det) (A) N
       b.   NP → NP's (A) N

The second rule is recursive: it characterizes an infinite number of strings: *the child's father, the child's father's new car, the child's father's new car's wheels,...* . Recursive rules help us capture the fact pointed out in Chapter I-1 that a language can construct infinitely many possible sentences.

We do not yet have rules that describe NPs containing Ps. There is evidence that substrings P+Det+N, or more accurately P+NP, form phrases, too: such sequences can be topicalized and coordinated.

(20)   a.   *To the woman, I talked.*
       b.   *To the woman with the red bag, I talked.*
       c.   *With the bag, I hit him.*

(21)   *In a clown's costume and with a red nose, you look funny.*

Accordingly, we add rule (22) for PPs: a prepositional phrase PP can consist of a preposition followed by an NP.

(22)   PP → P NP

The rules in (23) and (24) add the possibility of having a PP follow the noun in an NP to the rules in (19). (25) gives an example of an NP constructed with the rule in (24).

(23) NP → (Det) (A) N (PP)

(24) NP → NP's (A) N (PP)

(25) *Mary's pink trousers with blue flowers*

Notice that together, the NP rules and the PP rule are recursive, too. We can construct an NP that contains a PP. Since the PP contains an NP, we can construct another NP that contains a PP. And so on. That way, we can generate strings like *the park with the swings in the playground under the tall beech trees [...]*.

Exercise. Construct two examples illustrating recursive application of the second NP rule with the PP rule.   □

2.3. Other phrases

An NP is a group of words centered around a noun. In this subsection we see that there is evidence that groups of words centered around verbs form VPs, and analogously for APs.

Let us begin with **verb phrases**, VPs. Remember that distribution is one argument for considering a string to belong to a certain type of phrase. The characteristic distribution of VPs is that they can occur after a subject NP and after a modal auxiliary. The strings *visit Mary, talk to Mary, hit Bill with a stick* and *walk* are all VPs.

(26) a. *I visit Mary.*
      b. *I can visit Mary.*

(27) a. *John talked to Mary.*
      b. *John can talk to Mary.*

(28) a. *John hit Bill with a stick.*
      b. *John can hit Bill with a stick.*

28 *Categories, phrases and phrase structure rules*

(29) a. *We walk.*
     b. *We can walk.*

A further consideration is that grammatical processes like topicalization can affect these hypothesized VPs, but not arbitrary parts of our prospective VPs.

(30) a. *And walk, the woman will.*
     b. *And visit Mary, the woman will.*
     c. *And talk to Mary, the woman will.*
     d. *And hit Bill with a stick, he will.*

(31) a. ** and visit, the woman will Mary.*
     b. ** and talk to, the woman will Mary.*
     c. ** and hit Bill, he will with a stick.*

Coordination facts support the idea that these are phrases:

(32) *John visited Mary and talked to Bill.*

Pronominalization provides a further argument. The relevant form that we can use in this case is *do so*. *Do so* stands for the content of a previously mentioned VP and functions like a pronoun, but for a verbal category. Since 'pro-noun' isn't quite the right term, we say that *do so* is a pro-form for VPs.

(33) a. *John talked to Mary and so did Bill.*
     b. ** John talked to Mary and so did Bill to Kim.*

Another argument in favor of the strings we are considering being VPs is a certain kind of ellipsis. An ellipsis is an omission or deletion process. The ellipsis we look at here is **VP ellipsis**. Like pronominalization, ellipsis can target groups of words that form a unit. It cannot target random parts of sentences. Thus it gives us another reason to think that the relevant group of words 'belongs together' – it forms a phrase. Below we use strike-through in the examples to indicate the part that is not pronounced (i.e. is omitted), but is understood to be there semantically.

(34) a. *John visited Mary and Bill did [visit Mary], too.*

b. *John won't help me with the dishes, but his brother will* [~~help me with the dishes~~].
c. *Could you have a look at the car?*
   OK, I will [~~have a look at the car~~].
   * *OK, I will have* [~~a look at the car~~].

These are the ways of building VPs we have seen so far:

(35) a. VP → V NP
     b. VP → V PP
     c. VP → V NP PP
     d. VP → V

We simplify to (36):

(36) VP → V (NP) (PP)

Next, we turn our attention to phrases in the adjectival domain. In view of what we gathered so far, it is not surprising that linguists think that there are APs as well. Let us just mention that the material between a determiner and a noun comprises more than just an adjective.

(37) a. *a happy woman*
     b. *an extremely happy woman*
     c. *a happy and intelligent woman*
     d. *an extremely happy and very intelligent woman*

We limit ourselves for the moment to the PS rule in (38) for APs. We return to all the categories discussed here in more detail in the next chapter. This chapter concludes with a section on general properties of our syntactic theory.

(38) AP → (Adv) A

30 *Categories, phrases and phrase structure rules*

3. Phrase Structure Grammar and phrase structures

3.1. Phrase Structure Grammar

At this point, the syntax component of our grammar consists of a set of phrase structure rules. This is called a Phrase Structure (PS) Grammar. Let us collect the PS rules we have argued for above. In (39) we have added the information that a sentence S can consist of a subject NP followed by a VP, and we have updated the two NP rules to include APs, not As:

(39) S → NP VP
      NP → (Det) (AP) N (PP)
      NP → NP's (AP) N (PP)
      VP → V (NP) (PP)
      PP → P NP
      AP → (Adv) A

Coordination may be described by the following rule schema – constituents that are alike can be coordinated:

(40) X → X and X

In addition to these rules for phrases, we might assume lexical PS rules like the following:

(41) N → *woman*
      N → *bike*
      ...
(42) V → *see*
      V → *give*
      ...

But notice that that would double information already available in the lexicon. The lexicon of English contains for the word *woman* the information that it is a noun (just like it contains information about its phonetic representation etc.); and parallel facts hold for other words and categories. So instead of assuming lexical PS rules, we assume the following principle:

> **Lexicalization Principle**
> Any lexical item listed in the lexicon as belonging to a given category can be inserted in the syntax under any corresponding lexical category.

We will continue to add general principles to the grammar. We say that our grammar **generates** a sentence (a string of words) if it is possible to go from the symbol S for sentence to that string of words, using only rules in the grammar and conforming with all general principles. For example (43) shows that the set of rules in (39) plus the Lexicalization Principle generates the sentence *the woman left*:

(43) S
      NP VP
      Det N VP
      the N VP
      the woman VP
      the woman V
      the woman left

The set of all sentences generated by the grammar is the language generated by that grammar. Ultimately, for our enterprise, that should be English. At the moment, we are missing a few things (remember e.g. questions from Chapter I-1). This means that we will have to refine our rule system. Before we do so, we introduce some notions that will be helpful to us in our future work.

3.2. Phrase structure trees and constituency

As we uncover more syntactic regularities, we will see that it is central for us how syntactic units are hierarchically structured. A phrase structure grammar can be said to define a structure on the strings it generates. A standard way to represent syntactic structures is with graphs called **phrase structure trees.** The topmost node is called the **root** (so imagine the tree upside down). Every point in a tree is referred to as a **node** and the categorial information it has is its **label**. Nodes that only have the lexical items underneath are **terminal** nodes or **leaves**. For instance, in the tree for the NP *the woman* in (44) below, the two nodes with the labels Det and N,

32 *Categories, phrases and phrase structure rules*

respectively, are the terminal nodes. The NP has two **branches** in this example (Det and N), it is hence sometimes said to be binary branching.

(44)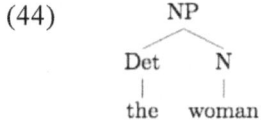

A node like the NP above is called the **mother** node of the two nodes it "branches off into", i.e. which it immediately **dominates**. Conversely, the nodes that are immediately dominated by it are its **daughters**. Nodes dominated by the same node are **sisters** (we do not normally talk about aunts or great grandmothers in syntactic theory). A local tree is a node with all its daughters.

A tree contains several kinds of information: the linear precedence (word order) facts (e.g. that the determiner precedes the noun), hierarchical structure (e.g. that the determiner and the noun form an NP), and the category of each word or group of words.

A tree is a special kind of graph. We rely on an intuitive understanding of trees. This includes that a node can only be dominated by one other node, that the tree must be connected, and that we do not have crossing branches. With the help of syntactic trees, we can also define more precisely what it means for a group of words to 'belong together'. Let us consider a larger tree now, one for an entire sentence. The PS grammar in (39) generates the sentence *the woman took the bike* and associates it with the PS tree in (45).

(45)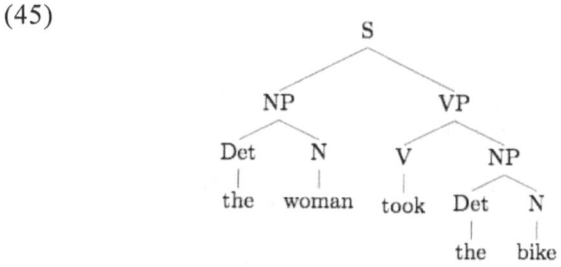

Notice that there is a correspondence between phrase structure rules and phrase structure trees. This is made explicit below (iff stands for 'if and only if'):

> A phrase structure grammar generates a **PS tree T for a sentence** iff
> (i) the root node is labeled with S,
> (ii) the leaves in the tree are the lexical items of the sentence,
> (iii) for every local tree [$_X$ a_1,...,a_n] in T, where X immediately dominates a_1,...,a_n, there is a rule in the grammar X → a_1,...,a_n.

The notion of a **constituent** defined below captures what we mean by saying that a sequence of words "belongs together" or "forms a unit".

> **Constituency**
> A group of words forms a constituent if there is a node in the tree that dominates all of them and nothing else.

Let us apply the definition to the tree in (45). According to the definition, *took the bike* is a constituent since there is a node (the VP) that dominates all of these words and nothing else. But *woman took* or *took the* are not constituents. There is no node in the tree that dominates them and nothing else.

So a grammar not only generates a language, it also provides us with a structure for the expressions of that language. It makes what we have said so far more precise. The regularities we have looked into when arguing for phrases are reflections of constituent structure. To put it differently, the phenomena we have used to argue for hierarchical structure are the empirical motivation for assuming that a sentence has a particular constituent structure. They are used to test a structure we might suggest: will the structure allow us to describe the phenomenon accurately?

☺ **Exercise.** Assign a tree structure to (E2) below according to the rules we have discussed.

(E2) *The woman in the grey suit left.* □

3.3. Structural ambiguities

One very important argument for structure comes from the ambiguity of examples like the following:

(46) *John saw the man with the binoculars.*

34 *Categories, phrases and phrase structure rules*

(47) *I like the woman next to Steve Pinker's pants.*

Each sentence has two possible interpretations, cf. (48) and (49), respectively:

(48) a. *John saw a man who had binoculars.*
      b. *John had binoculars with which he saw the man.*

(49) a. *I like the woman who is sitting next to Steve Pinker's pants (the pants are lying on a chair).*
      b. *I like the pants that belong to the woman who is sitting next to Steve Pinker.*

This is interesting because none of the words in the sentences seem to have two different meanings. That is, we do not have a lexical ambiguity in these examples. So why do they have two different readings? Our PS grammar in (39) allows us to assign two different structures to these two sentences. We illustrate this with the two structures generated for (46):

(50) a.

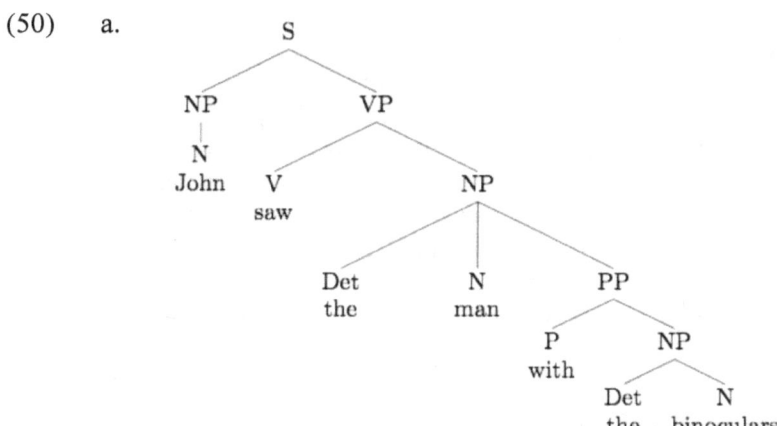

b.

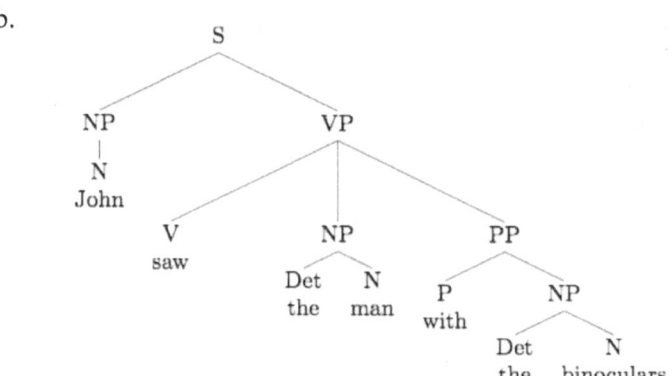

The words occurring in such sentences can be put together in different ways. The two ways reflect the two possible interpretations. In the first structure in (50), *the man with the binoculars* is a constituent. Let's say this means that this NP refers to a person (a man who has binoculars). In the second structure, this string is not a constituent. There is an NP, *the man*, and a VP *saw the man with the binoculars*. Let's assume this means there must be a person characterized as *the man*, and that the seeing happens with the help of the binoculars. The example is analyzed as a structural ambiguity.

☻ **Exercise**: Draw two different PS trees for (47), also according to the PS grammar in (39). Then, do the same thing for (E3) below. Paraphrase the two readings of (E3). Which tree reflects which interpretation?

(E3) *Bill's nephew repaired the radio under the sofa.* ☐

☕ **Exercise:**[1] The sentence in (E4) is ambiguous. Identify two major phrases in it and apply some of our constituency tests to them. Most likely, the linguistic processes you apply will disambiguate the sentence. Why?

(E4) *A linguist will interview the new manager in the library.* ☐

---

[1] We distinguish between exercises that consist of more or less routine transfer of main text discussions (☻) vs. more open ones (☕). This doesn't mean that you shouldn't be able to solve the latter tasks (even easily, depending on your background, angle etc.) or vice versa, that the more routine practice is disconnected from interesting theoretical points.

> ☞ THE BASICS BOX: *Rules and trees*
> - ✓ Syntactic rules make reference to category information.
> - ✓ Categories can be determined on the basis of distribution (what other words they keep company with syntactically) and morphological criteria.
> - ✓ Groups of words form phrases, and phrases are the building blocks of sentences.
> - ✓ Syntactic processes like topicalization and ellipsis affect constituents. Empirically, they help us detect constituents.
> - ✓ Phrase structure rules and phrase structure trees model these facts about language.

4. Selected references

A wealth of textbooks on generative syntax give excellent overviews on diagnosing categories in English, as well as on phrase structure and notions of phrasehood and constituency (e.g. Radford 1988, 2004, 2007; Haegeman 1994, Hageman and Guéron 1999); cf. Stowell (1981) for a critical advanced discussion of phrase-structure. Updated lecture-based introductions are Johnson (2004) and Santorini and Kroch (2006). Chomsky (1957, 1965) is a classic pair of references on the development of phrase structure or rewrite rules. Later versions of Chomskyan research abandon the use of rewrite rules as such, but they keep the insight of structure and syntactic trees in a more generalized syntactic theory (compare references on the so-called X-bar schema at the end of the next chapter).

Some specialized references on apparently unusual patterns of categories: Bayer (1984) is a classical paper on the syntax of words like *if* in Bavarian (the technical term for them is complementizers, to be discussed in Chapter I-4); see also Weiß (2005) for a discussion of the properties of such words in West Germanic. Inflection has been argued to appear on other categories on which it does not appear in English - see Napoli 1987 for discussion of Italian and McCloskey and Hale 1983 for Irish. You can find more on adjectival notions expressed through verbal stems in Young and Morgan (1987) and Bogal-Allbritten (2010).

We owe example (47) to William Snyder (p.c.). A special thank you to Kyle Johnson, whose lecture notes (see Johnson 2004 in the references) provided important conceptual and presentational input for us as early as

1996. Their influence on this textbook is still visible throughout in the presentation of syntactic issues.

We end this section on a practical note. If you are curious about glossing and abbreviations often used to convey grammatical information from different languages, see, e.g., the Leipzig glossing conventions: http://www.eva.mpg.de/lingua/resources/glossing-rules.php.

Chapter I-3
A systematic way of constructing phrases

If you can't explain it simply, you don't understand it well enough.
(Albert Einstein)

In this chapter, we examine the internal structure of phrases more closely. We find that there is additional – and more systematic – internal structure than our phrase structure rules capture so far, and we revise them accordingly (noun phrases in section 1, verb phrases in section 2, generalizing to all phrases in section 3). We do not give up the insight gained in the previous chapter, that words are grouped into phrases and phrases are the building blocks for constructing sentences. But we refine our understanding of how phrases are built. The most important outcome of this chapter is that there is a general pattern according to which all phrases are constructed. This is called the X' (read: x-bar) schema. This means that whatever phrase structure rules we propose must conform to the X' schema. We arrive at a more systematic view of the phrase structure rules that natural language permits as well as a more refined empirical picture. Sections 4 and 5 then deal with the connection between the lexicon and syntax, and with points of crosslinguistic variation, respectively. References are given in the final section of the chapter.

1. NPs revisited: more internal structure

So far we have found evidence for two kinds of categories: lexical and phrasal categories. There is evidence that we need still more hierarchical structure within phrases. We look at noun phrases first. Instead of the structure in (1) – a so-called "flat structure," with no sub-constituents below the NP level – we argue for the "hierarchical" structure in (2), which groups the noun and the prepositional phrase together before combining the result with the determiner.

(1) 'Flat structure' for the noun phrase *a student of physics*

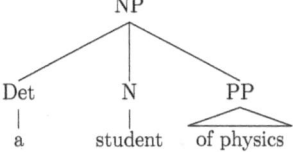

(2) 'Hierarchical structure' for the same noun phrase

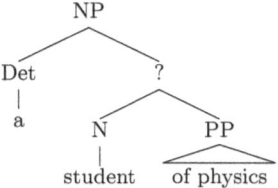

Before we proceed, two notes on presentation: instead of actual trees like (1) and (2), from here on we sometimes present the same structures as labeled bracketings like (1') and (2'). As you should be able to see easily, the labeled bracketings contain the same information and they take up less space. Occasionally, we don't spell out the structure of a constituent in full detail. In that case, we draw a triangle, as we did for the PP above.

(1') [$_{NP}$ a_{Det} *student*$_N$ [$_{PP}$ *of physics*]]
(2') [$_{NP}$ a_{Det} [$_?$ *student*$_N$ [$_{PP}$ *of physics*]]]

1.1. Intermediate levels: N'

In (2) above, there is a level between the phrasal level (the entire NP) and the lexical category (just the noun), which we have marked with *?* in the structure. What is the status of this intermediate level? We know it is not a lexical category because it contains more than the noun itself; hence, the appropriate label for the question mark cannot be N. Also, it is not the full phrase, i.e. the NP, because the determiner still needs to be added to this structure to yield the complete nominal phrase. Notice that if the category *?* were an NP, then it could contain a determiner, as e.g. in the NP *the cat*. But if we then add another determiner, we incorrectly generate structures with two determiners: **a the cat*.

We refer to such intermediate levels as N' (read: N-bar). The constituent N' is called a projection of N. While the noun itself is called the minimal or lexical projection, the N' constituent is an intermediate projection of the nominal head. The entire NP is then called the maximal projection. So, the NP is constructed in layers. First the head, then intermediate projection(s) (we will see that there can even be more than one), and finally the maximal projection, i.e. the full-fledged phrase.

What evidence is there for the intermediate level N'? Firstly, we can look at coordination. Intermediate projections can be brought together with conjunctions (and also with disjunctions):

(3) a. *Who would have dared to defy the [N' king of England] and [N' ruler of the empire]?*
b. *I bought Sam's [N' portrait of Billy] and [N' novel of his life].*

What we have in (3) above are neither just nouns coordinated nor entire phrases. Rather, intermediate projections are coordinated.

Secondly, what we have called the N' constituent can be the target of an ellipsis process, so-called N' deletion, in (4a-c). This process cannot target just the noun, so (4d) is unacceptable.

(4) a. *I painted Julie's car and sanded Bill's _ .*
b. *I liked Mary's long book, but hated John's _ .*
c. *I bought Sam's portrait of Billy and sold Jill's _ .*
d. * *I bought Sam's portrait of Billy and sold Jill's _ of Billy.*

Thirdly, let us consider the proform *one*, intuitively a relative of ellipsis:

(5) *I liked the [N' new novel about John], but you didn't like that [N' one].*

The proform *one* has the distribution of N' and picks up the meaning of a preceding N' in the discourse. Here are some more examples that illustrate *one* pronominalization:

(6) a. *The present [N' king of England] is more popular than the last one.*
b. *I liked the new [N' book about Lynn Hill], but Thilo preferred the old one.*
c. *I like the [N' picture] behind the sofa and Bill likes the one behind the chair.*

Not all instances of *one* pronominalization are accepabtle, cf. (7). Our grammar will need to explain these restrictions.

(7) a. * *The king of England defeated the one of Spain.*
     b. * *I like the student of physics and you liked the one of chemistry.*

According to the evidence provided by *one* pronominalization, *king of England*, *book about Lynn Hill*, and *picture* must be N's — they were pronominalized in good order in (6). On the other hand, *king* and *student* do not seem to be N's — they could not be pronominalized so well in (7). (6a,b) suggest that an N' can consist of an N and a PP. But this cannot be the entire answer: in *picture behind the sofa*, it seems that *picture* alone *can* be an N' - in contrast to *king* in *king of England*, which according to (7a) cannot be an N'. In order to understand the difference between the two, we need to answer the following question: what is the difference between two types of additions to the noun - namely the PPs *about Lynn Hill* or *behind the sofa* on the one hand, and the PPs *of physics* or *of England* on the other hand? Plain category information cannot help us to differentiate, given that we have prepositional phrases in both types of examples. Therefore, we next look more closely at the structural configurations, i.e. where the two types of constituents are attached within the noun phrase.

1.2. Complements vs. adjuncts

The question we have is: where do constituents such as the PPs and the APs in the sentences above go within the noun phrases they are part of? The key point made in this subsection is that we want to distinguish between two types of phrases that can be added to the head within a phrase. This is the complement/adjunct distinction. We will see that the former have a much tighter connection to the head than the latter.

First let us note that the problem we encountered above is not caused by the lexical choice of noun. Below we look at the noun *student* combined with two different types of PPs. The examples show that the PP *of physics* has a different status than the PP *with long hair*:

(8) a. *a student of physics*
     b. *a student with long hair*

(9) a. *Which student? The one with long hair?*

b. *Which student? The one of physics?

(10) a. a student of physics with long hair
b. *a student with long hair of physics

The PP *of physics* seems to belong to the noun *student* more closely than the PP *with long hair*. *Of physics* is called a complement, *with long hair* is called an adjunct. Interesting empirical differences are that (i) *one* pronominalization can be used so as to exclude the adjunct *with long hair*, while it must include the complement *of physics* (so (9a) is fine but (9b) is degraded); (ii) if an adjunct and a complement are present in the phrase, then the complement occurs closer to the head (i.e. as in (10a), and not as in (10b)).

In the phrase structure tree, complements are sisters to the lexical noun, so they are added to the N level. Their mother node is an N'. Adjuncts are added later to the projection, at the N' level – they are sisters to an N'. Their mother node is also an N'. The two NPs from (8) above have the following structures:

(11) a.

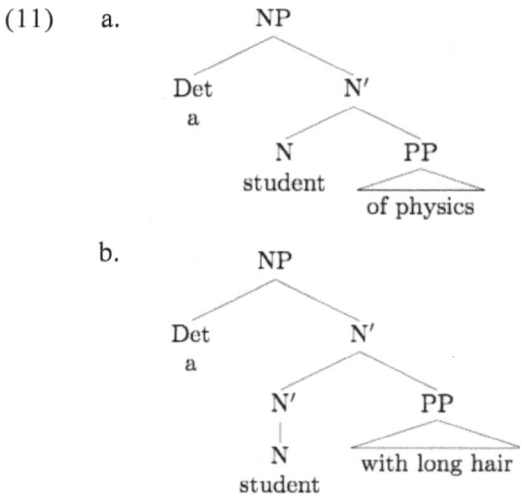

b.

The examples below illustrate some further properties of adjuncts. Adjuncts can also be attached to the left, not just to the right. Example (12a) with the APs *new* and *dark-haired* illustrates this. Adjuncts can be added recursively (i.e. several adjuncts are possible within one phrase), as in (12b) and (12c), and their order is flexible. The examples in (13) show that all the prospective N's in (12) behave as expected with respect to *one* pronominalization. For example, *student with long hair* is an N' and *student with long hair in the corner* is also an N'.

(12) a. the new dark-haired student
 b. the student in the corner with long hair
 c. the student with long hair in the corner

(13) a. *Which student? The one with long hair in the corner?*
 b. *Which student with long hair? The one in the corner?*
 c. *Which student with long hair in the corner? That one?*
 d. *Which stranger? The tall dark handsome one?*
 e. *Which handsome stranger? The tall dark one?*

We have seen the tree structures of NPs containing a complement or an adjunct in (11). In (14) we offer some further possible structures of NPs:

(14) a.

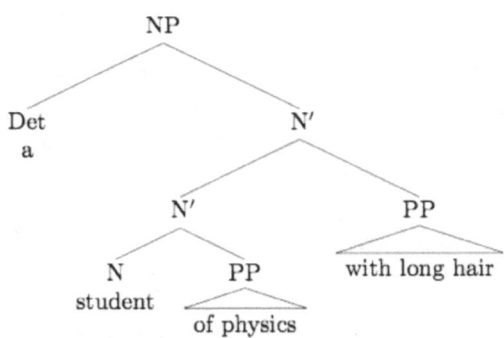

b.

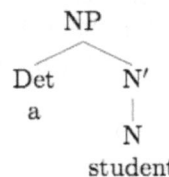

44   *A systematic way of constructing phrases*

c.

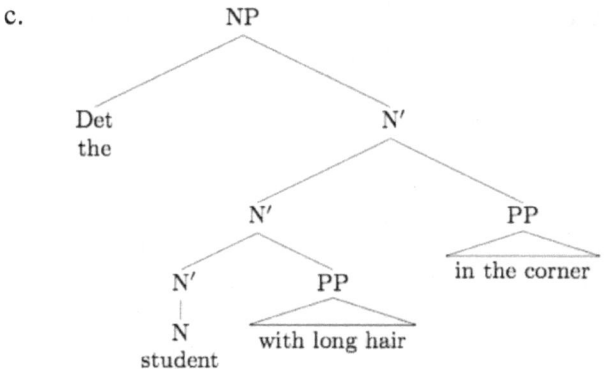

With these structures we make the right predictions for *one* pronominalization in (10'). The proform *one* pronominalizes all N's but no Ns — it can pronominalize *student* only when it is an N'.

(10')   a.   *The student with short hair is dating the one with long hair.*
        b.   *This student works harder than that one.*
        c.   * *The student of physics was older than the one of chemistry.*

Let us practice our understanding of the N' levels using coordination. The sentence in (15) is ambiguous.:

(15)   *Mary studied the classical descriptions of Rome and explanations of its downfall.*

Either just the descriptions of Rome are classical, or both the descriptions *and* the explanations of its downfall are. This ambiguity depends on where *classical* is adjoined. If it is an adjunct to the N' projected by the noun *descriptions* (which includes the noun and its complement *of Rome*), then we get the former interpretation. If it is adjoined to the coordinated N' (which contains both the N' projected by *descriptions* and the one projected by *explanations*), then the latter interpretation obtains.

⏺ **Exercise.** Draw the PS trees for both readings.   □

1.3. The new set of phrase structure rules

We have learned that adjoined APs and PPs form a new N' out of an N'. They do not change the category, as *one* pronominalization and coordination show us, and they can be added recursively. Complements, on the other hand, are added to an N and form an N'. Finally, determiners and possessive NPs combine with an N' and form an NP. Thus we have the following new set of phrase structure rules for NPs:

(16)   NP → (Det) N'
        NP → NP's N'
        N' → AP N'
        N' → N' PP
        N' → N (PP)

Further support for the complement/adjunct distinction can be drawn from the ambiguity of example (17). The PP can be an adjunct or a complement of *student*. To practice, draw the two PS trees and paraphrase the reading corresponding to each of the two configurations.

(17)   *a student of high moral principles*

When we revisit coordination, we find that the combination of our assumption (18) together with the PS rules above makes the desired predictions. In order to generate the examples in (19), take X in the rule to be N'. Any N' constituent can be coordinated. By adding N' levels, we add hierarchical structure, but no new type of phrase is created.

(18)   X → X and X

(19)   a. *the students of physics and professors of chemistry*
        b. *the students with long hair and professors with short hair*
        c. *the students of physics and professors with long hair*
        d. *the students of physics and new professors*

We have not used topicalization in this section to gather evidence about constituency (remember that this process has provided an important argument for phrasal constituents). Why not? It seems that topicalization is constrained in that only phrases can be topicalized, not constituents of other

46   *A systematic way of constructing phrases*

types. In particular intermediate projections cannot undergo topicalization. Thus no argument for N' can be gleaned from this syntactic process.

(20)   **pineapple with mold, John ate this.*

🕒 **Exercise**. Draw the PS trees for the following NPs using the rules in this chapter.

(E1)   a.   *a woman with an umbrella with a red handle*
       b.   *her dislike of men with big egos*
       c.   *a woman with three children with ginger hair*   ☐

☕ **Exercise**. The NP in (E2) is ambiguous, while the NP in (E3) is not. Why?

(E2)   *former presidents with long hair =*
       a.   *people who used to be long-haired and used to be presidents*
       b.   *people who used to be presidents and who are now long-haired*

(E3)   *former presidents of the US*
       = people who used to be US presidents   ☐

2.   Evidence for intermediate projections within verb phrases

Now that we have found evidence that there is more structure within NP than we first thought, we might wonder whether the same is true of other categories. Let's examine the internal structure of VPs first. Can we find a category analogous to N' – let's call that category V' - within the VP?

2.1.   First evidence for V'

Consider the sentence in (21). Its verb phrase contains two constituents following the verb *bought*, an NP and a PP. We want to take a closer look at the internal structure of this VP.

(21)   *John bought the book on Tuesday.*

In analogy to *one* pronominalization in the NP domain, we employ pronominalization in the VP domain using the proform *do so*. The entire string *buy the book on Tuesday* can be substituted by the proform *do so*, as in (22a) below. The example in (22b) shows that *do so* can also stand for *buy the book*. (22c) shows that *do so* cannot stand for *buy* in this example.

(22)   a.   *John will buy the book on Tuesday, and Paul will do so as well.*
       b.   *John will buy the book on Tuesday, and Paul will do so on Thursday.*
       c.   **John will buy the book on Tuesday, and Paul will do so the game console on Friday.*

Let us suppose that *do so* is a proform for V'. Then example (22a) shows us that the string *buy the book on Tuesday* is a V'. As we can see from (22b), the smaller constituent *buy the book* (containing just the verb and the NP) seems to be the same kind of unit V'. What goes awry, however, is trying to use *do so* pronominalization for the verb *buy* alone, excluding the object NP. So *buy* is not a V'. (22) gives us some indication that, similar to the case of NPs, there is more internal structure in VPs than we had first assumed.

The following example shows that we need to examine the status of the constituents in the VP, not just their category:

(23)   *Paul put the book on the table.*

(24)   a.   *John will put the book on the table and Paul will do so as well.*
       b.   **John will put the book on the table, and Paul will do so on the chair.*

The string *put the book on the table* seems to be a V', but not *put the book*. That is, *do so* pronominalization cannot strand the PP in the *put* example, unlike the *buy* example. Why should there be this difference between (21) and (23)?

2.2. Complements vs. adjuncts again

Consider the following contrast:

(25) a. *Mary put it on the table after dinner.*
b. * *Mary put it after dinner on the table.*

The PP *on the table* must come closer to the verb *put* than the PP *after dinner*. This is similar to **a student with long hair of physics*.

We may hypothesize that these are really the same facts as in the NP case – one kind of PP belongs closer to the verb than the other. The PP *after dinner* is an adjunct, but *on the table* is a complement. Complements are sisters to the lexical category, hence *on the table* in (23) is a sister to V. There is a level of V' to which adjuncts can be recursively added, just as in the case of N'. The proform *do so* can replace a verb + complement(s), or a verb +complement(s) + adjunct(s), but not a verb to the exclusion of its complement(s).

Adverbs are another kind of adjunct to our newly discovered V' level:

(26) a. *I [V' visited Mary] yesterday and Julie will do so tomorrow.*
b. *I [V' visited Mary yesterday] and Julie did so, too.*

Coordination supports this analysis. The examples below are ambiguous in a way that is analogous to (15).

(27) a. *I talked to Mary and played with John on the street.*
b. *I visited Mary and played soccer yesterday.*
c. *Hermione often meets with Harry or goes to the library.*

The adjunct in each case can, but need not, modify both conjuncts. Hence the adjunct does not change the category of its sister - it combines with a V' and yields a V'. We thus arrive at the following PS rules for VPs:

(28) VP → V'
V' → AdvP V'
V' → V' AdvP
V' → V' PP
V' → V (NP) (PP)

In (21') we provide the PS tree for (21) according to our current set of PS rules:

(21')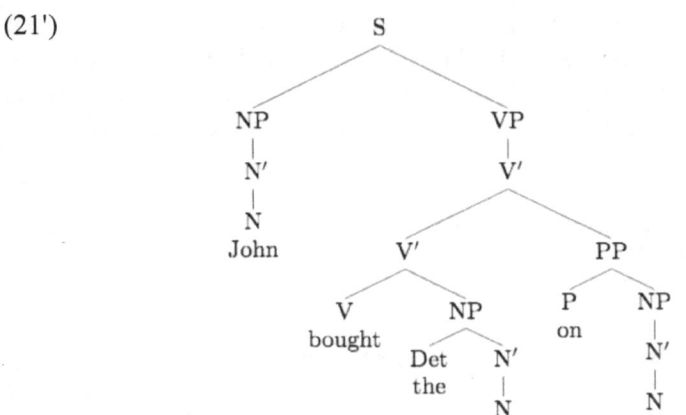

So far, we have not found expressions that turn the intermediate projection into the maximal projection in the case of VPs (in contrast to NPs). We will come back to the first rule in Chapter I-8.

3. Generalizing from nouns and verbs: the X' schema

3.1. Adjectives and prepositions

In the preceding chapter we used the following rules for PPs and APs:

(29)   a.   AP → (Adv) A
           b.   PP → P NP

We can formulate the following hypothesis. Since we have found an intermediate level X' for verbs and nouns, and since the major lexical categories seem to behave in parallel ways as far as we have seen, there should be an X' level (an intermediate projection) in the case of APs and PPs, too.
There is good evidence that this is correct for APs. Adjectives can take PP complements.

(30)   a.   *Mary is very proud of her son.*
           b.   *Sue is that fond of Mary.*

(31)   *John is extremely fond of Mary in some ways but less so in other ways.*

The little word *so* in (31) seems to stand for *fond of Mary*; hence, that must be a constituent that excludes both *extremely* and *in some ways*. The sequence consisting of the adjective with its complement (*fond of Mary*) is analyzed as A'. The PP *in some ways* is an adjunct, a sister of A'. What are adverbs like *extremely* or *severely*; cf. (32)?

(32)   Sue is extremely fond of Mary.

Another ambiguity helps us decide:

(33)   *severely personally critical of the president*

(33')   a.   [$_{AP}$ [$_{A'}$ *severely* [$_{A'}$ *personally* [$_{A'}$ *critical*$_A$ [$_{PP}$ *of the president*]]]]]
        b.   [$_{AP}$ [$_{A'}$ [$_{AdvP}$ *severely personally*] [$_{A'}$ *critical*$_A$ [$_{PP}$ *of the president*]]]]

The AP in (33) is ambiguous: *severely* can modify either *personally* or the entire A' *personally critical of the president*. Such adverbs must be sisters to A'. Words like *so* and *that*, on the other hand, seem to have a different status. Only one such word can show up in an AP:

(34)   a.   *Sue is so foolish.*
        b.   * *Sue is that so foolish.*

They seem to be more like determiners in the case of the NP. We may call them degree words and use the label Deg for them. The following set of PS rules for APs sums up the discussion:

(35)   AP → (Deg) A'
       A' → A' PP
       A' → Adv A'
       A' → A (PP)

Adjectives and adverbs share many characteristics. Adjectives show similar possibilities within NPs as adverbs within VPs. And their internal structure is also similar in that degree words (e.g. *so quickly*), complement PPs (e.g. *independently of her parents*) and further adverbs can be added to them (e.g. *amazingly well*). So for current purposes we can suppose that adverbial phrases have an internal structure similar to adjectival phrases, and we will not pursue their syntactic analysis further.

Lastly, we briefly look at the internal structure of PPs. It seems that prepositions take complements optionally; the following examples contain prepositions that don't need to take a complement:

(36) a. *John was there/out/in.*
b. *John put the book there/outside.*

That would make us revise our original PP rule as follows:

(37)   PP → P (NP)

There is also evidence that PPs have more internal structure. Expressions like *right* and *two miles* below can be added to preposition + complement. The coordination example in (39) provides evidence that preposition + complement forms a P' constituent.

(38) a. [PP *right* [P' *on the top shelf*]]
b. [PP [*two miles*] [P' *from Boston*]]

(39)   *The vase fell* [PP *right* [[*off the table*] *and* [*onto the floor*]]].

That means that we have roughly the PS rules in (40) for PPs:

(40)   PP → (XP) P'
           P' → P (NP)

We generalize what we have found for all major lexical categories (N, V, A, P): They have an intermediate projection and a maximal projection, centered around a lexical item or minimal projection. All phrases are thus built according to the following schema, the **X' schema**:

The X' schema
XP → (YP) X'
X' → ZP X'
X' → X' WP
X' → X (QP) (UP)

3.2. The four players: heads, complements, adjuncts, and specifiers

Let us examine the X' schema and its ingredients in more detail. We begin with the core of the phrase, the **head**, X in the schema. A phrase is centered around a lexical head, as stated in the following principle:

> **Endocentricity:** a phrase must have a head.

All other constituents are in principle optional. Each PP must contain a preposition, each NP a noun, and so on; and then there can be additional material in each phrase, which will lead to phrases of different sizes. The principle of endocentricity gives you a bit of practical help: when you draw syntactic trees, double-check whether you have identified the head of each phrase. (If, for example, you have a VP and no V in a syntactic tree, then there is usually something wrong.)

Heads, then, seem to be the most important and also the most straightforward ingredient of the phrase. But let us note that there is an apparent counterexample to the X' schema among the rules that we have discussed so far; remember (41) (from the previous chapter):

(41)   S → NP VP

The problem is that we do not (yet) know what the head of the sentence is. We will come back to this issue when we discuss clauses in some detail in Chapter I-4. Right now, note that the X' schema requires that we revise (41). All phrase structure rules that we propose should conform to the X' schema.

The next closest elements to the center of the phrase are the **complements**. A head may not require any complements (e.g. the example with the preposition *there*), or combine with one (e.g. the adjective *fond*), or with two such elements (recall the verb *put*) – hence the abstract optional QP and UP in the schema above. The crucial property of complements is the following: they are sister of the head (X) and their mother node is an intermediate bar level category (X'). All the complements we have seen follow the head of the phrase, and this is expressed by the rule as well. This is a feature of English, which we will put into perspective in section 5 below.

Adjuncts (cf. ZP and WP in the schema above) are added recursively and their relative order is generally not fixed. Their most important structural characteristic is that of being sisters to an intermediate level category and yielding another intermediate level category as their mother nodes.

Our fourth ingredient of the phrase is the **specifier** (cf. YP in the schema above). A specifier has an intermediate level X' as a sister (a structural property that it shares with adjuncts), but the specifier closes off the phrase: its mother node is the maximal projection XP. Notice that a phrase can have only one specifier according to the schema. In the case of NP, both determiners and possessive NPs are categories that occupy the specifier position. This correctly leads us to expect that an NP cannot have both in English:

(42) a. * *the Bill's book*
      b. * *Bill's the book*

Determiners and possessors are said to be in **complementary distribution** (we can have either one, but not both at the same time). This is typically taken to be evidence that two categories try to occupy the same slot in the phrase structure. We will see more examples in due course.

4. A loose end: subcategorization

We have left one aspect of phrase structure open: what does it mean, theoretically speaking, for a category to be a complement? And how do we ensure that the things we claimed to be complements end up where we want them to in the phrase structure – i.e. as sisters to the lexical head?

We approach these questions by observing that taking particular categories as complements depends on the particular lexical item:

(43) a. *a student of physics*
      b. * *a boy of physics*

Contrast this with adjuncts: it does not seem to matter which lexical noun we choose. They can all be modified.

(44) a. *a student with long hair*
      b. *a boy with long hair*

There is a closer relation between complements and the head than between adjuncts and the head. Lexical restrictions apply in a domain close to the head. We say that the head selects the complement.

It becomes even clearer that PS rules leave a gap regarding selection of complements when we look at verbs, which can have obligatory complements. This is not captured by the PS rule that introduces verbal complements.

(45)   V' → V (NP) (PP)

If we could insert any verb under any V node (as the lexicalization principle allows us to do at the moment), we should expect (46a) to be grammatical. Similarly in (47).

(46)   a. *John mentioned.
        b. John mentioned the book.

(47)   a. John put the book on the table.
        b. *John put the book.
        c. *John put on the table.
        d. *John put.

Some verbs can only be expanded to VPs with an NP, others with NP and PP. These categories are complements. How do we insure that they are obligatory? We analyze this as a lexical property of the verb in question. It is not information that should be incorporated into the syntax component directly. We assume that the lexical entry of a head tells us which complements it requires. This is called subcategorization. Thus the lexical entries for the heads considered above look as follows:

Subcategorization features
mention: [V, + _NP#]
put: [V, + _NP PP#]
student: [N, + _(PP) #]

The notation [+_NP#] can be read as follows: "there must be an NP in the context of the word." The hash sign (#) limits the context to the immediate context, i.e. the NP must be a sister to the lexical item.

Subcategorization is not taken care of by the lexicalization principle as presented in the preceding chapter. Here is the necessary revision:

Lexicalization Principle (revised)
When a lexical item is inserted in a PS tree, lexical properties (inluding category and subcategorization information) must be satisfied.

Interpretation seems to play a part in the selection of complements by heads. For example, a complete sentence with a verb meaning 'put' must include an object that is moved and a location where the object ends up. These complements look like they are semantic arguments that the verb requires. This is a valid intuition, and we will come back to this point in the semantics part. But there is more to subcategorization than semantics: lexical items can be quite picky about their subcategorized complements. For example, they can demand that the complement be headed by a particular head. We incorporate this requirement in the lexicon as indicated in (49).

(48) a. *fond of / *in Bill*
       interested in / *of Pat
    b. *king of / *to England*

(49) *king*: [N, +_(PP(of)) #]

Note that some aspects of subcategorization can vary randomly between languages for words that are direct translations of each other. In (50) the German adjectives require a different head preposition in the complement PP from the corresponding English adjectives. In (51) we see that whether a complement is obligatory or optional also varies.

(50) a. *interessiert an/*in Pat*
       interested at/ in Pat
    b. *allergisch gegen/*zu Steuerformulare*
       allergic   against/to tax forms

(51) a. *We have released a new version this year.*
    b. *We have released twice this year.*
    c. *Wir haben dieses Jahr eine neue Version herausgebracht.*
       we have this   year a   new version released
    d. * *Wir haben dieses Jahr zweimal herausgebracht.*
         we have this   year twice   released

Such properties of individual words cannot in any obvious way be traced to more general properties of the language, or to word meaning (which makes them quite a stumbling stone for the language learner!). The lexicon is therefore a good place for this kind of information.

So how exactly does our richer notion of lexical knowledge relate to complements vs. adjuncts in the syntax? Remember that we need to be able to predict two things:

(i) Complements must appear as sisters to the lexical head.
(ii) No non-complements must appear as sisters to the lexical head.

These are our generalizations. How do we technically ensure that (i) and (ii) hold? Essentially, this is the issue of how lexical properties are mapped into the syntax. This matter is taken care of by a principle called the projection principle in syntactic theory. A very simple version of the principle that basically states (i) and (ii) is given below.

Projection Principle (simplified)
If A and B are sisters and A is a head then B must be subcategorized by A. The subcategorization properties of a head can only be satisfied by sisters.

In sum, we can keep our phrase structure rules simple because specific information is contained in the lexicon, and general principles ensure that lexical information is transferred into the syntax correctly.

5. Universal and variable aspects of syntactic structure

Remember that linguists model knowledge of language. This chapter and the preceding one have begun to develop a model of people's knowledge of syntax (i.e. their ability to build sentences), specifically for English. Ultimately, that is not all we want to do: we also want to understand how other languages differ from English and what languages have in common. This means that our model needs to say something about variable and stable properties of human languages. Only then is it a model of people's knowledge of language, rather than a model of the knowledge of *a* language.

The X' schema is a good starting point for discussing this enterprise. It exemplifies both structural aspects that are universal, i.e. shared by all human languages, and aspects that differ between languages in a systematic way (so-called parametric variation).

The X' schema itself is suggested to be **universal.** This means that all phrases in all human languages are built according to this schema. This seems to be a strong generalization. Let's consider what it entails. For one thing, all phrases in human languages must have a head (recall the principle of endocentricity). Furthermore, we expect that phrases may also contain complements, adjuncts and specifiers in all human languages. Note, once more, that this does not mean that all actual phrases look exactly the same. Rather, the same building blocks are generally available.

An aspect of the X' schema that is subject to crosslinguistic **variation** is word order within phrases. While we have noted that syntactic phrases need a head, the position of the head may vary relative to the next closest potential building block in the phrase, namely the complement. The head may either precede or follow its complement(s). For example, while in English, French or Tagalog the verb precedes its object(s), in Basque, Burmese, Japanese or Korean the verb follows its object(s). The same type of variation holds within prepositional phrases: prepositions may also precede or follow their complements (prepositions following their complements are also called postpositions). To illustrate this, consider the following examples from Burmese (the realis mood marker $t\varepsilon$ can be ignored for current purposes), and Japanese (ignore the topic marker *wa*, too). In both languages, heads systematically follow complements, in the VP as well as the PP.

(52) a. [$_{VP}$ *kà màun-tɛ*]   [Burmese]
  car   drive-REAL
  'drive a car'
 b. [$_{PP}$ *Yankon ko*] *θwà-tɛ*
  Rangoon to go-REAL
  'go to Rangoon'   (adapted from Whitman 2008: 239, (8))

(53) *Watashi-wa kyooju-to   a-tta.*   [Japanese]
   I-TOP   professor-with met
   'I met the professor.'

In some languages, headedness is very systematic. In English, all heads precede their complements. In Japanese, all heads follow their complements. This has been called a parameter of crosslinguistic variation, which we may express as follows:

> **Headedness Parameter**
> In a given language, heads {precede/follow} their complements.

For us, a parameter is a choice point in the grammar, the setting of which has consequences for a set of grammatical phenomena. In the example at hand, the setting of the headedness parameter to "precedes" determines that verbs come before their objects in English, that English has prepositions rather than postpositions, that adjectives precede their PP complements, and so forth.

To wrap up our discussion of headedness, it should be noted that there are also languages that show a mixed behavior. German is a good example of a less uniform language. For one thing, we find prepositions as well as postpositions. For another, it sometimes looks as if it depends on the environment in the clause whether a head follows or precedes its complement.

(53) a. *auf dem Tisch*
 on the table
 'on the table'
 b. *dem Zug entgegen*
 the train towards
 'towards the train'
 c. *den Strand entlang*
 the beach along
 'along the beach'
 d. *Der Trainer ist* [$_{AP}$ *stolz auf Paul*].
 The coach is proud of Paul.
 'The coach is proud of Paul.'
 e. *der* [$_{AP}$ *auf Paul stolze*] *Trainer*
 the of Paul proud coach
 'The coach proud of Paul'

> ☞ THE BASICS BOX: *Constructing phrases: The X′ schema*
> ✓ All phrases contain a head.
> ✓ Complements combine with a head to yield an intermediate projection.
> ✓ Adjuncts combine with and yield intermediate projections.

> - ✓ The specifier closes off the phrase.
> - ✓ Lexical information like subcategorization is mapped into the syntax by the projection principle.
> - ✓ The X' schema is universal; word order within the phrase is variable.

6. Selected references

The early introduction of X' theory is sometimes credited to Chomsky (1970); cf. Stowell (1981: 65). Jackendoff (1977), Chomsky (1981) and Pesetsky (1982) are comprehensive references regarding the development of the X' schema. Introductions to this syntactic theory can be found in Radford (1988), among others - see once more the references in Chapter I-2, including the concepts of subcategorization, the projection principle etc. We have recapitulated the GB theory in a compact, simple form here.

The search for language universals has been important in much linguistic research (going back at least to Humboldt; cf. Johnson 2004) and notably also in the typological work of Greenberg (1963). See e.g. Whitman (2008) for a scrutiny of Greenberg's key, posited universals (including a review of the validity of some of them) together with their relationship to universals posited in the syntactic literature.

The term parameter was introduced into syntactic theory in the 1980s. A parameter can be thought of as a switchbox in a circuit, i.e. it has a small number of options to which it can be turned. With the setting chosen during the language acquisition period, the syntactic choices available in human languages will be regulated quite systematically. The switchbox metaphor pertaining to parameter theory is credited to James Higginbotham by Chomsky (1986). Syntacticians have since criticised both the concept and its empirical applications. The headedness parameter, specifically, has been subject to controversy. Kayne (1994) is a syntactic theory claiming strong universals with regard to the order of heads and complements. Kayne's position has been influential, but it is not shared by everyone.

We adopt a theoretically less loaded notion of parameter here. Our notion of a parameter is simply that of a decision point that the grammar of human language provides. Such a decision point determines a bundle of poperties in the grammar of a particular language, depending on how the parameter is set. Discussion of this concept of parameter can be found e.g. in Snyder (2007), Beck et al. (2009). It follows from the goal of providing principled and systematic analyses of linguistic phenomena across languages.

Much further empirical and analytical work is needed before we can understand what all human languages have in common, and how they may differ. But it is important to develop our model of the grammar with this goal in mind.

Chapter I-4
Clause structure and movement

> *What do you think what's in the box?*
> (Matthew, three-year old, in Thornton 1990)

The preceding chapter has pointed us towards an important open question for our syntactic analysis: the structure of clauses. This chapter examines clause structure and develops an analysis that conforms to the X' schema (section 1). In the course of developing the analysis further, we encounter another component of syntactic theory: transformations (sections 2 and 3). We end up with a model of syntax that includes a phrase structure component and, on top of that, a transformational component. The final section provides a selection of references.

1. Clausal structure

1.1. Finding the head of the clause

Remember that the following rule, which we use so far to generate sentences, violates the X' schema:

(1)   S → NP VP

Also, notice that we cannot account for sentences of the type in (2), which contain a modal auxiliary. The simple rule in (1) only generates sentences like (3). So obviously we have to improve and extend our analysis of English clauses.

(2)   a. *John might buy a turtle.*
        b. *John can buy a turtle.*
        c. *John will buy a turtle.*

(3)   *John bought a turtle.*

As a first step towards an improved analysis, notice that the modal auxiliaries in (2) are in **complementary distribution** to tense and agreement morphology, i.e. the finite inflection on the verb. That means that we can have one or the other, but not both. (4) illustrates this.

(4) a. *John might bought a turtle.
     b. *John might buys a turtle
     c. *John cans buy a turtle.
     d. *John wills buy a turtle.

An important syntactic fact about (today's) English is that there can only be one modal auxiliary verb per clause (5a); a related fact is that there can only be one agreement marking element per clause, (5b):

(5) a. *John can must buy a turtle.
     b. *John has buys a turtle.

Let us also consider in this vein the infinitival clause that is the complement of *believe* in (6) (the clause is called infinitival because there is no finite inflection on the verb for person, number etc.):

(6) John believes [Mary to like Hildegard].

The reason for considering it is that the element *to* is, in turn, in complementary distribution with modals and agreement:

(7) a. *John believes Mary to can like Hildegard.
     b. *John believes Mary to likes Hildegard.

When we find items that are in complementary distribution, we account for this by putting them in the same structural position. Now, we have to create a position for modals in the structure of English. The simple rule in (1) does not provide one at the moment. Let's call these elements **Inflection** (also Infl or I for short). Exactly one of them may occur between the subject NP and the VP, so there appears to be a reserved position for one such element. Hence we should revise our sentence rule to the following:

(8) S → NP I VP

This is progress insofar as we have a place where modals and *to* can be accommodated, as well as a structural position for the finite inflection on the verb. But the rule still does not conform to the X' schema. Also, we make the silly prediction that *Mary walked home* should really sound like *Mary -ed walk home*. This is obviously false, but it will take us a little while to repair it. First, we need to understand how clauses are compatible with the X' schema by identifying the head of the clause.

To this end, let's look at clauses that are slightly larger than the ones that we have looked at so far. The examples in (9) contain embedded clauses.

(9)   a.   *John believes [that Mary bought a turtle].*
        b.   *John wonders [whether/if Mary bought a turtle].*

Such clauses are the complements of the verbs *believe* and *wonder*. They contain a **complementizer** (words like *that, whether, if*). These elements introduce the embedded clause. They occur to the left of the subject. Since we have no room for complementizers so far, we introduce a new rule (10) that describes the facts in (9): a complementizer C can combine with a sentence S to form a (larger) clause. This larger clause we call CP, complementizer phrase, in keeping with Endocentricity (cf. Chapter I-3, section 3.2.).

(10)   CP → C S

This means that C is the head of the larger clause, the CP. Is this plausible? Remember that heads select their complements, and they may be picky about the head of their complement. Hence, a verb that subcategorizes for a CP might select a CP headed by a particular C head, if our rule is on the right track. This is confirmed when we look at (11): *wonder* subcategorizes for a CP headed by *whether* or *if* and does not accept a CP complement headed by *that*. On the other hand, *think* requires a CP headed by *that* and does not like a CP complement headed by *whether*. (The short-hand notation with the brackets {} means that you should choose each of the items listed in turn to form the sentence. The judgment is given per item.)

(11)   a.   *I wondered {whether/if/*that} Mary had bought chocolate.*
         b.   *I thought {that/*whether} Mary had bought chocolate.*
         c.   *I know {that/whether} Mary had bought chocolate.*

(12)   Example of a subcategorization frame:
       thought: V, [_CP (*that*)#]

It is plausible, then, that C is indeed the head of the larger clause, the CP. There is evidence that a particular C in turn selects a particular kind of S:

(13)   a.   *I wondered* [$_{CP}$ *whether to leave*].
       b. * *I wondered* [$_{CP}$ *if to leave*].

The C element *whether* accepts a complement S that contains *to* in the I position, while *if* doesn't. Similarly for *that* versus *for*:

(14)   a.   *I want* [$_{CP}$ *for Bill to leave*].
       b. * *I want* [$_{CP}$ *that Bill to leave*].

The picture that emerges from such data is that C imposes selectional requirements on the I element, e.g. whether it can be *to* or not. Hence, we should view I as the head of the S that is selected by the C element. If what we have called S so far is headed by I, this means that it is in fact an IP. We revise (8) to (15):

(15)   IP → NP I VP

This rule, like the one we have for CPs, at least gets endocentricity right. I is the head of 'smaller' clausal structures, which we call IPs; and C is the head of 'larger' sentential units, the CPs. However, the rules in (10) and (15) still do not conform to the X' schema. Here is a pair of rules that generates IPs with the same number of constituents in them, but matching the X' schema:

(16)   a.   IP → NP I'
       b.   I' → I VP

The rules in (16) generate structures in which I together with the VP forms a constituent, I'. There is some evidence for this structure in terms of coordination:

(17)   *Mary* [$_{I'}$ *will go to Boston*] *and* [$_{I'}$ *might visit Janina*].

There is thus evidence for I'. Subjects are the specifiers of IP. That is, they combine with I' to yield IP. The CP rule should be similarly revised:

(18) a. CP → C'
      b. C' → C IP

Notice that we do not have a specifier of CP. We will come back to this later in the chapter. But before we do, we offer a contrastive excursus for those interested.

1.2. Excursus: Mood selection in Romance and Balkan languages

Remember that while we are concerned with the syntax of English, specifically, we want to have a more general perspective in mind. Regarding the structure of clauses and their heads, there is interesting evidence from other languages that we look at briefly in this subsection. We have already seen differences in selection between complementizers of the *whether* and *that* types in English. Many languages show additional effects when it comes to selection. Here, we consider both the selection of complementizers (C) by verbs from matrix clauses and the selection of inflection (I) by complementizers. Consider first Portuguese, a Western Romance language, and focus on what inflection is selected:

(19) (*Eu*) *quero*   ***que*** (*tu*) ***venhas***   *cá*.
      I   want.PRES.1SG.IND. that you come.PRES.2SG.SUBJ. here.
      'I want you to come here.' (Lit. 'I want that you come here.')
(20) (*Eu*) *sei*   ***que*** (*tu*) ***vens***   *cá*.
      I   know.PRES.1SG.IND. that you come.PRES.2SG.IND. here.
      'I know you're coming here.'

(Subjects can often be omitted in the Romance languages, but we leave this aside.) The embedded clause following *want* requires a different form of the verb from the embedded clause following *know* (exchanging them would be ungrammatical above). Why?

The difference is one of mood. One inflection is the subjunctive (another term used to describe such moods in Portuguese and elsewhere is *conjunctive*), and the other is the indicative, the 'normal' finite verb form. While the morphological forms of the subjunctive virtually died out in English (with the exception, for example, of the form *if I were...*), subjunctive-like verb forms are widely available crosslinguistically. It has been proposed that the indicative involves more speaker commitment regarding the truth of the complement than the subjunctive. This fits with the two types of embedding verbs illustrated by (19) and (20) above: one class of the 'want' type, the other of the 'know' type. The latter intuitively involves more speaker commitment regarding the truth of the complement than the former.

The Portuguese facts look as if one and the same C element, the complementizer *que* 'that', can select different forms of the inflected element in the embedded clause. But looking at Romanian, we can see the connection between embedding verb, complementizer, and inflection even more clearly.

Romanian is a language from the same family (Romance), but it belongs to the group of languages spoken on the Balkan Peninsula (languages from different families which developed common properties including more specialized complementizers). Consider the following examples:

(21)   *Vreau   să vină*.
        want.PRES.1SG.IND. that come.PRES.3SG.SUBJ.
        'I want her/him to come.' (Lit. 'I want that s/he come(s).')
(22)   *Știu   că vine*.
        know.PRES.1SG.IND. that come.PRES.3SG.IND.
        'I know s/he is coming.'

The complementizer positions in the embedded clauses in (21) and (22) are occupied by two different items in the same contexts as above. Thus the 'want' verb selects CPs headed by the complementizer *să*, which in turn selects the subjunctive I as the head of its IP complement. Verbs of the 'know' type, on the other hand, select *că* which in turn selects the indicative. These facts about mood selection, illustrated especially transparently by the Romanian examples, strengthen the theory that I and C are the heads of (smaller and larger) clauses.

Exercise. Conduct a comparative investigation on how mood inflection is selected in another language (e.g. German, Spanish, French).

Identify two groups of embedding predicates according to the distinct mood inflections selected. Can you find embedding verbs that allow both moods? Is an overt complementizer always required? What, if any, are the conditions under which it can be omitted? Is embedding always required for subjunctive inflection?

Further suggestion: you may consider a factor that influences mood selection in many languages of the world: negation in the main clause. If you have found such a language (you'll discover this quickly, by testing if negating the main clause can shift mood in the complement), describe the effect of negation on the complement as precisely as possible, too. □

2. Head movement

Section 1 has provided us with an understanding of the structure of clauses, but it has left us with an open question: how do verbs combine with their inflectional morphology? This section addresses this question. In the course of developing our answer, we encounter the first kind of transformation we talk about in this textbook: head movement.

2.1. V-to-I movement and affix hopping

Remember that we wrongly generate strings like *Mary -ed walk to school* with the IP rules from the preceding section. That is, inflection and verbs occupy separate positions in the clause structure, and we appear to have gotten the word order wrong. We now address this puzzle with inflection and verbs.

The auxiliary verbs *have* and *be* are particularly relevant when we consider verbs and inflection in the syntax of English. So first we answer the question: how do *have* and *be* combine with the inflectional endings they bear? We begin with a basic observation. As auxiliaries, *have* and *be* select verbal complements:

(23) a. *Mary has eaten chocolate.*
 b. *Sally had been working.*
 d. *The finder was rewarded.*
 c. *Peter is changing diapers.*

(24) have: V_{aux}, [_ VP(past part)#]
 be: V_{aux}, [_ VP(past/pres part)#]

We observe the following distribution in such sentences. A VP selected by *have* is headed by a past participle. VPs selected by *be* can be either past or present participles.

Next, consider the sentences in (25). The I position is occupied by a modal auxiliary. The complement of I is a VP, and in these examples, it is a VP headed by *have* and *be* respectively.

(25)   a.   *Mary should have eaten chocolate.*
         b.   *Ibrahim might be eating chocolate.*

Let us now bring in negation. When we negate (25), *have* and *be* obligatorily follow negation (the versions in parentheses with the asterisk show unacceptable structures, i.e. places where negation can**not** go):

(26)   a.   *Mary should **not** have (*not) eaten (*not) chocolate.*
         b.   *Ibrahim might **not** be (*not) eating (*not) chocolate.*

The order is modal > *not* > VP – a that is, more technically: I > not > VP. Empirically, we have now found a way to demarcate the territory between the verb and the I node. We assume that sentential negation is adjoined to VP, as indicated in (27) below. (This is a simplification - the syntax of negation is interesting in its own right, but we won't be concerned with it here.). What is important is that we can use *not* as a signpost to determine the relative position of auxiliaries and verbs.

(27)

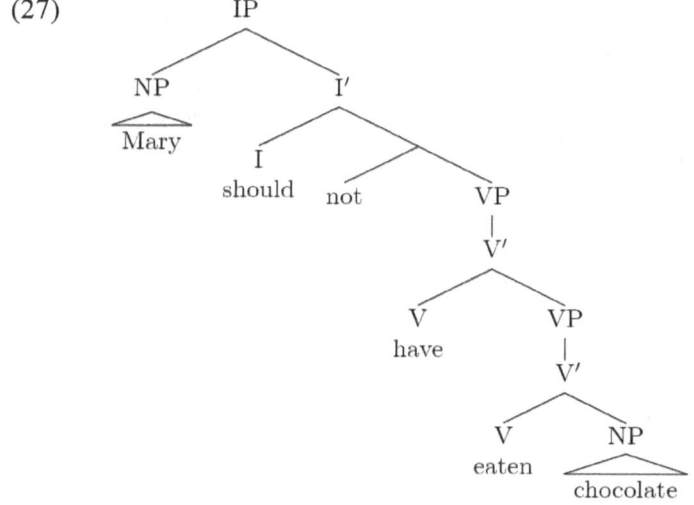

Let us now consider word order when there is no modal:

(28) a. *Mary (*not) is **not** eating (*not) chocolate.*
 b. *Mary (*not) has **not** eaten (*not) chocolate.*
 b. *Mary (*not) has **not** been (*not) eating (*not) chocolate.*

In this case, *have*/*be* bear inflectional morphology; and they must appear to the left of negation. Neither inflected auxiliary, *be* or *have*, can stay to the right of *not*. This is interesting. According to our reasoning above, the element to the left of *not* is in the I position (like the modal in (27)). Therefore *have* and *be* in (28) occupy the I position. But they were born into the syntax as heads of their own VP. To reconcile our findings, we propose that the auxiliary verb moves: it raises from its original V position to the I position.

> **Verb Raising**
> Move an auxiliary verb to I.

This allows us to see how inflection is combined with verbs for auxiliary verbs.

We now have a PS component and a transformational component to our grammar. The latter defines transformation rules, including movement rules. Transformations manipulate PS trees. So far, we have seen only one example of a transformational rule, verb raising. But we will see more examples shortly.

First, let's see what happens with main verbs. They also need to combine with inflectional morphology. However, they do not seem to rise to I. This is straightforward to test with the signpost of negation. Notice where the verb cannot appear in (29): preceding negation, in the I position.

(29) a. ** Mary likes not chocolate.*
 b. ** Sam went not to the store.*

Since the verb does not seem to be raised to I, we assume that the affix in I moves down to the verb instead. This is called affix hopping.

> **Affix hopping**
> Move I onto the following main verb if they are not separated by *not*.

70   *Clause structure and movement*

The presence of negation interferes with affix hopping, as seen in (30). So the rule has to be formulated with this proviso.

(30) a. *Mary not likes chocolate.*
     b. *Sam not went to the store.*

The rule of affix hopping allows us to combine inflection with main verbs, but not when negation is present. What happens then with main verbs and inflection? English has a special syntax for such cases:

(31) a. *Mary does not like chocolate.*
     b. *Sam did not go to the store.*

A semantically empty verb *do* is inserted to bear the inflectional morphology. We formulate the corresponding transformational rule as simply as possible:

Do-support
Attach *do* to the I node.

This rule only applies if all else fails (that is, when we can have neither affix hopping nor verb raising). We cannot have *do*-support when there is an auxiliary that could raise to I:

(32)   *Mary does not have eaten.*

None of these transformational rules always applies. When there is a modal auxiliary verb in the I position, none of them applies. However, something must force an affix to combine with a verb, otherwise we would generate *Mary -ed like chocolate*. Intuitively, it's the stray morpheme *-ed* sitting in I that is the problem. As a bound morpheme, the inflectional ending needs a host. The following filter states this intuition.

Stray Affix filter
A bound morpheme must be attached to a stem when the sentence is pronounced.

☙ **Exercise**. It seems unsatisfactory that *not* is outside the X' schema. And in fact, a detailed syntactic analysis of negation reveals that there are good reasons to think that negation falls under the X' schema like all other categories: it is a head which projects its own phrase, the negation phrase NegP. Syntacticians have argued that a proper analysis of negation in the English clause structure should look as in (E1):

(E1)

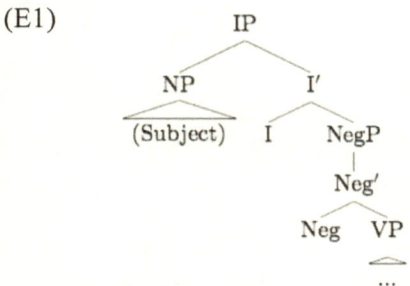

Data like (E2) can be used in support of the richer structure for negation in **Old English** (OE). Provide an analysis of (E2a) in terms of the structure in (E1). *Hint.* Remember head movement. Assume that the head of NegP undergoes movement to I together with the finite verb. (Example (E2b) is not needed to complete the task, but it provides background if you are interested: (i) negation could be marked via just one element; (ii) the combination *ne*+verb could move even beyond the subject position – the latter structures were common in OE declaratives, alongside structures like (E2a); come back to (E2b) after the next section; state where *ne+cuðe* is in it precisely.)

(E2) a. *He ne cuðe na þa boc.*
he NEG knew NEG the book
'He didn't know the book.' (Adapted after Fischer et al. 2000)
b. *Ne cuðe he boclice stafas.*
NEG knew he bookish characters
'He didn't know (any) letters.'
(YCOE corpus, cocathom2,+ACHom_6:58.175.1165)   ☐

2.2. I-to-C movement

This subsection introduces another movement transformation. This movement is involved in question formation in English. Notice the relative position of subjects and auxiliaries in (33)–(35):

72 *Clause structure and movement*

(33) a. *Should Mary eat chocolate?*
 b. *Mary should eat chocolate.*

(34) a. *Has Bill eaten spinach?*
 b. *Bill has eaten spinach.*

(35) a. *Is Mary eating Reeses?*
 b. *Mary is eating Reeses.*

The (a)-examples involve what is traditionally called Subject-Auxiliary Inversion; we can describe it informally as follows:

(33') **Subject-Auxiliary Inversion (SAI)**
 The auxiliary verb and the subject are inverted in yes-no questions.

In terms of our syntactic analysis, it looks like the content of the I node has moved across the subject. This is supported by the fact that main verbs cannot undergo this movement in (today's) English:

(36) a. * *Ate Mary chocolate?*
 b. * *Went Sam to the store?*

We wouldn't expect them to because they are not in I. Main verbs remain under V and are joined there by the affix. Since they do not rise to I, grammatical processes that apply to I cannot affect them. What actually happens is that *do*-support is once more involved:

(37) a. *Did Mary eat chocolate?*
 b. *Did Sam go to the store?*

This fits with what we have noted so far: the content of I moves across the subject in question formation. Apparently, the distance between verb and inflection is then too great for affix hopping to apply. Remember that that is a sensitive process that wants things close together (cf. the interference of negation). The only thing that can rescue us from a violation of the Stray Affix filter is *do*-support.

So where does the content of I move to? What is there to the left of the subject? The only position that our PS rules make available is C. Now notice that when there is a complementizer, SAI can't apply:

(38) a. *I wondered whether Mary has eaten the chocolate.*
b. **I wondered whether has Mary eaten the chocolate.*

It seems that a moved auxiliary and a complementizer are in complementary distribution. Here is an interesting fact that lends further support to this conclusion:

(39) a. *If I should die, give all my money to Greenpeace.*
If I had known, I wouldn't have participated.
b. *Should I die, give all my money to Greenpeace.*
Had I known, I wouldn't have participated.
c. **If should I die, give all my money to Greenpeace.*
**If had I known, I wouldn't have participated.*

Either there is a complementizer (*if*) or an inverted auxiliary in the position preceding the subject. But an attempt to have both at the same time yields an ungrammatical sentence. Hence we analyze SAI as the following transformation rule:

I-to-C movement
Move the content of I to C.

V-to-I and I-to-C movements are called head movement because it is the head of the phrase that moves. Notice that head movement can only take a head to the nearest empty head position:

(40) a. * *Read you have the book?* b. * *Been you have eating cookies?*

Examples such as those in (40) would represent movement of V to C, skipping the I head position. They are ruled out by the following constraint:

Head movement constraint
A word level category may be moved no farther than the head of the immediately dominating category.

2.3. Differences in head movement: The case of French

Once more it is interesting to consider a language that is slightly different from English - here, in the domain of head movement. Let us compare our findings for English with the situation in French:

(41) a. *Tu as donné le ballon à ton ami.*
you have given the balloon to your friend
'You gave the balloon to your friend.'
b. *As-tu donné le ballon à ton ami?*
have you given the balloon to your friend
'Did you give the balloon to your friend?'
c. *Vous travaillez dans le jardin.*
you work in the garden
'You work in the garden.'
d. *Travaillez-vous dans le jardin?*
work you in the garden
'Do you work in the garden?'

Here it looks like the main verb can rise past the subject. Did the main verb come from I or from inside VP?

(42) a. *Alphonse (ne) (*pas) travaille pas dans le jardin.*
Alphonse (NE) (*NOT) work NOT in the garden
'Alphonse doesn't work in the garden.'
b. *Alphonse (n)'a pas travaillé (*pas) dans le jardin.*
Alphonse (NE) has NOT worked (*NOT) in the garden
'Alphonse hasn't worked in the garden.'

Let's treat *pas* as the relevant negation and let's assume that its position is between the subject and VP, like in English. Then (42b) with an auxiliary is just like English – negation occurs between I, occupied by an auxiliary, and the VP. But (42a) isn't: negation occurs after the main verb rather than before. This suggests that in French (as in many other languages), the raising of the verb to I is not restricted to auxiliary verbs. Main verbs can do it too. Hence, main verbs can also undergo I-to-C movement. The difference between French and English can be narrowed down to just one small parameter within the verb raising rule. An idea that syntactic research has explored is that the reduced inflectional paradigms of English make the setting of the language more rigid, i.e. disallow movement in this domain.

Earlier stages of English allowed movement of main verbs too (not just of auxiliaries), i.e. they behaved like French.

🕒 **Exercise.** We have noticed a difference between French and English, but they are also similar e.g. in that they both have verb raising and I-to-C movement. Check by constructing both grammatical and ungrammatical examples whether they both obey the **head movement constraint**. You may also do this with another language you have access to. ☐

2.4. An intermediate summary and a note on the model of grammar

We have begun to introduce rules that change the trees that the PS component of the grammar generates: do-support, affix hopping, V-to-I movement, I-to-C movement. Such rules are called transformations (they 'transform' trees). Rules that move things about in the tree are called movement transformations. The movements produced by the V-to-I movement and I-to-C movement rules are called head movement: the head of a phrase moves to a position that is the head of the higher phrase in the tree. The input to a transformation is a tree, and its output is also a tree. For our tree representations, we assume the X' schema, as before. The input tree is called the **Deep Structure** or underlying structure (D-Structure for short). The output tree is called the **Surface Structure** (S-structure). This model of syntax is considerably more complex than a plain phrase structure grammar. It is also arguably more general. For example, verb raising and I-to-C movement allow us to capture the fact that the complement of *have* is a VP headed by a past participle, no matter whether *have* occurs in the V position, the I position, or the C position of the clause.

We will encounter further movement operations below. They will allow us to account for the dislocation of elements in natural language. Sometimes syntactic elements appear in places where we would not expect them to be – they seem to be "inverted", or disconnected from the elements with which they would normally form constituents. We have encountered one such phenomenon already with topicalization in Chapters I-2 and I-3. We consider it and other movements in the sections and chapters to come.

Right now, let us take a look at our model of grammar after these updates:

76 *Clause structure and movement*

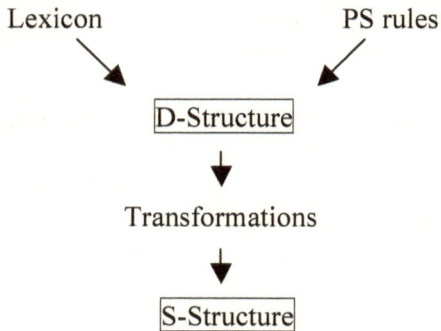

In addition, general principles like the projection principle and the Stray Affix filter constrain the grammar. Let us be precise about our representation of what happens when a movement transformation takes place. We now associate a sentence like *Has Mary eaten chocolate?* with two structures: a Deep Structure and an Surface Structure; cf. (43a,b).

(43)   a.

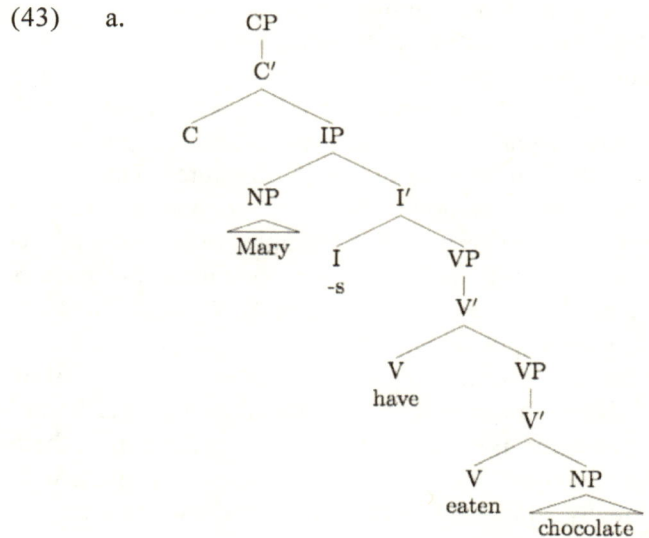

b.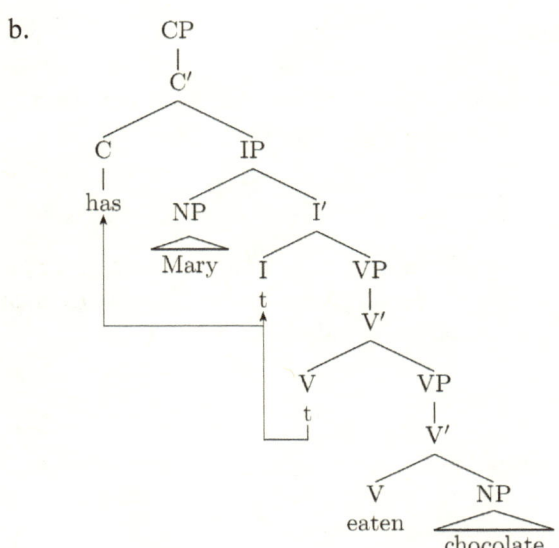

When we remove a category from a place in the tree, we leave the symbol *t* for "trace". This element is silent, i.e. it is not pronounced.

☻ **Exercise**. Offer tree representations for the following sentences (depending on whether or not a movement has taken place, this may be one PS tree only, or a Deep Structure and a Surface Structure):

(E3)   a.   *I may have been being selfish.*
        b.   *Could Jennifer solve the problem?*
        c.   *Is the new prime minister doing his job properly?*   ☐

3. Wh-movement

We consider one final transformation in this chapter, wh-movement. This movement is involved in question formation in English. It is not head movement, and it will introduce us to further properties of movement transformations.

3.1. Basic wh-questions

Among the syntactic structures that our grammar does not describe yet is another type of question. Consider the example in (44).

(44)   *What will Sue buy?*

Notice that SAI, that is, I-to-C movement, has applied here, just like in yes-no questions like (45). (*Sue* is the subject. The auxiliary *will* occurs to the left of the subject; hence it must have undergone SAI.)

(45)   *Will Sue buy ice cream?*

But in addition, *what* occurs at the very beginning of the sentence. That is, there is something to the left of the fronted auxiliary – to the left of C. *What* is a so-called wh-phrase. We revise our old CP rule (CP → C'), in which the CP only had the C' as its daughter, to include a specifier of CP, as in (46). This gives us a slot for the wh-phrase:

(46)   a.   CP → (XP) C'
        b.   C' → C IP

So the word *what* is sitting in the specifier of CP in (44). How did it get there? One possibility would be that the wh-phrase was generated in that position:

(47)   CP → (WhP) C'

The other option is to say that like the auxiliary, it started out elsewhere and got moved to Spec-CP (the specifier of CP). We argue for the second option:

If the wh-phrase were generated in Spec-CP, we would expect the IP of that clause to look just like any other IP. But this means that we expect sentences like (48):

(48)   a.   **Which book did Molly read the magazine?*
        b.   **What will Sue buy the pineapple?*

Verbs like *read* and *buy* select a complement.

(49) a. *read*: [_(NP)#]
 b. *buy*: [_NP#]
 c. * *Sue will buy.*

The verb *buy* seems to violate its subcategorization frame in (44). But intuitively, it doesn't: the complement of *buy* in (44) is the wh-phrase in the beginning of the sentence. And providing the verb with the object it would normally require, as in (48), leads to ungrammaticality.

(48) shows that we cannot have a complement next to the verb and, at the same time, the wh-phrase. Intuitively, we have too many read things or bought things. The wh-phrase wants to fulfill the role of the complement. The same point (that the wh-phrase fills the role of the complement) can be made in a slightly different way too. Consider (50).

(50) a. $^{??}$*Molly read the pineapple.*
 b. $^{??}$*Joe ate the magazine.*

These are odd (hence the question marks) because the complement NP is semantically unsuitable. Verbs are selective in that the verb meaning has to combine with the complement meaning in a sensible way. The sentences in (51) are odd in exactly the same way.

(51) a. $^{??}$*Which pineapple did Molly read?*
 b. $^{??}$*Which magazine did Joe eat?*

So the wh-phrase acts as the complement of the verb, except it appears in the wrong place: all the way to the front instead of as a sister to the verb. Movement allows us to reconcile the complement status of the wh-phrase with the word order. We assume the following rule:

Wh-movement
Move a wh-phrase to the specifier of CP.

Intuitive support for the movement analysis comes from so-called echo-questions: (52) is acceptable e.g. in a context in which you didn't hear what somebody just said.

(52) *Molly bought what?*

In such structures, the wh-phrase does occur in the complement position.

Note that generating *What will Sue buy?* involves two transformations. A derivation of the sentence (a series of tree structures) is given below. There is an intermediate step between Deep Structure and Surface Structure.

(53) a. [$_{CP}$ [$_{C'}$ [$_{IP}$ *Sue will* [$_{VP}$ *buy what*]]]]
     b. [$_{CP}$ [$_{C'}$ *will* [$_{IP}$ *Sue t* [$_{VP}$ *buy what*]]]]
     c. [$_{CP}$ *what* [$_{C}$ *will* [$_{IP}$ *Sue t* [$_{VP}$ *buy t*]]]]

We put a *t* for "trace" in the place in which a constituent started its movement. Since more than one thing may move, as in (53), we put an index on a trace (t_1, t_2 etc.) and the same index next to the corresponding moved constituent (to indicate the connection). A proper representation of the S-Structure of our example is thus (54). (We discuss such structures in more detail in Part II.)

(54) [$_{CP}$ *what* 2 [$_{C'}$ *will*$_1$ [$_{IP}$ *Sue* t_1 [$_{VP}$ *buy* t_2]]]]

Above, we have chosen an example with an auxiliary. Note that if we choose one without an auxiliary, SAI in wh-questions behaves in exactly the same way as in yes-no questions: do-support is used.

(55) *What did Sue buy?*

Wh-movement is a well studied transformation that will occupy us for a little while longer. Let's first make the rule a bit more precise: we need to know what counts as a wh-phrase.

3.2. Wh-phrases

Which expressions can be affected by the transformation wh-movement? First, so-called wh-pronouns (*who, what, where, when, why, how*) can be moved to Spec-CP. Second, the movement can affect an NP with a wh-phrase in its specifier position (*which book, whose coat, which woman's son*). Third, a PP whose NP complement is a wh-phrase (*in which book, from whom, about whose brother*) can also be found in the Spec-CP position in questions.

Other things are not wh-phrases. In particular, not everything that contains a wh-word can be moved to Spec-CP to form a question:

(56)   a.   * *A rumor that Bill loves who did you overhear?*
         b.   * *Buy which coat will Molly?*
         c.   * *That Bill loved who does Molly believe?*

That should make clear how the rule applies in simple wh-questions. Next, we discuss more complex cases of wh-questions, which involve embedded clauses.

3.3. Embedded wh-questions

Consider some examples of embedded clauses that are not questions first:

(57)   a.   *Sally heard that Bill failed the exam.*
         b.   *Sally said that Sue got an A.*

We now know that the complements of these verbs are CPs. The PS rule below describes the structures in (57).

(58)   V' → V CP

The above examples are embedded statements. There are also embedded questions, in particular embedded wh-questions:

(59)   a.   *Sally asked which exam Bill failed.*
         b.   *Sally wonders what Sue will buy.*

The sentences in (59) are called embedded questions because the embedded clauses (the complements of the verbs *ask* and *wonder*) are questions. The main or matrix clauses in (59) are not questions (the overall sentences are statements). There is an important syntactic difference between these embedded questions and matrix questions: I-to-C movement does not apply. We get neither an auxiliary moving across the subject nor do we get do-support.

(60)   a.   * *Sally knows which exam did Bill fail.*
         b.   * *Sally wonders what will Sue buy.*

82   *Clause structure and movement*

There is also an important parallel between embedded and unembedded questions: wh-movement takes place in both cases.

🕒 **Exercise**. What is the derivation of (59b)? Can you extend the syntactic analysis developed in this section to the relative clauses below?

(E4)   *Pat likes the man* [CP *who Sally will invite*].
(E5)   *The fruit* [CP *which Sally will buy*] *is expensive.*   ☐

3.4. Complex wh-questions: an analysis and corroborating evidence from German

Next, consider a sentence like (61).

(61)   *What will Sally say that Sue bought?*

The whole structure above is a question. We have a fronted wh-phrase *what* and I-to-C movement has applied in the matrix clause. We also have an embedded clause, and the movement of the wh-phrase must have started out there: note that *what* is the complement of *bought*. This is called a "long distance wh-question" because the wh-phrase has moved 'a long distance' out of an embedded clause. How does wh-movement derive this question? We consider two possibilities:

(i)   wh-movement applies once and moves *what* from the complement position of *bought* to the specifier of the matrix CP (**long movement**)
(ii)   wh-movement applies twice: first *what* moves to the specifier of the embedded CP, and then from there to the matrix CP (**step-by-step movement** – there are two CPs, hence two steps)

The two trees below represent the Surface Structures according to the two possibilities.

(62)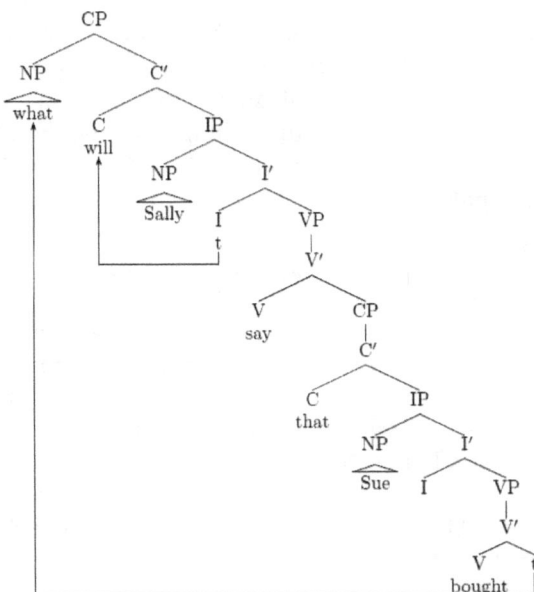

(63)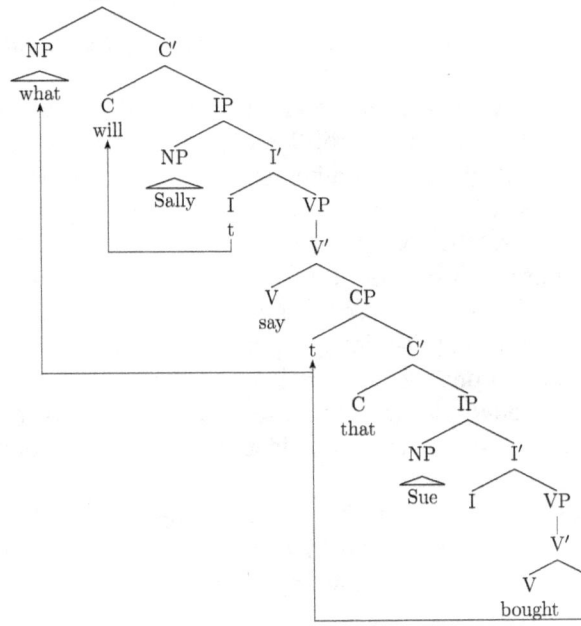

84 *Clause structure and movement*

We argue here for the second option. First we show that the second option must exist, and then we show that the first option cannot exist. We begin by showing that the second option is available. To do so, we look at so-called partial wh-movement. Partial wh-movement is a question type that exists in many languages including Hindi, Iraqi Arabic, Hungarian and German. We consider examples from German. Many speakers from Southern Germany can produce the following patterns of wh-questions:

(64)   a.   *Wen   glaubt   Maria, dass Hans eingeladen hat?*
               who.ACC believes   Maria   that   Hans   invited   has
         b.   *Was glaubt   Maria, wen   Hans eingeladen hat?*
               what believes Maria   who.ACC Hans invited   has
         c.   *Wen   glaubt   Maria, wen   Hans eingeladen hat?*
               who.ACC believes   Maria   who.ACC Hans invited   has
             'Who does Maria believe that Hans invited?'

Was is a question marker. All examples in (64) are matrix questions and synonymous with the English long distance question. But in (64b,c), we see a wh-phrase occurring inside the embedded clause. At the same time, that wh-phrase is fronted inside the embedded clause. It is not in the complement position of the verb. A structure for (64c) is sketched in (65).

(65)   [CP *wen* [C' *glaubt Maria* [CP *wen* [C' *Hans t eingeladen hat*]]]]

One difference between German and English is that there is no do-support although we have a main verb. We will discuss this aspect of German syntax in Part II. Right now, another aspect of (65) is more important. In the embedded Spec-CP a wh-phrase *wen*, 'who', occurs that looks just like the wh-phrase in the matrix Spec-CP. We may think of this as a copy of the fronted wh-phrase. It occurs in just the place where option (ii) from above (in (63)) would put a trace. We suggest that this copy is just a pronounced trace. Traces are syntactically present but normally not audible. This one actually gets pronounced. This is evidence that a wh-phrase that starts out in the embedded clause, aiming to undergo wh-movement to the matrix clause, moves through the embedded Spec-CP. We conclude that option (ii) exists.

We now introduce an argument that makes it implausible that option (i) is available (recall, this is the option that involves one long movement of the wh-phrase as in (62)). Consider the ungrammatical sentence (66):

(66) * *What does Mary wonder where John bought?*

What would the two options predict about generating (66)? Option (i) would involve movement of *what* from the complement position of *buy* directly to matrix Spec-CP. If option (i) existed, the sentence should be fine.

(67)   Long movement of wh-phrase skipping embedded Spec-CP (ungrammatical):

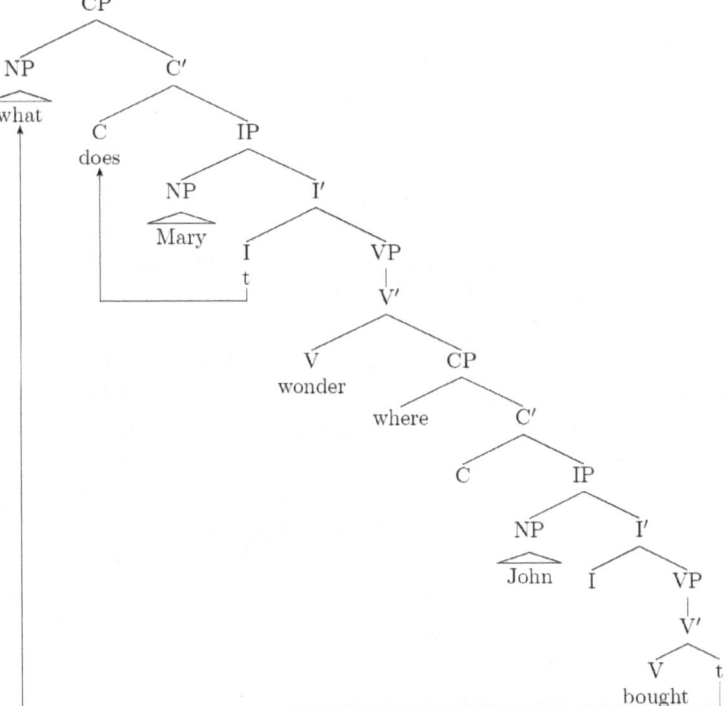

Option (ii) involves movement of *what* to the embedded Spec-CP first; however, that position is occupied by *where*. We cannot fill the same position twice. The prediction here is that the sentence should be unacceptable because the trace of *what* and *where* cannot both occupy the embedded Spec-CP at the same time. This is confirmed by the intuitions that speakers of English have for such sentences: they are unacceptable. Only the second option correctly predicts that the sentence is bad. Therefore, long wh-movement must be excluded. We must make sure that all wh-movement is local, i.e. that it passes through intermediate relevant positions. These are Spec-CPs. We revise the rule as specified below and keep in mind that it can apply in repeated steps.

> **Wh-movement** (revised)
> Move a wh-phrase to the nearest specifier of CP.

A terminological note: A structure out of which we cannot move is called an **island,** and the one just discussed is a wh-island.

🕒 **Exercise.** Offer tree representations for the sentences in (E6). A Surface Structure tree will suffice – but include both head and wh-movements as well as all traces.

(E6) a. *Which route did you climb?*
 b. *Which candidate did the delegates vote for?*
 b'. *For which candidate did the delegates vote?*
 c. *What colors did Faye say she liked?* ☐

🕒 **Exercise.** *All* is a so-called **floating quantifier.** It belongs to the wh-phrase *what* in the West Ulster English examples in (E7) (cf. McCloskey 2000) and requires you to spell out all the things asked for completely in your response. Other than that, the questions in (E7) are the same as questions without *all*. Determine if the examples in (E7) lend support to the step-by-step or the long-movement version of wh-movement.

(E7) a. *What all do you think that he'll say that we should buy?*
 b. *What do you think all that he'll say that we should buy?*
 c. *What do you think that he'll say all that we should buy?*
 d. *What do you think that he'll say that we should buy all?* ☐

> ☞ THE BASICS BOX: *Clauses and movement*
> ✓ The head of sentences in English is I, and the sentence is analyzed as an IP. I is occupied by modals, *to* and inflection.
> ✓ Larger clauses in English are CPs, and the complementizer C is their head.
> ✓ Auxiliary verbs *have/be* move from V to I. Affix hopping combines main verbs with inflection. If all else fails, do-support applies.

> ✓ The content of I undergoes I-to-C movement in questions.
> ✓ Languages may vary w.r.t. the expressions that a movement transformation applies to (e.g. V-to-I movement in French vs. English).
> ✓ Movement transformations allow us to understand the displacement we observe in wh-questions. Wh-movement moves a wh-phrase to Spec-CP in a stepwise fashion.

4. Selected references

This chapter introduces part of what is called the T-model of the grammar. An interface with semantics and one with phonology are usually attached to it (cf., e.g., Haegeman and Guéron 1999). The interface with semantics is discussed below. Unlike some of the early literature, we do not attach anything 'deep' to Deep Structure. We use the term for the PS structure before transformations have been applied. Surface Structure is the structure after such transformations have been applied.

Wh-movement (cf. Chomsky 1977) is a much studied area in syntax. One focus in the literature is its step-by-step character. One of the interesting empirical pieces of evidence we have seen, wh-copying, is not available in English adult language. But developmental stages in language acquisition include the option; cf. Thornton (1990), Crain and Lillo-Martin (1999), Snyder (2007). See Lutz, Müller and von Stechow (2000) on partial wh-movement. There are many further aspects of variation between languages in wh-clauses. While English displaces exactly one wh-phrase, other languages do not move their wh-phrases at all (so called *in-situ* strategy, cf. Bayer 2007 for a recent overview), and yet others can front multiple wh-phrases (see Dayal 2007 for an overview article on yet another large topic).

Influential readings on head movement differences (English vs. French) are Emonds (1978) and Pollock (1989). For earlier stages of English and French as well as reference to the Scandinavian languages see Roberts (1993). Bobaljik (2002) explores the idea that rich inflection and verb movement may be related; cf. e.g. Heycock and Wallenberg (2013) for recent discussion. The major reading for the head movement constraint is Travis (1984). Baker (1985) discusses the relationship between inflections and so-called functional heads (I and C in our inventory) in the languages of the world. It proposes the so-called 'Mirror Principle': when there are several functional items, their linearization is claimed to be – by and large – the inverse of the realization of corresponding inflectional morphemes.

The idea that auxiliaries and inflections are in complementary distribution has been around for as long as the generative tradition. Let us note that the label adopted here (I) corresponds to much of the GB tradition. Aux would be a more old-fashioned label, and T (from "tense") a more fashionable one today, perhaps. There have also been versions with multiple such heads (Pollock 1989). We will approach some of the semantic issues of temporality in Chapter II-7.

In addition to being in complementary distribution with inflection on verbs, the modals have no productive inflection on themselves. This is due to the origin of the modals as a special class in Old English (see Roberts 1993, Warner 1993, Gergel 2009, among many others, for the syntax of the modals in the history of English).

We have considered *not* as the sentence negation and have not distinguished it here from *-n't,* the reduced form. A classic is Zwicky and Pullum (1983). A key issue there is whether this is really just a reduced (clitic) form or inflection. Haegeman and Guéron (1999) offer an interesting syntactic proposal. On the syntax of negation in Old English, Fischer et al. (2000) is a textbook with pointers to further literature.

If you are interested in the patterns of mood inflection we have discussed: Siegel (2009) offers a discussion of selectional patterns in Romance and Balkan languages. See also Villalta (2008) and Portner (2011) for further semantic considerations for some of the data (ideally after you have taken more semantics).

A point that is minor here, but with connections to upcoming chapters, is the complementary distribution of complementizers and I-to-C movement (**If had I known,* ...). Movement to C is prominent in Germanic, and we discuss this in the second part (see references on verb-second in Germanic including early English in Chapter II-2). Today's English is more complex. Examples of the type which we noted in the main text are much more restricted than e.g. in German; and they have a hypothetical, often counterfactual flavor. This fact is observed in Iatridou and Embick (1995). English also has other constructions involving subject-auxiliary inversion which require more structural refinement than we have now. If you are interested, a starting point is the VP internal subject hypothesis introduced in Chapter I-8; you can find further references there.

Chapter I-5
Goals and methods in semantics

> ... 'Tis wisdom to conceal our meaning.
> (Edward in Shakespeare's *Henry VI*)

This chapter gets us started on developing the semantics component of the grammar. In the first section, we introduce the concept of sentence meanings that we will use from here on. We also introduce a centerpiece of modern semantics, Frege's principle of compositionality. The second section is a mini-tutorial on set theory. Selected references are given in the final section.

1. What we have to account for

It is part of our knowledge of language that we associate linguistic expressions with meanings. We normally take this for granted, in the same way as we take our ability to produce and parse linguistic expressions for granted (to recognize things as part of a language, or as not part of it). In the preceding chapters, we have taken a step back from that unreflected attitude and asked what being able to produce and understand linguistic structures actually implies. We have looked at the formal part of our ability, i.e. the syntax. From now on, we will think about what it means to associate linguistic expressions with a particular meaning. For this, we need to know what meanings are, and what it means to know the meaning of sentences and phrases.

1.1. Elements of reasoning: contradiction and consequence

A first clue towards the meaning of sentences is to be found in the notion of consistency which we discussed informally in Chapter I-1. We introduce an informal definition below (remember that *iff* stands for "if and only if"):

> **Consistency**
> A set of sentences is consistent iff the members of the set could all be true together in some possible situation.

An example of something that is not consistent is (1):

(1) *Sally was born in Tübingen and Sally was not born in Tübingen.*

Below we offer a slightly more formal definition of consistency. We use the standard notation for sets (e.g. {Homer, Marge} is the set consisting of Homer and Marge, the sign $\cap$ stands for "intersected with", and the sign $\emptyset$ is used for the empty set (we remind you in more detail of the necessary background on sets in section 2)).

> **A more formal version of consistency**
> Consider a set of sentences $A = \{\alpha_1, \ldots \alpha_n\}$. For any sentence α, $[[\alpha]]$ is the set of possible situations in which α is true. The set of sentences A is consistent iff $[[\alpha_1]] \cap \ldots \cap [[\alpha_n]] \neq \emptyset$.

In (2) there is a set of sentences which is not consistent, as a further example:

(2) *I have invented an amazing new sedative which makes people faster and more excited.*

Example (2) is not consistent (we say that it is contradictory), because there is no situation in which everything claimed in (2) is true. Notice how your knowledge of when a sentence would be true guides your intuitions.
Another application of the same concept - the set of situations in which a sentence is true - is used in the following definition:

> **Logical consequence**
> A set of sentences $A = \{\alpha_1, \ldots \alpha_n\}$ logically implies a sentence β iff there is no possible situation in which all the members of A are true, but β is false.

The sentences in A are called the premises, and β is called the conclusion. We also say that β (logically) follows from A. An example of logical consequence is the following, where (3)–(5) are the premises and (6) the conclusion:

(3) *The Earth is either round or not round.*
(4) *If the Earth were round, then many things would just fall off it.*
(5) *Things do not just fall off the Earth.*
(6) *The Earth is not round.*

A more formal definition of logical consequence is once more given below (where $\subseteq$ stands for "is a subset of"):

A more formal definition of logical consequence
A set of sentences $A = \{\alpha_1, \ldots \alpha_n\}$ logically implies a sentence β iff $[\![\alpha_1]\!] \cap \ldots \cap [\![\alpha_n]\!] \subseteq [\![\beta]\!]$.

We offer two more simple examples of logical consequence below. The conclusion (9) logically follows from (7)–(8) and the conclusion (12) is implied by the premises (10)–(11). (Notice that to say the conclusion follows from the premises is not the same thing as saying that it is true.)

(7) *All good skiers are Norwegian.*
(8) *Jan is a good skier.*
(9) *Jan is Norwegian.*

(10) *All good skiers are Norwegian.*
(11) *All Norwegians like salmon.*
(12) *All good skiers like salmon.*

Judgments about consistency and logical consequence are examples of our ability to reason. What is important about them for our purposes is that our reasoning starts from an intuition about what would have to be the case in order for the claims made to be true. And we go on to try to decide whether all claims could be true together, and whether whenever all premises are true, the conclusion is also true. Fundamental to such reasoning is our ability to associate sentences with the conditions under which they would be true. This ability can equivalently be described as the ability to understand which situations are described by a sentence, or in which possible situations the sentence would be considered true. The set of possible situations in which a sentence is true is so fundamental for all interpretive processes that semantic theory considers it to be the **meaning of a sen-**

tence. It is what we will call the meaning of a sentence from here on. We write this as [[S]].

> **Sentence meanings**
> The meaning of a sentence S, [[S]], is the set of situations in which S is true.

🕒 **Exercise.** Decide and justify for each of the sets of sentences in (E1) whether they are consistent, and whether in examples (E2)-(E4) the last sentences follows as a conclusion from the previous sentences (the premises) or not.

(E1) a. *It would be wrong to censor violent TV programs, because people's behavior isn't really affected by what they see on the screen. All the same it would be a good idea to have more programs showing positive things like community efforts and environmental activities, because it would help people to act in a more constructive way.*
 b. *The surface of the Earth is flat (apart from mountains, oceans and other relatively small bumps and dips). When people think they have sailed around the Earth, all they have done is set out from one place and finish up in another place exactly like the one they started out from, but several thousand miles away.*

(E2) a. *My car doesn't start.*
 b. *When Jones's car didn't start, the trouble was with the spark plugs.*
 c. *Cars like mine have this as a common problem.*
 d. *The fault in the car is the spark plugs.*

(E3) a. *I can go on holiday by car or by plane.*
 b. *If I go on holiday by plane, then I will get there faster, but cannot take much luggage.*
 c. *If I go by car, I can take more luggage.*
 d. *A successful holiday requires that I take the right clothing.*
 e. *I couldn't take the right clothing on the plane.*
 f. *If my holiday is to be a success, I must go by car.*

(E4) a. *If Sandy failed the course and he went to the professor's office hours before, then the professor was unhelpful.*
   b. *Sandy had been to that professor's office hours.*
   c. *That professor is commonly considered unhelpful.*
   d. *Sandy failed the course.* ◻

1.2. Several meanings: ambiguity

There is another type of fact that makes us consciously take note of how we associate sentences with meanings. That is when expressions can be associated with more than one meaning: ambiguity. We have seen instances of ambiguity in the preceding chapters. We return to it briefly here because it makes our semantic ability look less trivial.

To give an example, imagine somebody's will containing a bequest of:

(13) *five rings and rugs*

There could be considerable room for argument regarding how this is to be read! In fact, there have been court cases centered on such ambiguities with linguists as expert witnesses. Try to state precisely two different bequests that could have been intended.

Two further examples are given below. You should be able to see for both examples how the ambiguity arises from different syntactic structures that can be associated with the sentences.

(14) *We fed her chicken nuggets.*
   a. *To her chicken, we fed nuggets.*
   b. *To her, we fed chicken nuggets.*

(15) *We discussed the man on TV.*
   a. *We discussed the man who is on TV.*
   b. *On TV, we discussed the man.*

☺ **Exercise.** Each of the following sentences is ambiguous. Paraphrase the different readings. Try to identify what the source of that ambiguity is, i.e. whether it is lexical, structural, or whether it has to do with reference.

(E5) a. *Lisa talked to Molly about her grades.*
   b. *I didn't drop my linguistics class because it meets at 8:30 am.*

c. *The dean told the police to stop drinking on campus.*
d. *The inspector took a picture of the bank.*
e. *Who did the basketball coach want to shoot?*
f. *They seem to enjoy boiling champagne.* □

A sentence can be associated with more than one meaning – i.e. there can be different sets of situations in which it would be true. This is another part of our task: describe when and why this happens. How do we derive that some sentences can have more than one meaning?

1.3. Method: compositionality

According to what we have said so far, here is one way of stating the task of semantics: specify for each sentence exactly which set of situations it describes. Given that the language under investigation is English, this means that, if S is a well-formed sentence of English, we have to state what [[S]] is.

Why don't we just sit down and list, for all sentences of English, the meanings that they intuitively have?

Keep in mind that English has infinitely many sentences. For the purposes of syntax, we have concluded that we must find a systematic way of generating all English sentences. Syntax does that by defining rules that build all possible sentences up from their component parts. Well, similarly, we must find a systematic way of relating them to their meanings. A list will not work. What would work instead? We have the component parts already from our syntactic analysis – so here is the idea: We construct the meaning of the sentence on the basis of the meanings of the parts. This is parallel to how we construct the whole structure by putting together the structural parts. We identify the meanings of the constituents and combine them to form the meaning of the whole. This is, in essence, the principle of compositionality, which semanticists owe to Gottlob Frege:

The Principle of Compositionality
The meaning of a sentence is determined by the meanings of its parts and the way they are put together.

This leads to a refined formulation of our goal: The task of semantics is to predict the meanings of sentences on the basis of the meanings of the lexical items used and their syntactic structure. We have an idea now what the meaning of a sentence is: the set of possible situations in which it is true. We still need to find out what the meanings of other linguistic expressions are – nouns, verbs, phrases of various types, etc. It turns out they can all be characterized in set theoretic terms. Hence we need some basic set theory to proceed. The next section offers a tutorial on basic set theory.

1.4. Semantic and pragmatic meaning

Before we move on to the more technical material, there is one more point we should make. People mean rather different things when they talk about meaning. There are uses of the word *meaning* that we will not be concerned with here. Among them are uses we might call pragmatic. To illustrate, consider an utterance of *It's raining*. Smith can use *It's raining*, and so can Jones and Müller. Now Smith may use this as a piece of advice for her interlocutor to take his umbrella with him. But that is just one possibility, among many others. Jones may use such a sentence to make conversation. Müller may do so to try to come across as British.

But there is also a simple, literal meaning that can be associated with the sentence, independently of the particular pragmatic usage. This notion of meaning is the one we are interested in here. The meaning of the sentence in this sense is the set of situations in which it is raining, as we have decided in the preceding subsections. We also call this the semantics or the denotation of the sentence. We present it as in (16).

(16)   [[*It's raining*]] = {s: it is raining in s}

It is part of our linguistic knowledge that we are able to associate sentences with their truth conditions. The chapters to come model this aspect of our linguistic abilities. We do not want to pretend that this is all there is to linguistic meaning. But it is the aspect of linguistic meaning that we concentrate on in this book. We feel justified in selecting semantics, and in taking a constrained view of meaning, because semantics is the basis of everything else. Take another look at Smith: her intention may be to give advice. But she is able to do so on the basis of the literal meaning of the sentence, because the literal meaning allows an inferential process that leads to the intended piece of advice. Her interlocutor may reason roughly like this: "Smith says that it is raining. I can see that for myself, so why is she telling me this? She must have more in mind than she actually said. What could be relevant about the rain? I intend to go out. I might get wet. Smith must have intended to suggest I take an umbrella." The truth conditions of a sentence are the foundation upon which further notions of meaning are based.

2. Tutorial on sets

2.1. Sets and elements

We can define a set as a collection of unordered items called the members or **elements** of the set. Anything can be in a set; consider (17):

(17) $A = \{y, 6, \text{Jürgen Klinsmann}\}$

The set A as given in (17) is the set that contains the letter y, the number six, and the person Jürgen Klinsmann. A given object either is or is not an element of a given set; the notation for this is as follows:

(18) $y \in A$: y is an element of A
(19) $y \notin A$: y is not an element of A

Sets may be specified by listing their members:

(20) $\{3, 4, 5\}$: the set that contains 3, 4 and 5

or by specifying a criterion for membership. The second way of specifying what is in a set is especially useful for large or infinite sets.

(21)   a. $\{x: 3 \leq x \leq 5\}$: the set of all x such that x is larger than or equal to 3 and smaller than or equal to 5
        b. $\{x: x \text{ is a natural number}\}$: the set of all x such that x is a natural number
        c. $\{x: x \text{ is a person in room 027 of the Brechtbau}\}$: the set of people who are in 027 of the Brechtbau
            (This is a lecture hall in Tübingen where this course has been taught in the past; transfer the example to your own situation.)

Sets are identical iff they have the same members.

(22) {Woglinde, Wellgunde, Flosshilde} = {x: x is a Rhinemaiden}

The empty set is the set that has no members; the usual notation for it is ∅ or {}.

We can count how many things are in a set. This is called the **cardinality** of the set and the shorthand notation is card(A). For example, for the set S = {a, {2}, Ian Somerhalder}, card(S) = 3. Let us practice a bit and notice the following facts about S:

(23) a. 2 ∉ S
      b. {2} ∈ S
      c. a ∈ S
      d. ∅ ∉ S

2.2. Relations between sets

Sets can stand in different relationships to one another. We begin with set inclusion, the subset relation (which you have come across in our definition of logical consequence):

> A is a **subset** of B (A ⊆ B) iff every member of A is also a member of B.

Taking S to be once more {a, {2}, Ian Somerhalder}, the statements in (24) hold and those in (25) do not.

(24) a. {{2}} ⊆ S
      b. ∅ ⊆ S
      c. {3} ⊆ {3, 4, 5}
      d. S ⊆ S

(25) a. 2 ⊆ S
      b. {2} ⊆ S
      c. 3 ⊆ {3, 4, 5} (but: 3 ∈ {3, 4, 5} holds)

Note that the empty set is a subset of every set and every set is a subset of itself. We end this subsection with two more definitions:

> Two sets A and B are **identical** A = B iff A is a subset of B and B is a subset of A.
> Two sets A and B are **disjoint** iff there is nothing that is both a member of A and a member of B.

2.3. Operations on sets

If you remember the notion of intersection from our discussion of consistency above, you will realize that for the definition of disjointness, we can say that the intersection of two disjoint sets is the empty set. Intersection is one of the basic operations on sets defined below:

> The **union** of A and B, A ∪ B is the set that contains exactly those elements that are in A or in B or in both.
> The **intersection** of A and B, A ∩ B is the set that contains exactly those elements that are in A and in B.
> The **complement** of A in B, B \ A is the set that contains exactly those elements that are in B but not in A.

More formal definitions are given in (27)-(29) together with Venn diagrams to illustrate the three operations. Two arbitrary sets A and B are represented as a Venn diagram in (26). They each could contain any sorts of elements, it doesn't matter which.

(26)   a.   Sets A and B
        b.

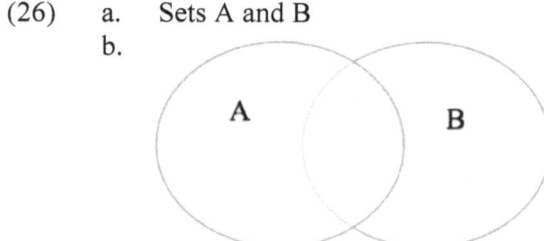

The union, the intersection, and the complement (of A in B) are given in (27)-(29). The set-theoretic notation is followed by the Venn diagram.

(27) a. Union of A and B: A ∪ B = {x: x ∈ A or x ∈ B}
b.

(28) a. A ∩ B = {x: x ∈ A and x ∈ B}
b.
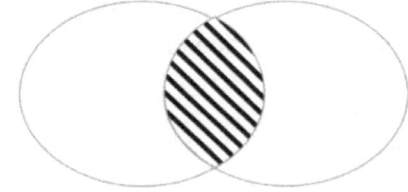

(29) a. B \ A = {x: x ∉ A and x ∈ B}
b.
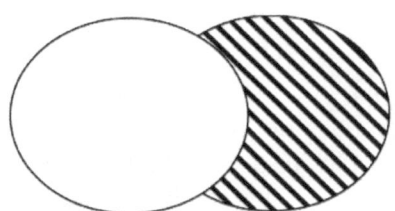

⊕ **Exercise.** *Set-theoretic operations.* Assume the sets in (E6) below and specify the following: M ∩ N, O ∩ M, M ∪ N, O ∪ N, M ∪ ∅, ∅ ∩ N.

(E6) a. M = {3, 4}
b. N = {7, a}
c. O = {4, 7}   □

⊕ **Exercise.** Do the following tasks for the sets in (E7) below: (i) list the members of P, Q and R; (ii) List P ∩ Q, P ∩ R, Q ∩ R, P ∪ Q, P ∪ R, Q ∪ R. Finally, state whether Q is a subset of P and whether R is a subset of P or Q.

(E7) a. P = {x: x is a woman and x is in this room}
b. Q = {x: x is a person and x is in this room
 and x is shorter than 1,70m}

c. R = {x: x is a person and x is in this room
and x's first name includes the letter *e*} □

☞ THE BASICS BOX: *Goals and methods in semantics*

✓ The meaning of a sentence is the set of situations in which the sentence is true.
✓ The task of semantics can be characterized as specifying for each sentence in the language under investigation its truth conditions.
✓ Since there are infinitely many sentences, truth conditions of sentences have to be derived compositionally: the meaning of a sentence is determined by the meanings of its syntactic components and the way they are combined.
✓ Meanings can be modeled with the mathematical tools of naive set theory.

---

3. Selected references

Gottlob Frege is credited with the principle of compositionality (cf. Szabó 2013 for recent discussion). Truth conditional semantics takes its starting point from Alfred Tarski's theory of truth (Tarski 1935). Richard Montague's work has been particularly influential on the modern tradition of formal semantics (Montague 1970, 1973 and much subsequent work; cf. also the papers in Montague and Thomason 1974 and Dowty, Wall and Peters 1981 for an introduction).

There is a large and lively area of research concerned with the interface between structure and interpretation in natural language (the syntax/semantics interface). Heim and Kratzer's (1998) introduction to compositional semantics (plus von Fintel and Heim's (2011) follow-up for the area of intensional semantics) probably comes closest to our own perspective. Other introductions to semantics include e.g. Grewendorf, Hamm and Sternefeld 1987, Chierchia and McConnell Ginet 2000 as well as Zimmermann and Sternefeld 2013. The edition of *Formal Semantics* by Portner and Partee (2002) offers a collection of original key readings in the study of meaning.

The tradition of investigating the logical properties of inferences goes all the way back antiquity. We refer here to Gamut (1991), Partee et al.

(1990), Krifka (2007) for discussion of issues in logic conducted in connection with the concerns of modern semantic theory. Portner (2005) and Krifka (2007) offer accessible introductions to the question of what meanings are, and what the place of semantics is in the bigger landscape of meaning related research. The investigation of pragmatic meaning is largely beyond the scope of this book, but that is not to say that it isn't an interesting and active area of research. Portner's and Krifka's introductions discuss some of the key issues. Useful resources on the interplay between pragmatics and semantics include Horn and Ward (2008) with a handbook collection regarding the topics in the field and Kadmon (2000) as an investigation into the connection between pragmatic phenomena and semantic meaning. On the semantics/pragmatics interface, see also Chierchia's (2013) monograph and Sauerland's (2012) overview article on the computation of scalar implicatures and the many references they contain.

An introduction to basic set theory can be found in Partee et al. (1990). Crain and Lillo-Martin (1999) is the source of some of the ambiguous examples above. Finally, this chapter owes a lot to Angelika Kratzer's lecture notes on semantics, both conceptually and in presentation. She generously shared them with us in 1997. Some of the original examples can still be found in the present discussion and their influence is visible in this and the following chapters.

Chapter I-6
Composing sentence meanings – first steps

Contrariwise, if it was so, it might be; and if it were so, it would be; but as it isn't, it ain't. That's logic.
(Lewis Carroll[1])

The chapter proposes a first rule of semantic composition: the combination of a referential NP with a predicate. In order to be able to state the rule, we decide what the meaning of a referential NP is and what the meaning of a predicate is.

1. Sentence meanings - some distinctions and a first composition rule

In the preceding chapter we have decided that the meaning of a sentence is the set of all possible situations that would make the sentence true. For a given sentence α, we write $[[α]]$ for {s: s is a possible situation in which α would be true}. Putting it slightly differently: If we know the meaning of a sentence and if we're then confronted with a particular situation, we know whether the sentence is true or false in that situation. Let's write $[[α]]^s$ for the meaning of a sentence in a particular situation. According to what we have just stated, this must be either *true* or *false* – a truth value. For true and false, we will write 1 and 0, as is standard practice in semantic theory and logic.

Wait: it seems we have called both $[[α]]$ and $[[α]]^s$ meanings of α. Is this a problem? No, this is a distinction that linguists and logicians have been making for a long time – the first is called the **intension** and the second the **extension** of α. The intension of α is the 'real' meaning of α (the linguistic knowledge that native speakers have), the extension is α's meaning relative to a given situation. If for every possible situation s we know $[[α]]^s$, then we also know $[[α]]$. And conversely, if we know $[[α]]$, then we can determine $[[α]]^s$ for any s. So intension and extension are two interdefinable notions of

---

[1] Read more at http://www.brainyquote.com/quotes/authors/l/lewis_carroll.html.

meaning. We will mostly look at extensions, i.e. the meanings that linguistic expressions have in particular situations.

As a first illustration of the idea behind compositionality, we take a look at coordination. Let us specify the intension of (1) (a conjunction) on the basis of the meanings of the simpler sentences it contains.

(1)   [$_{IP1}$ [$_{IP2}$ *There is a frog in my basement*] *and*
                [$_{IP3}$ *there is a wild turkey in the neighborhood*]].

[[[$_{IP2}$ *there is a frog in my basement*]]]
= {s: a frog is in the speaker's basement in s}
[[[$_{IP3}$ *there is a wild turkey in the neighborhood*]]]
= {s: a wild turkey is in the speaker's neighborhood in s}

For the meaning of (1), we will want to consider situations which include both a frog in the speaker's basement and a wild turkey in the neighborhood. That is the set of situations which is the intersection of the meanings of the two conjuncts. This can be illustrated with the following Venn diagram:

(2)
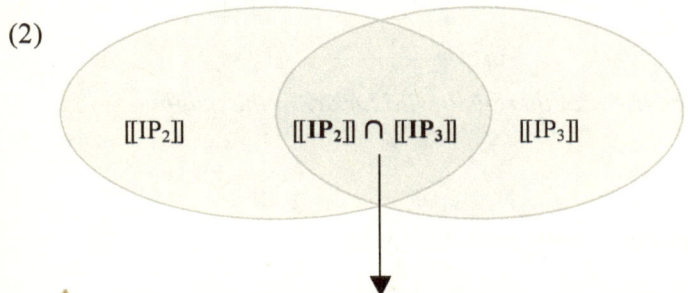

Situations with frog in the speaker's basement
and a wild turkey in the neighborhood

We can formulate a first rule of composition for the case of conjoined sentences:

If Z = [X1 *and* X2] then [[Z]] = [[X1]] ∩ [[X2]]

This gives us a first idea regarding the composition of sentence meanings. The meanings of the sentence parts (the two smaller IPs) contribute to the meaning of the whole in a systematic way (namely via intersection).

Rules like the one for conjunction model native speakers' subconscious knowledge of how the combination of the meanings of the individual words and phrases proceeds. Recall the goal of compositional semantics: we want to be able to derive the meanings of all possible English sentences in this manner. This entails that we also need to know the meanings of the parts of the sentence (for example *a frog* and *in the basement*) and the ways in which they are combined (for example to derive the meaning of *there is a frog in my basement* compositionally). We turn to this enterprise in the next section.

☺ **Exercise. Disjunction** (*or*) and **negation** (*not, it is not the case that, no way,* ...) also systematically operate on sentence meanings. Write composition rules parallel to the one for conjunction in the text. Illustrate how they apply to (E1) and (E2). Explain this in your own words, and subsequently draw corresponding Venn diagrams. (As an aside: can you identify two different uses of *or* in English?)

(E1)   *There is a frog in my basement or there is a wild turkey in the neighborhood.*

(E2)   *It is not the case that there is a wild turkey in the neighborhood.*
□

2. Meanings of parts of sentences: first steps

We have, with the previous sections, subscribed to what people call a referential theory of meaning: meanings are things. In the case of sentences, we can view sentence meanings either as truth values (the extension of a sentence) or as sets - sets of possible situations (the intension of a sentence). Meanings are out there in the world. Meaning relates language to the the things talked about. Noun phrases give a simple example of what we mean by that, and we turn to their semantics next. This is followed by a semantics for predicates and a rule that compositionally combines NP meanings with predicates to yield sentence meanings.

2.1. Referential NPs

Many NPs (though not all; see Chapter I-8 for NPs with a different semantics) can be used to **refer**, i.e. stand for an individual in the world. Let us give some examples of referential NPs. Proper names constitute a prime example of referring expressions:

(1)   a.   *Sir Edmund Hilary*
        b.   *Mount Everest*
        c.   *Barbara Partee*
        d.   *Edinburgh*
        e.   *Barack Obama*

"Individuals" is the standard term used in semantics for entities such as the ones above. Notice that the term is not restricted to persons, or even animate objects. *Mount Everest* and *Edinburgh* are names of places. The term "individual" simply stands for any kind of entity, including mountains, particular objects in the world, etc.

Definite descriptions are also referential NPs. Below are some examples:

(2)   a.   *the highest mountain in the world*
        b.   *the tallest student in this course*
        c.   *the author of "North and South"*
        d.   *the president of the US*
        e.   *the printer in my office*

Definites have more internal structure – a topic to which we return in Chapter I-8. But as far as their overall semantic contribution goes, definite descriptions also denote individuals. So do demonstrative NPs and pronouns:

(3)   a.   *this pen*
        b.   *those papers*

(4)   a.   *she*
        b.   *we*

Demonstrative NPs are traditionally called deictics: you can point to the object they refer to. Pronouns can have deictic uses, too. If you imagine such a use in (4a), for example, it is intuitively very clear that the meaning of the pronoun is an individual. We'll come back to the analysis of pronouns in Chapter II-7; but for current purposes, we note that reference to individuals can also be made with demonstrative NPs and pronouns.

Let us make our suggestion regarding the meaning of referential NPs precise: the meaning of the name *Sir Edmund Hilary* is the person Sir Edmund Hilary. This is stated in (5). Note that the expression from the language under investigation (English) is written in italics (as it has been throughout the book). We call this the **object language**. The English words show up inside the meaning brackets '[[.]]' because this is what we interpret. Note that the expression outside the meaning brackets to the right of the '=' sign is not an expression of the object language. It is an expression of the language that we (the authors) use to talk to you (the readers). This is called the **metalanguage** – the language we communicate in. This happens to be English as well. In order to keep the two apart, the object language is always in italics and the metalanguage never is.

(5) $[[$*Sir Edmund Hilary*$]]^s$ = Sir Edmund Hilary (for any situation s)

The referent of a proper name will always be the same individual – it does not depend on the situation. But this is not always the case with referential NPs. Clearly, the referent of *the president of the US* varies from one situation to another. If you pick a situation in 1998, for example, the referent of the same NP is Bill Clinton. Similarly in (7), and most of our other examples, the extension of an expression will vary from one situation to another.

(6) $[[$*the president of the US*$]]^s$ = Barack Obama (if s is our world in 2014)

(7) $[[$*the highest mountain in the world*$]]^s$ = Mount Everest (if s is here and now)

When nothing else is explicitly said, we will generally assume that the situation s relative to which we determine the extension of an expression (i.e. the superscript in the notation $[[...]]^s$) is the actual situation. That is, roughly speaking, the "here and now".

To sum up, we say that an NP refers to an entity if the extension of the NP is that entity. For example $[[$*New York*$]]^s$ is the actual city on the East coast of the US; [[*the highest mountain on Earth*]]^s refers to Mount Everest, and so on.

2.2. Predicates

Remember: we are trying to construct the meaning of an entire sentence from its syntactic parts. Suppose we have a sentence like (8):

(8)   *Mount Everest is covered in snow and ice.*

The meaning of (8) can be rendered as in (9):

(9)   a. [[(8)]] = {s: Mount Everest is covered in snow and ice in s}
        b. [[(8)]]^s = 1 (i.e. the sentence is true in the here and now; it could be false e.g. in a different situation with extreme global warming)

What do we have to assume about [[*is covered in snow and ice*]]^s to derive (9) from its components?

The sequence *is covered in snow and ice* denotes a **predicate** or a property. An individual either has or does not have that property. We identify properties (their extensions) with sets: *is covered in snow and ice* denotes the set of all those individuals that are covered in snow and ice. The meaning of the predicate will look as follows:

(10)   [[*is covered in snow and ice*]]^s = {x: x is covered in snow and ice in s} = {Mount Everest, Mount Cook, Mont Blanc, Anapurna, Antarctica ...}

Now, the sentence (8) is true if and only if the denotation of the subject NP is a member of the set denoted by the predicate. The predicate is rest of the clause, I' in our syntactic analysis. We can state the truth conditions as follows:

(11)   [[*Mount Everest is covered in snow and ice*]]^s = 1 iff
        [[*Mount Everest*]]^s ∈ [[*is covered in snow and ice*]]^s iff
        Mount Everest ∈ {x: x is covered in snow and ice in s}

108   *Composing sentence meanings – first steps*

We will be more explicit about how the grammar derives (11) in a moment. First, here are a few other examples of predicates:

(12)   a.   *is a student*
            $[[\textit{is a student}]]^s = \{x: x \text{ is a student in } s\}$
       b.   *loves Mary*
            $[[\textit{loves Mary}]]^s = \{x: x \text{ loves Mary in } s\}$
       c.   *is French*
       d.   *is present*
       e.   *paints watercolors*

Such properties can be used to form sentences together with individual-denoting NPs:

(13)   a.   *Judith is a student.*
       b.   *She loves Mary.*
       c.   *The dark-haired male student in my class is French.*
       d.   *The tallest student in this class is present.*
       e.   *Lindsey paints watercolors.*

We observe that the pattern of combining the subject NP with the predicate is quite general. For the sentence to be true, the individual denoted by the subject must be a member of the set denoted by the predicate. We have thus arrived at our first composition rule. We call the rule the Subject-Predicate Rule and it is stated below. We first state the actual rule in formally correct terms. Underneath, we describe what it says informally.

Subject-Predicate Rule (SUBJPRED)
If $X = [_{IP} \text{ NP I'}]$, then for any s: $[[X]]^s = 1$ iff $[[\text{NP}]]^s \in [[\text{I'}]]^s$

For a sentence X consisting of NP and I', the meaning of X in any situation s is the truth value 'true' iff the meaning of the NP in s is a member of the meaning of the I' in s.

🕒 **Exercise.** Calculate the truth conditions of (13d). Determine the extensions of NP and predicate as well as the sentence's truth value for the situation you are in.   □

Sentence meanings - a first composition rule 109

This is progress: we have made a specific proposal for how the truth conditions of a sentence IP depend on the meaning of the subject and the predicate. But it is only a first step. In our examples above, we have just assumed that we know the interpretations of NP and I'. However, those interpretations really have to be determined compositionally, too. We have to calculate them from the subparts they contain (ultimately from the lexicon upwards according to syntactic structure). So, more rules of composition will be required.

We have set our research agenda for the chapters to come. But we have also achieved something else: We know a bit more about meanings. Meanings can be individuals, as in the case of referential NPs, but also more abstract entities like sets. Let's keep that in mind, and proceed with our research program.

✏ **Exercise.** Some of the predicates we have seen contain the copula, i.e. the verb *be*. You should have a clear idea from the previous chapters how *be* behaves syntactically in English. But we do not yet know what its semantic contribution is. Try to establish a preliminary answer by making use of a small, crosslinguistic investigation. If you have access to a language such as **Russian, Hungarian,** or **African-American English**, make a list of examples which correspond to simple Standard English sentences and contain the copula (e.g. 'That tree *is* very tall.'). What do you observe? Focus solely on the present tense (in order not to get involved with issues of tense). Taking your findings into account, suggest a simple hypothesis regarding the contribution of the copula in such examples.

☐

☞ THE BASICS BOX: *Composing sentence meanings*

- ✓ Referential NPs denote individuals.
- ✓ Predicates denote sets of individuals.
- ✓ A sentence consisting of a referential NP subject and a predicate is true iff the individual denoted by the NP is a member of the set denoted by the predicate.

3. Selected references

The division between two types of semantic meaning (for which we have used 'extension' and 'intension') has a long tradition in logic with repercussions both in philosophy and linguistics. The classical reading is Frege's (1892) *Über Sinn und Bedeutung* ('sense' and 'reference' in the English translation; cf. also Russell 1905, Carnap 1947, and Lewis 1970 for foundational literature as well as Szabó 2013 and Zimmermann and Sternefeld 2013 for interesting recent discussion, the latter in a more accessible format for the beginner level). The recent *Handbook of Semantics* (Maienborn, von Heusinger and Portner 2011) contains an article specifically concerned with Frege's notions of sense and reference. Discussion of proper names as rigid designators can be found in Montague (1970) and Lewis (1986).

We use situations in this book informally in the place of a proper intensional semantics with both times and worlds. (Von Fintel & Heim 2011 is a good introduction to intensional semantics, with references to the classical work in this area.) We stay with an intuitive understanding of situations. But our use of them should be compatible with Kratzer (1989). See also Kratzer (2011) for how situations may feed into standard intensional semantic theories.

The semantics for conjunction (and also disjunction and negation) is intended to be the classical one, which can be found in any standard introduction to logic. See, e.g., Partee et al. (1990).

There is a large body of literature on referential noun phrases. A good starting point might be the section on NP semantics in the recent Handbook of Semantics (2011, ed. Maienborn et al.). Heim's (1991) "Artikel und Definitheit" is a great discussion of the semantics of definites, with many classical references (cf. also Heim 2011's overview). Demonstratives are analyzed in particular in Elbourne (2005). His analysis is extended to pronouns.

If you are interested in the realization of non-verbal predicates without the copula, e.g. in African American English and Hungarian, Green (2002) and É. Kiss (2002) are theoretically informed grammatical descriptions.

Interesting information on Sir Edmund Hilary's life and mountaineering accomplishments is available at the DOC visitor center and the Hermitage hotel in Mount Cook village, NZ.

Chapter I-7
Extending the theory

Compositionally I do not exclude the building across the road;[...]
(From an interview with Frank Gehry[1])

This chapter adds rules of interpretation to the semantics component which allow us to handle simple sentence structures compositionally, in keeping with the goal laid out at the end of the preceding chapter. In addition, we discuss the semantic topic of modification, and we add transitive verbs and other relation denoting categories to the picture.

1. Step by step composition – some trivial steps

We saw in the previous chapter how the meanings of subjects and predicates can be combined to derive the truth conditions of a sentence: the individual denoted by the subject NP needs to be a member of the set denoted by predicate, in order for the sentence to be true. This is a rule of composition in keeping with the Fregean program: the meaning of a complex expression, IP, is defined in terms of set membership on the basis of the meanings of its component parts, NP and I'. But the NP and the I' are themselves complex expressions. Their meanings need to be derived from the meanings of their component parts as well.

This section adds further rules of composition to the semantics component of the grammar. Those rules enable us to compositionally interpret simple sentences like (1) below. (1) is 'simple' in that what needs to be added to the subject-predicate rule is not very interesting semantically. Let us be precise about what we have to do in order to spell out a compositional semantics. For each constituent in (1b) that is not a lexical item, we require a rule that states how its meaning is determined from the meaning(s) of its daughter(s). The meanings of the words come from the lexicon – they are

---

[1] Retrieved via http://www.interviewmagazine.com/art/new-again-frank-gehry/#_.

the smallest building blocks in the composition. But all other meanings are composed.

(1)   a   *John is present.*
        b.

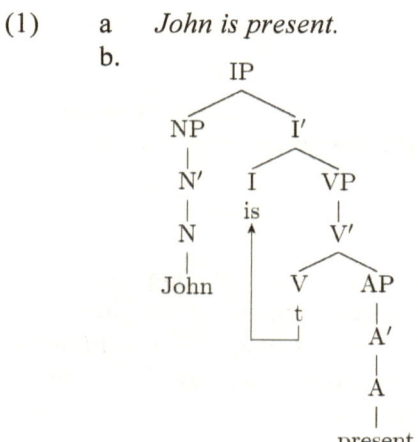

Let's first look at the subject NP. The syntactic structure for *John* has NP, N' and N dominating *John*. NP and N' don't seem to add any information to the lexical noun *John*. We could state this in terms of a rule along the following lines:

(2)   If you are looking at a tree X = [$_{NP}$ N'], then for any relevant s:
       [[NP]]^s = [[N']]^s

We would need a parallel rule for N' and N. You might have a suspicion that what is relevant is the fact that the trees are non-branching. There is in each case only one daughter node and we are not adding anything that could make a contribution. Your suspicion will be confirmed when we look at the predicate in (1), *is present*.

First, let us decide on how composition proceeds with regard to the role of *is* in *is present*. That concerns the role of I. The tense information contained in I is certainly meaningful: if you exchange *is* in (1) with *was*, a different interpretation results. Rather counterintuitively, we are going to ignore tense information throughout Part I in order to simplify things (we return to tense in Chapter II-8 and remedy this omission). Apart from tense, the auxiliary verb *be* doesn't seem to add anything. So we will assume that [[*is present*]]^s = [[*present*]]^s. The meaning of lexical items comes from the lexicon. The lexicon tells us that for any s, [[*present*]]^s = {x: x is present in s}. Hold on though: What we come across as the sister of *is* is not actually the lexical adjective *present*. It's the AP dominating the A' and then the adjective as you see in (1b). All these non-branching nodes seem to make no difference.

Let's therefore adopt the following composition rule:

> **Non branching trees** (NONBR)
> If X = [$_Y$ Z], then for any s: $[[X]]^s = [[Z]]^s$
> In a non-branching tree, the denotation of the whole tree is the same as the denotation of the only daughter.

Now, our reasoning above has actually been a little sloppy. We have pretended that the sister of *is* is the AP consisting of *present*. That is not quite accurate: *is* occupies the I position in (1b). The auxiliary verb is moved there from the V position, and the AP is actually the sister of the V position filled by the trace of *is*, as shown in (3):

(3)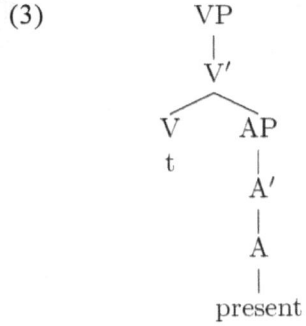

What are we going to do with the trace in the semantics? In the example at hand, it does not seem to do anything semantically. (There is more to say about the role that traces play for interpretation, but let us postpone this.) For now, we adopt the following rule of composition to be able to deal with trees like (3):

> **Ignore traces** (IT)
> If X = [$_Z$ t Y], then for any s: $[[X]]^s = [[Y]]^s$
> If a tree consists of a trace and its sister Y, then the denotation of the whole tree is the same as the denotation of Y.

That is, we treat traces as semantically vacuous elements.

We have looked at *be* above in a parallel way. *Be* doesn't add to the interpretation of its sister in any way, so that the meaning of the larger constituent is simply the meaning of the sister of *be*. There are a few more words like that: words that have to show up in the structure for some reason, but seem to be semantically vacuous. Recall that we said *is a student* denotes the set {x: x is a student in s}. But this is simply the interpretation of *student* (same as *present* denotes the set of all individuals who are present, the meaning of *student* is the set of all individuals who are students). So neither *is* nor *a* seem to add anything. Similarly, the auxiliary *do* of do-support: It has an important function syntactically, but it does not add anything to the meaning. The following rule of composition takes care of semantically vacuous items:

Ignore semantically vacuous elements (SEMVAC)
If X = [$_W$ y Z] and y is a semantically vacuous element, then for any s: $[[X]]^s = [[Z]]^s$
If a tree consists of a meaningless daughter and its sister Z, then the denotation of the whole tree is the same as the denotation of Z.

We will encounter further examples of semantically empty words below.

With these rules, we are able to compute the meanings of simple sentences like *Molly is tall*, *Robin is a woman* etc., making use of only the following three things:

1. Syntactic structure
2. Lexical information
3. Rules of compositional interpretation

That is, we can carry out Frege's semantic program for a very small fragment of English. From here on, we will work on making the fragment bigger, but the examples we have illustrate the program: We need to be able to compositionally interpret every structure that our syntax component generates.

Let us practice, by compositionally calculating the truth conditions of the sentence in (4) below. We perform this task in the subsequent (5). We compositionally interpret the syntactic structure of (4). At each step, we apply one of our rules of composition. We indicate the rules that allow us to get to the next step in brackets.

(4)   *Molly is a student.*

(5) $[[[_{\text{IP}} [_{\text{NP}} [_{\text{N'}} [_{\text{N}} Molly]]] [_{\text{I'}} \text{ is } [_{\text{VP}} [_{\text{V'}} t [_{\text{NP}} a [_{\text{N'}} _{\text{N}} student]]]]]]]]^s = 1$ iff
(SUBJPRED)
$[[[_{\text{NP}} [_{\text{N'}} [_{\text{N}} Molly]]]]]^s \in [[[_{\text{I'}} \text{ is } [_{\text{VP}} [_{\text{V'}} t [_{\text{NP}} a [_{\text{N'}} _{\text{N}} student]]]]]]]^s$ iff
(2x NONBR)
$[[[_{\text{N}} Molly]]]^s \in [[[_{\text{I'}} \text{ is } [_{\text{VP}} [_{\text{V'}} t [_{\text{NP}} a [_{\text{N'}} _{\text{N}} student]]]]]]]^s$ iff   (LEX)
Molly $\in [[[_{\text{I'}} \text{ is } [_{\text{VP}} [_{\text{V'}} t [_{\text{NP}} a [_{\text{N'}} _{\text{N}} student]]]]]]]^s$ iff   (SEMVAC)
Molly $\in [[[_{\text{VP}} [_{\text{V'}} t [_{\text{NP}} a [_{\text{N'}} _{\text{N}} student]]]]]]^s$ iff   (NONBR)
Molly $\in [[[_{\text{V'}} t [_{\text{NP}} a [_{\text{N'}} _{\text{N}} student]]]]]^s$ iff   (IT)
Molly $\in [[[_{\text{NP}} a [_{\text{N'}} _{\text{N}} student]]]]^s$ iff   (SEMVAC)
Molly $\in [[[_{\text{N'}} _{\text{N}} student]]]^s$ iff   (NONBR)
Molly $\in [[_{\text{N}} student]]^s$ iff   (LEX)
Molly $\in \{x: x \text{ is a student in } s\}$

(6)   The sentence *Molly is a student* is true in a situation iff the individual Molly is an element of the set of students in that situation.

The last line we obtain in (5) is the result of a step-by-step compositional interpretation. The calculation proves (6). That is, according to our rules, the sentence *Molly is a student* is true in a situation iff the individual referred to by the name *Molly* is a member of the set of individuals who are students in that situation. This is intuitively correct. Hence the calculation above can be seen as a proof that the rules of composition we have proposed make the correct predictions about the meaning of the sentence.

2. Modifiers

2.1. Intersective modifiers

We are ready to move on and consider the interpretation of further types of structures. We begin with the interpretation of certain adjuncts. The rules we have so far can interpret *Kaline is gray* and *Kaline is a cat* – but how about *Kaline is a gray cat*? Our intuition tells us that the sentence is true if and only if Kaline is gray and she is a cat. How do we predict this?
We know the syntactic structure – the AP *gray* is an adjunct within the NP *a gray cat*. And we also know the individual meanings of *gray* and *cat*. Both denote sets.

(7) a. For any s: $[\![gray]\!]^s = \{x: x \text{ is gray in } s\}$
b. For any s: $[\![cat]\!]^s = \{x: x \text{ is a cat in } s\}$

So what about their combination? An intuitive way to combine the two meanings is to form their intersection. That is the set of individuals that have both properties, i.e. are in both sets. The following rule implements the intuition:

Predicate Modification (PM)
If $X = [_W Y Z]$ and both Y and Z denote sets, then for any s:
$[\![X]\!]^s = [\![Y]\!]^s \cap [\![Z]\!]^s$

The structure of our NP *a gray cat* (8a) can now be interpreted, (8b):

(8) a. $[_{NP} a [_{N'} [_{AP} [_{A'} A\ gray]] [_{N'} N\ cat]]]$
b. $[\![[_{NP} a [_{N'} [_{AP} [_{A'} A\ gray]] [_{N'} N\ cat]]]]\!]^s =$
$[\![[_{N'} [_{AP} [_{A'} A\ gray]] [_{N'} N\ cat]]]\!]^s =$
$[\![gray]\!]^s \cap [\![cat]\!]^s =$
$\{x: x \text{ is gray in } s\} \cap \{x: x \text{ is a cat in } s\} =$
$\{x: x \text{ is gray in } s \text{ and } x \text{ is a cat in } s\}$

Here is a description in words of what is done in (8b): (8b) is a compositional calculation of the meaning of the NP in (8a) with the rules of composition that we have introduced. The meaning of the NP in a given situation s is the same as the meaning of the N' *gray cat* in s (by virtue of the rule for semantically vacuous elements). The meaning of that N' is composed of the meanings of the AP *gray* and the N' *cat* as their intersection, via the rule Predicate Modification. By virtue of several applications of the rule for non-branching trees, this amounts to the intersection of the meaning of the word *gray* in s and the meaning of the word *cat* in s. Ultimately, the meaning of the NP in a given situation is the set of all individuals that are both gray and a cat in that situation.

The same rule Predicate Modification is used in the interpretation of PP adjuncts like (9).

(9) a. *Oamaru is a town in New Zealand.*
b. *Bill is a student from Sweden.*

⏲ **Exercise.** Compositionally interpret (9a) step by step. For the PP, you can assume that for any situation s: [[*in New Zealand*]]^s = {x: x is in New Zealand in s}. □

Consider (10). This sentence is syntactically ambiguous. Why isn't it semantically ambiguous?

(10) *Molly is a blond woman from Europe.*
   a. [$_{NP}$ *a* [$_{N'}$ [$_{N'}$ *blond woman*] [$_{PP}$ *from Europe*]]]
   b. [$_{NP}$ *a* [$_{N'}$ [$_{AP}$ *blond*] [$_{N'}$ *woman from Europe*]]]

The reason is that intersection – the set-theoretic operation that interprets modification – is associative: (A ∩ B) ∩ C = A ∩ (B ∩ C). This is obvious when you draw the Venn diagram. The order in which we combine the modifiers with the noun does not matter. With predicate modification this is not a surprise. No matter in which order the sets are intersected, the result is in either case the set of elements that are contained in all three sets:

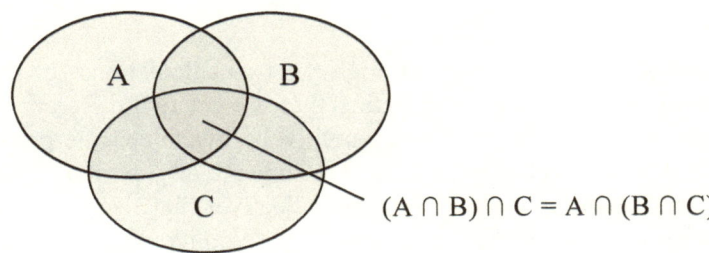

2.2. Adjuncts with non-intersective meanings

But now consider (11). Note that the sentence is structurally parallel to (10). So why is (11) semantically ambiguous?

(11) *Sally is a former president with long hair.*

The explanation lies in the semantics of *former*. *Former* can't be an intersective adjective, in contrast to *French*, *gray*, etc. You can see this in (12).

(12) *Joe is a former teacher.*   ≠
   **Joe is former and Joe is a teacher.*

118 *Extending the theory*

Former is an intensional adjective. That means that it is sensitive to the meaning of its sister constituent not in the present, actual situation, but in other situations. Within our set theoretic framework, we can describe the effect of modification by *former* by the following semantic rule:

> ***former***
> If X = [$_{N'}$ *former* N'] then for any s: $[[X]]^s$ = {x: there is an s' before s such that x ∈ $[[N']]^{s'}$}

Let's apply this to a simple example first:

(13) $[[\textit{former teacher}]]^s$ =
{x: there is an s' before s such that x ∈ $[[\textit{teacher}]]^{s'}$} =
{x: there is an s' before s such that x ∈ {z: z is a teacher in s'} } =
{x: there is an s' before s such that x is a teacher in s'}

We can now explain why in (11) there is a semantic ambiguity along with the syntactic one.

🕒 **Exercise.** Show this; i.e., go through the two calculations for the two possible trees of (11) above, illustrating that we get two different sets of truth conditions reflecting the two intuitively available interpretations. Then, try to think of other words that are semantically similar to *former*. (*Hint*. You can begin by looking for other adjectives that also make us look at situations other than the here and now. When you have found some such adjectives, you can think about words belonging to other categories, but doing something similar semantically). ☐

3. Relations

3.1. Transitive verbs

So far, we are unable to interpret transitive verbs like *kick*, *like* etc. Consider (14):

(14)   *Molly kicked Bill.*

We know that the names *Molly* and *Bill* refer to individuals. What is the contribution of the verb? The verb seems to express a relation between individuals. This becomes clearer in the slightly artificial example (15):

(15) a. *2 precedes / is smaller than 4*
      b. *2 < 4*

We know that < is a relation between numbers, namely the "smaller than" relation. Mathematically, a relation is a set of ordered pairs. The relation < for the natural numbers contains the following pairs:

(16) {<1,2>, <1,3>, <1,4>, ..., <2, 3>, <2, 4>, <2, 5>,...}

where the first number in each ordered pair is smaller than the second. The same relation is better identified by specifying the criterion for membership:

(17) {<a, b>: a < b}
      The set of all ordered pairs <a, b> such that a is smaller than b

The *kick* relation can be modeled in a parallel way. What is different is that this is not a relation between numbers, but a relation between individuals. Here is the lexical entry for *kick*:

(18) For any s, [[*kicked*]]^s =
         {<a, b>: a kicked b in s}
         The set of all ordered pairs <a, b> such that a kicked b in s

We now need to specify how the verb combines with the object NP. Here is the composition rule that takes care of that:

Objects of relations (OBJREL):
If X = [$_w$Y Z], where Z denotes an individual and Y denotes a relation, then for any s: [[X]]^s = {v: <v, [[Z]]^s> ∈ [[Y]]^s}

Note that the result of combining a transitive verb with its object yields a set of individuals. This is as desired, since the result, the meaning of verb + object, needs to be a predicate. It combines with a subject via the subject-predicate rule.

120   *Extending the theory*

🕒 **Exercise**. Compositionally interpret (14).   □

3.2. Transfer to prepositions

What we have just found out can be applied to prepositions and prepositional phrases. Consider (19):

(19)   *Robin is from Trenton.*

The denotation of *from Trenton* is a property; that is, a set of individuals. The subject individual must have this property if the sentence is to be true. But how does the internal composition within the PP proceed? This is in fact identical to the situation with transitive verbs. The preposition denotes a relation. Just like a transitive verb, it relates two individuals (e.g. Robin and Trenton above). The meaning of *from* is as follows:

(20)   For any s: $[[from]]^s = \{<a, b>:$ a is from b in s$\}$

The combination of the preposition with its object can be modeled with the rule Objects of relations. Applying (OBJREL), we get:

(21)   For any s:
$[[from\ Trenton]]^s =$ (OBJREL)
$\{v: <v, [[_{NP} Trenton]]^s> \in [[_P from]]^s\} =$ (2x NONBR, 2x LEX)
$\{v: <v, Trenton> \in \{<a, b>:$ a is from b in s$\}\} =$ (SIMPL)
$\{v:$ v is from Trenton in s$\}$

3.3. Three-place relations

Let's take another look at verb meanings. We have ascertained that an intransitive verb like *leave* denotes a set of individuals, and a transitive verb like *kick* denotes a set of ordered pairs. What about verbs that have two objects, like *show*, *give* and *introduce* in (22)?

(22)   a.   *Sue showed Bill Sandy.*
       b.   *Molly gave Bill the book.*
       c.   *Heidi introduced Sigrid to Darcy.*

Relations 121

The analysis of transitive verbs can be extended to verbs with two objects (such verbs are called ditransitives). The difference is that these verbs relate three individuals rather than two. So instead of two-place relations, they denote three-place relations. For instance, *give* denotes a set of ordered triples as in (23):

(23)   For any s, $[[give]]^s$ = {<a, b, c>: a gives b to c in s}

Notice that there is a connection to subcategorization and what we informally called arguments in Chapter I-3: A verb with two argument positions denotes a two-place relation, one with three a three-place relation. Notice also that *introduce* can receive the same analysis as *show* and *give* if we take *to* to be semantically vacuous.

⊕ **Exercise**. Propose a rule of composition that allows you to compositionally interpret the VP *show Bill Sandy*. In order to write the rule, remember that the syntactic structure is [VP [V' show$_V$ Bill$_{NP}$ Sandy$_{NP}$]]. Use your rule to demonstrate that you are able to predict the correct truth conditions for (22a).   ☐

3.4. Interpretability

On the basis of the denotations introduced, we can raise the question why a sentence such as (24) is ungrammatical:

(24)   *Sue kicked Bill Sandy.*

Sentence (24) is uninterpretable because we cannot integrate three individuals into a two-place relation. Notice that we can thus use uninterpretability to explain some unacceptable sentences of English.

⊕ **Exercise**. Explain the ungrammaticality of the sentences in (E1) below by capitalizing on the lexical entries of the predicates involved.

(E1)   a. * *Homer snored Marge.*
        b. * *Lisa gave Bart.*   ☐

122 *Extending the theory*

> ☞ THE BASICS BOX: ***Rules of compositional interpretation***
> - ✓ The interpretation component of the grammar must be able to interpret all acceptable structures generated by the syntax component.
> - ✓ It includes rules that specify what happens with semantically empty material and non-branching trees.
> - ✓ Many modifiers are interpreted intersectively with the category they modify. The rule Predicate Modification handles them. Some modifiers have a different semantics. An example is the intensional adjective *former*.
> - ✓ Verbs and prepositions denote relations; in a sentence, the number of places in the relation must match the number of individuals.

4. Selected references

We continue to follow the perspective in standard semantics textbooks, especially Heim and Kratzer (1998), with the noted difference that we use a set theoretic framework rather than functions. Again take a look at the references given at the end of Chapter I-5.

The distinction between different types of adjectives, with the rough subdivision between intersective and non-intersective ones, can be traced back to Montague's work (cf. the papers in Montague and Richardson 1974 and Dowty, Wall and Peters 1981), but see especially also Kamp (1975), Parsons (1970), Kamp and Partee (1995). In this connection, Partee offers an interesting discussion of the issues in a research historical context (Partee 2007). You might want to read Partee's recent work if you are interested in the differences between the interpretive possibilities of adjectives – e.g. further subdivisions amongst the non-intersective adjectives – and the article contains, alongside the English data, further and more complex data sets from Polish. A proper handling of intensional phenomena requires a proper intensional semantic framework, e.g. von Fintel and Heim (2011) (cf. also Partee 1973, Kratzer 1998, 2011, Portner 2009). We have merely provided an impression, with *former*, of what it is supposed to do. We provide a basic interpretation of tenses in Chapter II-7 (cf. also the references there on the topic).

Chapter I-8
NP semantics

> *I'm Nobody! Who are you? Are you - Nobody – too?*
> (Emily Dickinson, *I'm Nobody! Who are you?*)

In this chapter, we extend the semantic theory to NPs with the definite determiner *the* and to NPs with quantificational determiners like *every*, *most* and *some*. Definite NPs are presuppositional. With the notions presupposition and quantification, we introduce two central topics in semantics.

1. Definites: referential NPs with presuppositions

We decided in chapter 6 that definite NPs like *the president of the US* denote an individual, e.g. Barack Obama at the time of writing this textbook. How does this meaning arise? Remember once more that we are committed to compositionality. The interpretation of definite NPs comes about by combining their syntactic components, which are the definite determiner *the* and its N' sister. We have analyzed nouns and N's as denoting sets of individuals. Thus, we know that *president of the US* is the set of all individuals that are US presidents. The question is how such a set combines with *the* to yield the referent of the NP.

Here are some more examples of definite descriptions and their referents:

(1)   a.   *The opera by Beethoven* : Fidelio
         b.   *The capital of New Zealand:* Wellington
         c.   *The positive square root of 4 :* 2
         d.   *The first woman to climb Mt Cook* : Freda du Faur

A pattern emerges from these examples. The denotations of all the N' constituents above are sets containing just one element. There is only one opera composed by Beethoven; New Zealand has exactly one capital; there is only one positive square root of four; and the predicate *first woman to climb Mt Cook* is true of just one individual. The following generalization can be established:

(2) For any constituent N' and any situation s:
If $[[N']]^s$ is a set M that contains exactly one element,
then $[[\textit{the } N']]^s$ is the unique element of M.

But what if M is a set that does not contain anything, or more than one thing? Let us consider some such examples:

(3) a. *The opera by Mozart*
b. *The capital of South America*
c. *The square root of 4*
d. *The king of Boston*

In these examples, you do not know who or what would be referred to by the NP. In our terms, all of these expressions seem to have no denotation. There is nothing ill-formed in their syntactic structure, but their semantics is not well-defined. The difference from the previous examples is that the denotation of the N' is a set that has either more than one element (in (3a,c)) or no element at all (in (3b,d)). Our semantics needs to take this restriction into account. The following rule of composition interprets definite NPs:

---
the
If $X = [_{NP} \textit{the } N']$ then for any s: $[[\textit{the } N']]^s$ is only defined if there is exactly one z such that $z \in [[N']]^s$. Then, $[[\textit{the } N']]^s$ is that z.

This rule reflects the Fregean interpretation for *the*. When the definedness condition in the rule is met, the definite NP refers to an individual. However, the rule can also lead to an undefined interpretation: it is possible for a definite NP not to have a referent. This happens when the definedness condition in the rule is not met. What about a full sentence that contains a definite NP which does not have a denotation? Consider the following sentence.

(4) *The capital of South America lies at a high altitude.*

The sentence is just as odd as the NP (3b). Our system of compositional interpretation leads us to expect that when the interpretation of a daughter constituent is undefined, then the denotation of the mother will also be undefined. In the example, we would wish to apply the Subject-Predicate rule, but the subject *the capital of South America* does not have a denotation. Hence we cannot determine whether or not its denotation is an element of the predicate, rendering the denotation of the whole sentence undefined. Therefore (4) is neither true nor false.

The condition that there be exactly one element in the N'-denotation is a **presupposition** (PSP for short) A presupposition needs to be true for the sentence to be either true or false. When the presupposition is false, the sentence is not false, but undefined. A presupposition is a definedness condition. We model the intuition that a sentence like (4) is inappropriate as undefinedness.

Let us look at the motivation for this in more detail. It is clear that (4) is not true (and neither are further examples like *The king of Boston enjoys Reese's Peanut Butter Cups* – you can think about further relevant data yourself). But why don't we just say that (4) is false? An important argument comes from negation. When we negate a false sentence, we get a true outcome. (5b) is true iff (5a) is false.

(5)   a.   *It is raining.*
         b.   *It is not raining*

But negating (4) above yields a result that is judged as odd as (4) itself. (6) is not a true sentence. If (4) were simply false, then (6) should be true. The judgement that neither (4) nor (6) are true is modeled in the analysis as both their denotations being undefined.

(6)   *The capital of South America doesn't lie at a high altitude.*

Let us look at a second example of presupposition (example taken from Heim and Kratzer):

(7)   *John is absent again today.*
        (i)   PSP: John has been absent before.
        (ii) Assertion: John is absent today.

(8)   *Today is not the first time that John is absent.*
        (i)   PSP: John is absent today.
        (ii) Assertion: John has been absent before.

(9)   *John is absent today and that has happened before.*
        (i) no PSP
        (ii) Assertion: John is absent today and
                        John has been absent before

(7)–(9) are appropriate in different contexts. Imagine yourself walking into your friend Robin's room and uttering (7). This is ok if Robin knows that John has been absent in the past; but if she doesn't know this, (7) is not quite appropriate. (9) would have been a better choice. Similarly with (8): (8) is a decent way to inform Robin that John has been absent in the past if she already knows that he is absent today. But if she doesn't know this, then (8) is an odd thing to say. Once again, (9) would have been more appropriate. Intuitions about appropriateness are part of native speakers' knowledge. The grammar thus needs to capture them. Such intuitions motivate the distinction between assertion and presupposition.

Similar intuitions can be observed in examples with the definite determiner. Consider (10) vs. (11):

(10)   *The excursion to the semantics labs at MIT will be on April 20th.*

(11)   *There will be an excursion to the semantics labs at MIT, which will be on April 20th.*

The sentence in (10) is not appropriate to inform people that there will be an excursion to the MIT semantics labs. It can only be used appropriately if this is already known. If it isn't, (11) would be the way to convey this information. (10) presupposes that there will be an excursion to the semantics labs at MIT, while (11) asserts it. Consider also:

(12)   *John didn't go on the excursion to the semantics labs at MIT on April 20th.*

If the condition that there be an excursion to the semantics labs at MIT was asserted, not presupposed, then we would expect the sentence to be true if there was no excursion. (Remember what we said about negation: a negated sentence is true iff the sentence without the negation is false.) However, intuitively, the sentence is inappropriate in that case. Our other example of a presupposition introducing element from (7), *again*, allows us to see the same thing:

(13)   *John isn't absent again today.*

This denies that John is absent today, not that he had been absent before. (13) is true in a situation in which John had been absent before and he is not absent today. So when we negate (7), the presupposition still has to be true. Only the assertion of (7) is negated. This is generally the case when sentences that have presuppositions are negated. The presupposition survives the negation. This is a characteristic behavior of presupposition, which also motivates distinguishing it from assertion.

To sum up, the definite article has introduced us to the notion of presupposition. A presupposition is a meaning component that has to be distinguished from assertion. The following types of intuition motivate the distinction: A sentence with a presupposition can only be appropriately used if the presupposition is known. When such a sentence is negated, the presuppostion still has to be true. It seems unaffected by the negation. Presuppositions are modeled in our grammar as definedness conditions.

One more remark has to be made regarding the uniqueness condition in the definition of *the:* the element fullfilling the description of the N' sister of *the* has to be unique in the context of the disourse, not in the entire world. Otherwise, we would never be able to say perfectly normal things like *the cat is asleep*. We can say *the cat is asleep* if in the context of the utterance, there is a unique cat (for example the only cat in the house). We will read the *the* rule in this way.

To see the rule at work, let's go through a sample calculation:

(14)   For any s:
$[\![[_{IP} [_{NP} \text{ the } [_{N'} \text{ president}]] [_{I'} \text{ left}]]]\!]^s$ is defined only if
$[\![[_{NP} \text{ the } [_{N'} \text{ president}]]]\!]^s$ is defined. This is the case only if there is a unique z such that z is president in s. If this is the case, then:

For any s:
$[\![[_{IP} [_{NP} \text{ the president}] [_{I'} \text{ left}]]]\!]^s = 1$ iff
$[\![[_{NP} \text{ the president}]]\!]^s \in [\![[_{I'} \text{ left}]]\!]^s$ iff
for the unique z such that $z \in [\![[_{N'} \text{ president}]]\!]^s$: $z \in [\![[_{I'} \text{ left}]]\!]^s$ iff
for the unique z such that $z \in [\![\text{president}]\!]^s$: $z \in [\![[_{I'} \text{ left}]]\!]^s$ iff
for the unique z such that $z \in \{x: x \text{ is president in } s\}$: $z \in [\![[_{I'} \text{ left}]]\!]^s$ iff
for the unique z such that z is president in s: $z \in [\![[_{I'} \text{ left}]]\!]^s$ iff
for the unique z such that z is president in s: $z \in \{x: x \text{ left in } s\}$ iff

128 *NP semantics*

for the unique z such that z is president in s: z left in s

🕀 **Exercise.** Caculate the definedness and truth conditions of the sentence below.

(E1)   *The French student loves Pat.*   □

There are lots more expressions (besides *the* and *again*) that introduce presuppositions. These expressions are called **presupposition triggers.** We give a few examples below.

(15)   Factive verbs:
   a. *Vera **regrets** upsetting the editor.*
   b. PSP: Vera has upset the editor.

(16)   Aspectual verbs:
   a. *Konstantin has **stopped** smoking.*
   b. PSP: Konstantin has smoked in the past.

(17)   Cleft sentences:
   a. ***It was** in May that Nadine left Harvard.*
   b. PSP: Nadine left Harvard sometime.

(18)   Pseudoclefts:
   a. ***What** Sonja destroyed was her juicer.*
   b. PSP: Sonja destroyed something.

(19)   Too:
   a. *ANNA went to 'Sinn und Bedeutung', **too**.*
   b. PSP: Someone other than Anna went to 'Sinn und Bedeutung'.

🕀 **Exercise.** Convince yourself that the (a)-sentences really have the presuppostions under (b). You can use intuitions on appropriateness, and you can also negate the sentences to see which meaning components are stable under negation. Negation is actually one of a family of environments that can be used to detect presuppositions. Identify those environments from the examples below and apply them to (15)-(19) as well.

(E2) a. *Is John absent again today?*
 b. *Maybe John is absent again today.*
 c. *If John is absent again today, Pritty gets to eat Polina's chocolate.* ◻

☕ **Exercise.** An important topic in the research on presupposition is the so-called **projection problem for presuppositions**. The problem can be formulated as follows: How are the presuppositions of a sentence determined by the presuppositions of its parts? To take a specific (and important) example, recall negation and the examples in (7) and (13). There, the presupposition "survives" when the sentence is negated. Or, in other words: The presupposition of the sentence as a whole, (13), is inherited from the non-negated sentence contained in it, (7). Such observations have led some linguists in the early days of research on presupposition to postulate the following hypothesis:

The Cumulative Hypothesis (Langendoen & Savin)
Complex sentences inherit all of the presuppositions of their constituent clauses.

Which of the following examples support the Cumulative Hypothesis? Which examples falsify it?

(E3) a. *It wasn't Pat who solved the problem.*
 b. *If there is a king of France, then the king of France is in hiding.*
 c. *If it wasn't Pat who solved the problem, then I wonder who will be awarded the Nobel Prize.*
 d. *If the problem was difficult, then it wasn't Pat who solved it.*
 e. *Either it is Pat who solved the problem or they have awarded the Nobel Prize to the wrong person.*
 f. *If the problem has been solved, it wasn't Pat who solved it.*
 g. *It isn't likely that it was Pat who solved the problem.*
 h. *Either it is Pat who solved the problem or the problem hasn't been solved.* ◻

2. Quantifiers

2.1. Quantifiers: non-referential NPs

In contrast to definites and names, NPs like *nothing, every boy* etc. don't refer to any individual. They are quantificational NPs. In order to understand their semantics, we consider (20):

(20) a. *Every turtle has back problems.*
b. *No turtle has back problems.*
c. *Some turtle has back problems.*
d. *Exactly 5 turtles have back problems.*
e. *Most turtles have back problems.*

We know the denotations of *turtle* and *has back problems*. Those are sets: $[[turtle]]^s = \{x: x \text{ is a turtle in } s\}$ and $[[has\ back\ problems]]^s = \{x: x \text{ has back problems in } s\}$. In (21) we describe the claims made by the sentences in (20) in terms of those sets.

(21) a. $[[turtle]]^s \subseteq [[has\ back\ problems]]^s$
b. $[[turtle]]^s \cap [[has\ back\ problems]]^s = \varnothing$
c. $[[turtle]]^s \cap [[has\ back\ problems]]^s \neq \varnothing$
d. $\text{card}([[turtle]]^s \cap [[has\ back\ problems]]^s) = 5$
e. $\text{card}([[turtle]]^s \cap [[has\ back\ problems]]^s) > 0.5 \times \text{card}([[turtle]]^s)$

(21) shows that the determiners in (20) have the job of relating two sets (the N' meaning $[[turtle]]^s$ and the meaning of the I' $[[has\ back\ problems]]^s$). Different determiners express different relations between sets.

The interpretation component of the grammar has to predict the truth conditions in (21) compositionally. Remind yourself of the syntactic structure of these sentences, e.g. (22) for (20a):

(22) [$_{IP}$ [$_{NP}$ *every* [$_{N'}$ *turtle*]] [$_{I'}$ *has back problems*]]

Compositionality requires that we define the meaning of the NP *every turtle* on the basis of the meanings of *every* and *turtle*. The resulting NP meaning then has to be combined with the predicate *has back problems* to give us the truth conditions of the sentence, i.e. (21a) for this example.

In order to get an idea of the meaning of quantified NPs, consider (23), where the quantified NP is just one word:

(23) a. *Nothing is dusty.*
      b. *Everything is dusty.*
          etc.

The morpheme *-thing* seems to be the set of all entities in the context. We call this the domain of discourse, and we write D for domain of discourse. We can identify the contribution of the quantified NP as follows:

(24) a. For any s: $[[nothing]]^s = \{P: P \cap D = \emptyset\}$
                      the set of all properties that no entity has
      b. For any s: $[[everything]]^s = \{P: D \subseteq P\}$
                      the set of all properties that every entity has
          etc.

This helps us to figure out what the meaning of the quantified NP *no turtle* is. Just like *nothing* denotes the set of all properties that no entity has, *no turtle* denotes the set of all properties that no turtle has. That is the set of all those sets whose intersection with the turtles is empty. In (25) we spell out the meanings of the NPs from (20) according to this reasoning. Quantified NPs denote sets of sets.

(25) a. $[[every\ turtle]]^s = \{P: [[turtle]]^s \subseteq P\}$
      b. $[[no\ turtle]]^s = \{P: P \cap [[turtle]]^s = \emptyset\}$
      c. $[[some\ turtle]]^s = \{P: P \cap [[turtle]]^s \neq \emptyset\}$
      d. $[[exactly\ 5\ turtles]]^s = \{P: card(P \cap [[turtle]]^s) = 5\}$
      e. $[[most\ turtles]]^s = \{P: card(P \cap [[turtle]]^s) > 0.5 \times card([[turtle]]^s\}$

What you see in (25) are the subject NP meanings that want to combine with the predicate. Note that our Subject-Predicate rule needs to be revised. The version from chapter I-6 says that the meaning of the subject needs to be an element of the meaning of the predicate for the sentence to be true. In the case of quantifiers, it's the other way around: the predicate that needs to be a member of the subject denotation. Let's revise the Subject-Predicate rule by dividing it into a part that handles non-quantificational subjects (the old rule), and adding a second part that handles quantified subjects:

> **Subject-Predicate rule** (SUBJPRED 1 and 2, respectively)
> **Part 1**
> If X = [$_{IP}$ NP I'] and NP is not a quantifier, then for any s:
> $[[X]]^s = 1$ iff $[[NP]]^s \in [[I']]^s$.
> **Part 2**
> If X = [$_{IP}$ NP I'] and NP is a quantifier, then for any s:
> $[[X]]^s = 1$ iff $[[I']]^s \in [[NP]]^s$.

We still need to address composing the NP meanings in (25) from the determiner meaning and the meaning of its N' sister. What do the quantified determiners mean? Their sister denotes a set, and that set needs to play the same role that D plays in the case of *nothing* etc. This leads us to the meanings in (26) for the quantified determiners contained in the sentences in (20).

(26) a. For any s: $[[every]]^s = \{<P, Q>: P \subseteq Q\}$
 b. For any s: $[[no]]^s = \{<P, Q>: P \cap Q = \emptyset\}$
 c. For any s: $[[some]]^s = \{<P, Q>: P \cap Q \neq \emptyset\}$
 d. For any s: $[[exactly\ 5]]^s = \{<P, Q>: card(P \cap Q) = 5\}$
 e. For any s: $[[most]]^s = \{<P, Q>: card(P \cap Q) > 0.5 \times card(P)\}$

Thus, as we had intuitively anticipated, quantified determiners denote relations – relations between sets, not individuals.

The first set restricts the claim made by the quantifier. It is often called the restriction. We also need to specify a composition rule that combines the restriction with the quantified determiner. The rule below makes the N' restriction take the place of the first set in the relation denoted by the determiner. This rule should remind you of verbs denoting relations between individuals and combining them with their syntactic objects.

> **Quantified NPs** (QUANTNP)
> If X = [$_{NP}$ Det N'] and Det is a quantified determiner, then for any s:
> $[[X]]^s = \{Q: <[[N']]^s, Q> \in [[Det]]^s\}$

We are now able to go through a complete calculation of the truth conditions predicted for our examples in (20) and similar data. An example calculation is presented below. Remember: the point of the calculation is to show that we have done our job properly. We have developed an interpretation component for our grammar (with lexical entries for the quantifiers and other items, and rules of composition that follow the syntactic structure), which is suitable to account for the intuitive truth conditions that these examples have.

(27) $[\![\, [_{IP} \, [_{NP} \, no \, student] \, [_{I'} \, is \, [_{VP} \, [_{V'} \, t \, [_{AP} \, French]]]] \,]\!]^s = 1$ iff (SUBJPRED 2)
$[\![\, [_{I'} \, is \, [_{VP} \, [_{V'} \, t \, [_{AP} \, French]]]] \,]\!]^s \in [\![\, [_{NP} \, no \, student] \,]\!]^s$ iff (SEMVAC)
$[\![\, [_{VP} \, [_{V'} \, t \, [_{AP} \, French]]] \,]\!]^s \in [\![\, [_{NP} \, no \, student] \,]\!]^s$ iff (NONBR)
$[\![[_{V'} \, t \, [_{AP} \, French]] \,]\!]^s \in [\![\, [_{NP} \, no \, student] \,]\!]^s$ iff (IT)
$[\![\, [_{AP} \, French] \,]\!]^s \in [\![\, [_{NP} \, no \, student] \,]\!]^s$ iff (2x NONBR)
$[\![\, [_{A} \, French] \,]\!]^s \in [\![\, [_{NP} \, no \, student] \,]\!]^s$ iff (LEX)
$\{x : x \text{ is French in } s\} \in [\![\, [_{NP} \, no \, student] \,]\!]^s$ iff (QUANTNP)
$\{x : x \text{ is French in } s\} \in \{Q : <[\![\, [_{N'} \, student] \,]\!]^s, Q> \in [\![no]\!]^s\}$ iff (SIMPL)
$<[\![\, [_{N'} \, student] \,]\!]^s, \{x : x \text{ is French in } s\}> \in [\![no]\!]^s$ iff (LEX)
$<[\![\, [_{N'} \, student] \,]\!]^s, \{x : x \text{ is French in } s\}> \in \{<P, Q> : P \cap Q = \varnothing\}$ iff (SIMPL)
$[\![\, [_{N'} \, student] \,]\!]^s \cap \{x : x \text{ is French in } s\} = \varnothing$ iff (NONBR)
$[\![\, [_{N} \, student] \,]\!]^s \cap \{x : x \text{ is French in } s\} = \varnothing$ iff (LEX)
$\{x : x \text{ is a student in } s\} \cap \{x : x \text{ is French in } s\} = \varnothing$

⊕ **Exercise.** Suggest lexical entries parallel to (26) for *many*, *less than four* and *few*. □

⊕ **Exercise.** Calculate compositionally the truth conditions of the sentence *Every English sailor admires Captain Cook*. □

2.2. No simpler meaning is possible for quantified NPs

Quantified NPs denote sets of sets. This may be surprising because other kinds of NPs denote simpler kinds of things: the meaning of a referential NP is an individual. But it can be shown that there is no simpler kind of object that quantifiers could denote. In particular, they cannot be individuals. In this subsection, we go through some of the reasoning that shows this. Heim and Kratzer (1998) is our source for this presentation.

We first consider **inferences.** (28a) with a referential subject is a valid inference: every situation in which the first sentence is true is a situation in which the second sentence is true. In fact, it will be a valid inference with any referential subject, not just *John*. This is because the predicates in the two sentences stand in a subset relation, (28c). Every individual that is in the set $[\![arrived\ yesterday\ morning]\!]^s$ is also in the set $[\![arrived\ yesterday]\!]^s$. But (28b) with the quantified subject NP *at most one letter* is not a valid inference. Since we have just convinced ourselves that the inference is valid for any referential NP, it follows that *at most one letter* is not a referential NP. A parallel point can be made for further quantified NPs like *no letter, exactly two postcards, few visitors*.

(28)   a.   *John arrived yesterday morning.*
              => *John arrived yesterday*
       b.   *At most one letter arrived yesterday morning.*
              ≠> *At most one letter arrived yesterday.*
       c. $[\![arrived\ yesterday\ morning]\!]^s \subseteq [\![arrived\ yesterday]\!]^s$

=> $[\![at\ most\ one\ letter]\!]$ is not an individual.

We can use **contradictions** to extend the argument. Recall that contradictions are sentences which are not true in any situation. While (29a), which contains an individual-denoting NP, is a contradiction, (29b), with a quantifier instead, is not. (29b) is a so-called contingent statement – it is true in some situations and false in others.

(29)   a.   *Picton is on this side of the Cook Strait and Picton is on the other side of the Cook Strait.*
       b.   *More than two towns are on this side of the Cook Strait and more than two towns are on the other side of the Cook Strait.*
       c. $[\![be\ on\ this\ side]\!]^s \cap [\![be\ on\ the\ other\ side]\!]^s = \emptyset$

The reason for (29a) being contradictory is that the two properties in the respective conjuncts of the sentence have the empty set as their intersection, cf. (29c). No individual can be in both sets. Thus the structure in (29a) will be a contradiction with any individual denoting subject. But (29b) with the quantified subject *more than two towns* is not a contradiction. Therefore, the meaning of *more than two towns* cannot be an individual. A parallel point can be made e.g. for *some beautiful bays, several cities, many parks*.

A third area in which we can see differences between referential and quantified NPs are **tautologies**. Tautologies are sentences that are true in any situation. An example is (30a):

(30) a. *I am over 30 years old or I am under 40 years old.*
 b. *Every woman in this room is over 30 years old or every woman in this room is under 40 years old.*
 c. $[\![be\ over\ 30]\!]^s \cup [\![be\ under\ 40]\!]^s = D$

(30a) is true for any referential subject NP. Why? The union of the two predicates is the entire universe of discourse D, i.e. the set of all (relevant) individuals. So an individual will necessarily be in one set or in the other (or in both). But once more, a quantified NP such as *every woman in this room* does not lead to a tautology in (30b). Therefore, the meaning of the quantified NP cannot be an individual.

In sum, for all the quantified NPs an argument can be made that their meaning is not an individual. We are justified in giving them a different kind of denotation than referential NPs.

3. Scope ambiguity ambiguity

3.1. Interpreting negation

Quantifiers are different in another respect from referential NPs: they give rise to a type of ambiguity called scope ambiguity. In order to approach this topic, we need to discuss negation first.

Let us begin by asking when a sentence such as (31) is true.

(31) *It didn't snow yesterday.*

Intuitively, (31) is true iff (32) is false:

(32) *It snowed yesterday.*

So here is a meaning rule for negation that captures this intuition:

136   *NP semantics*

> **not$_{sent}$**
> If X = [*not* Y] and Y denotes a truth value, then for any s: $[[X]]^s = 1$ iff $[[Y]]^s = 0$.

The rule is intended for the negation of sentences (as indicated by the subscript *sent*). It obviously works well for the expression *it is not the case that*, and also for sentences like the one above with a semantically vacuous *it* as the subject. But what about (33)?

(33)   *Bill does not snore.*

Even though we ignore *does* as semantically vacuous, we have a problem: the sister of *not* is a predicate, *snore*, not a truth value. But the rule above requires a truth value. We explore two possible ways of dealing with this problem.

The first approach takes the following observation as its starting point: while we clearly have sentential negation, as in *it is not the case that*, we can just as clearly negate things that aren't sentences. Examples would be the prefix *un-* in *uninspiring* and *non* in *non-resident*. What happens here? We negate a property, i.e. set. The operation involved seems to be forming the complement of the set. The set of uninspiring entities is the complement of the set of inspiring entities. Similarly, the set of non-residents is the complement of the set of residents.

A fact that goes together with this analysis is the following type of coordination, where a non-negated and a negated predicate are coordinated:

(34)   *Bill is tired and not interested.*

Here is a rule for this *not*, predicate negation, which yields the complement of its input set:

> **not$_{pred}$**
> If X = [*not* Y] and Y denotes a set, then for any s: $[[X]]^s = D \backslash [[Y]]^s = \{x: x \notin [[Y]]^s\}$

This rule allows us to interpret the S-structure of (33).

🕐 **Exercise.** Show this.   □

There is also a second approach to the problem posed by (33): Syntacticians have proposed that Spec-IP, where we find the subject at S-Structure in English, is not really the place where the subject originates. Instead, at the underlying level (D-Structure), the subject is in Spec-VP. (Notice that this is theoretically pleasing in that VPs have a specifier after all.) Assuming that the subject originates in Spec-VP is known as the **VP-internal subject hypothesis**. What is the motivation for it?

One bit of evidence is that sometimes we seem to be able to see the subject in Spec-VP, for example in contexts such as (35):

(35)   *I saw* [$_{VP}$ *Bill run*].

In an intuitive sense, *Bill* is the subject of the embedded verb *run*. And since there is no evidence for a category I (no modal or inflection), *Bill run* could very well be a VP. Another bit of evidence is that sometimes, it looks like part of the subject gets left behind in Spec-VP when the subject moves to Spec-IP. In (36a), the word *all* (which is called a floated quantifier) intuitively belongs to the subject NP. We see this in (36b). But in (36a), it does not occur together with the NP, but rather in a position below I.

(36)   a.   *The students must all leave.*
       b.   *All the students must leave.*

(37)   [$_{IP}$ [$_{NP}$ *the students*] [$_{I'}$ *must* [$_{VP}$ ***all*** _ *leave*]]]
       |_____|

This may be explained by saying that the subject is in Spec-VP at D-Structure and moves to Spec-IP on the way to S-Structure. It may leave behind elements like *all*. This idea is sketched in (37). Let us suppose that this is so and adopt the VP internal subject hypothesis. Then, the derivation of (38) contains a movement transformation that we have so far been unaware of. Let's call this movement subject movement.

(38)   *Bill snores.*
       a.   D-Structure: [$_{IP}$ _ [$_{I'}$ *-s* [$_{VP}$ *Bill snore*]]]
       b.   S-Structure: [$_{IP}$ *Bill* 1 [$_{I'}$ _ [$_{VP}$ t_1 *snore+s*]]]

> **Subject Movement**
> Move the subject from Spec-VP to Spec-IP.

With this syntactic analysis in place, notice that one might then say that the VP starts out as a truth value denoting expression. It no longer seems to be one because the subject has moved out. But what if we interpret the structure before movement, not after movement? Perhaps we can simply ignore this syntactic maneuver and interpret *Bill* in Spec-VP. VP is interpreted via the Subject Predicate rule (which, notice, requires a change in the phrasing of where the rule applies), and *not* is sentential negation. In (39) and (40) below, we provide the key steps in the interpretation of the sentence based on the D-Structure (*does* in the inflectional layer of the sentence is ignored – recall that it is a semantically vacuous element).

(39)   *Bill does not snore.*
      a.   D-Structure: $[_{IP} \_ [_{I'} \text{-}s [\textit{not} [_{VP} \textit{Bill snore}]]]]$
      b.   S-Structure: $[_{IP} \textit{Bill}\, 1 [_{I'} do\text{+}\text{-}s [_{VP} \textit{not} [_{VP} t_1 \textit{snore}]]]]$

(40) $[\![[\textit{not} [\textit{Bill snore}]]]\!]^s = 1$ iff   (NEG)
          $[\![\textit{Bill snore}]\!]^s = 0$ iff   (SUBJPRED)
          $[\![\textit{Bill}]\!]^s \notin [\![\textit{snore}]\!]^s$ iff   (LEX)
          Bill $\notin \{x: x$ snores in $s\}$

> **Subject-Predicate rule**
> **Part 1:**
> If $X = [_Y \text{ NP } Z]$ and Z denotes a set and NP is not a quantifier, then for any s:
> $[\![X]\!]^s = 1$ iff $[\![NP]\!]^s \in [\![Z]\!]^s$.
> **Part 2:**
> If $X = [_Y \text{ NP } Z]$ and Z denotes a set and NP is a quantifier, then for any s:
> $[\![X]\!]^s = 1$ iff $[\![Z]\!]^s \in [\![NP]\!]^s$.

This second solution, then, relies on interpreting the subject in a different position than where it surfaces. At this point this may seem a bit contrived. But we will see more evidence for it from the interaction of negation and quantifiers in the next subsection.

3.2. Negation and quantifiers

A final point we make here concerns the interaction between syntax and semantics. Empirically, it involves a certain type of ambiguity called scope ambiguity. Theoretically speaking, we reexamine the role of movement for interpretation. It might have seemed that the movements we have assumed for syntactic purposes just kind of got in the way semantically. But this is not really true in general. The scope ambiguity below is one way to see that syntax and semantics work together very closely. We look at the interaction of a quantifier with negation in this chapter. Scope ambiguity is investigted more generally and in more detail in Part II of the textbook.

Notice that the sentences in (41) are ambiguous:

(41) a. *More than 3 students didn't answer question 2.*
b. *One of my friends didn't invite Joey.*

Let's focus on (41a). This can mean either (41'a) or (41'b):

(41') a. *There are more than three students such that they didn't answer question 2.*
b. *It is not the case that there are more than three students who answered question 2.*

Suppose that we have 8 students. Suppose that four of them did not answer question 2. Then (41'a) is true (because there are four students who didn't answer question 2) and (41'b) is false (because there are four students who did answer). In (41"a,b), the two interpretations are formalized using our semantics of the quantified determiner *more than three*.

(41") a. card({x: x is a student in s} ∩ {x: x didn't answer question 2 in s}) > 3
b. NOT: card({x: x is a student in s} ∩ {x: x answered question 2 in s}) > 3
i.e.: card({x: x is a student in s} ∩ {x: x answered question 2 in s}) ≤ 3

How does the grammar create this ambiguity? Notice that none of the words are ambiguous. This is the type of case that we would then analyze as a structural ambiguity. But for this sentence, we have only one S-

140 *NP semantics*

Structure (unlike obvious examples of structural ambiguity such as *We discussed the man on TV*). This is where the second proposal from above comes in. In a sense, we do have two structures for the sentence: one with the subject moved, and one with the subject in Spec-VP. Those two structures correspond to the two meanings described above. This can be seen intuitively: In the first structure (42), the first element contributing to interpretation is the negation, which we interpret with the rule for sentential negation. Sentence negation is applied to *more than 3 students answer question 2*. Thus here we negate the statement that the intersection of the students with the individuals that answered question 2 has more than three members. This corresponds to reading (41'b) = (41"b). When we interpret the structure in (43), on the other hand, we consider the cardinality of the intersection of the students with the complement of those who answered question 2. The complement of the set of individuals that answered question 2 is derived by application of the rule for predicate negation to the set of individuals who answered question 2. The resulting interpretation is (41'a) = (41"a).

(42)

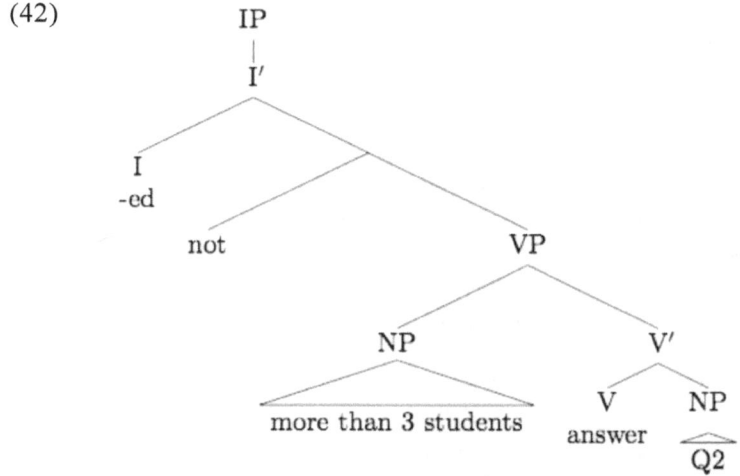

(43)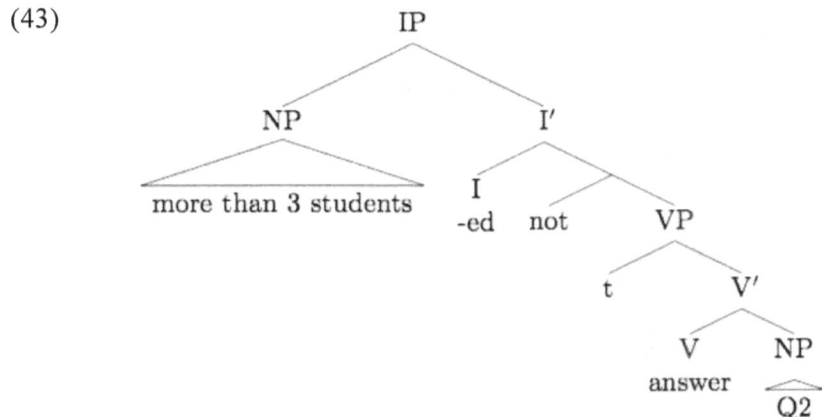

We have thus revised our beliefs about movement: It may be relevant for interpretation where an expression started out. Even though that position is not where the expression is in the Surface Structure of English, it can be relevant for the purposes of interpretation.

Also note that the contrast between (33) and examples with quantifiers like (41) motivates a different semantics for quantifiers vs. referential noun phrases. The two different structures do not lead to two different interpretations in the case of a referential subject, as we have seen.

🕒 **Exercise.** Show that the truth conditions described above are derived, by doing a step by step calculation of (42) and (43). To practice the use of paraphrases, go back to (41b) and provide unambiguous paraphrases for the readings available. ☐

☕ **Exercise.** While the presence of a quantified NP and negation creates the potential for scope ambiguity, not all sentences containing the two ingredients are always ambiguous. Try to create sentences with negation and quantifiers that fall into three categories (you may do this with English sentences or with sentences in another language): (i) two meanings are available (as above); (ii) one meaning is particularly prominent; (iii) only one meaning is available due to grammatical factors. Try to describe those factors as precisely as you can – we will return to this issue in our discussion of scope in Part II. ☐

> **THE BASICS BOX: *NP semantics***
> - ✓ Definite descriptions are referential NPs with a presupposition: the property denoted by the sister of the definite determiner has to be true of just one individual. The NP then refers to that individual.
> - ✓ Presuppositions are appropriateness conditions: a sentence with a presupposition can only be used appropriately if the presupposition is true. Presupposition is different from assertion in that it is unaffected by negation and other embedding contexts.
> - ✓ Quantified NPs denote sets of sets, quantified determiners denote relations between sets. Quantified NPs cannot have the same kind of meaning as referential NPs.
> - ✓ Quantifiers can give rise to scope ambiguities, for instance, when they occur with negation. Scope ambiguities have interesting consequences for the interface between syntax and semantics; for example, they support the VP internal subject hypothesis.

4. Selected references

Frege (1892), Russell (1905) and Strawson (1950) are classic references on the denotation of the definite article. Heim (2011) discusses both the classical beginnings and the recent developments in the semantics of definites in comparison to indefinites. Schwarz (2013) offers a recent overview of the types of definites with interesting crosslinguistic differentiation.

Presupposition is a large topic in semantics and pragmatics. A standard reference is Stalnaker (1972). Kadmon (2000) offers a general introduction. A recent overview is Beaver and Geurts (2012).

Montague (1973), Barwise and Cooper (1981), Keenan and Stavi (1986) are cornerstones in the development of the field's understanding of quantifiers – the so-called Generalized Quantifiers Theory. See Keenan's (2011) contribution in the recent edition of the *Handbook of Semantics* and Szabolcsi's (2010) monograph for recent surveys. We will return to the issues of quantification and scope in more detail in Part II (Chapter II-3).

The interpretation of sentential negation is standard and can be found in any textbook on propositional logic (see e.g. Partee et al. (1990)). Logical operators like negation can occur in different syntactic environments in natural language. This is handled by a 'family of types' approach. See Partee and Rooth (1983) and also Partee (1987), and de Hoop (2012) for recent discussion. In Quine's work (1960), many of the basic things about predicates or negation that we have observed here are available, though in a different system. Frege (1906) interestingly refers to a debate between two views regarding negation – whether it attaches to the predicate or to the 'whole', a debate which he himself finds *unfruchtbar,* roughly: 'useless', (i.e. the two views are quite equivalent - as indeed a type shifting approach would suggest).

We have used the VP internal subject hypothesis to facilitate the interpretation of negation in accordance with the position it has in a language like English. The hypothesis was proposed by several researchers in the 1980s and 1990 (cf., e.g., Zagona 1982, Diesing 1990, Koopman and Sportiche 1991).

The revision of the Subject-Predicate rule in the last section of this chapter gets rid of category information in the application of the rule. Instead, application of the rule is dictated by the kinds of denotations that the two expressions have whose meanings are combined. This is a step towards type driven interpretation. See Heim & Kratzer (1998) for such a theory of compositional interpretation, as well as older references. The way we proceed in this textbook is a rule-by-rule approach: we formulate a large set of semantic rules each of which applies under particular circumstances. It is easy to see that such an approach misses generalizations. Modern semantic theory has basically replaced rule-by-rule approaches by more general, type driven theories of compositional interpretation, as you will see when you pursue the study of semantics further.

The idea that different levels of syntactic representation can be the input to interpretation can be traced to the work of Robert May in the late 1970s and early 1980s (cf. May 1985 for the relevant monograph). See Heim and Kratzer (1998) for how the idea may be used in compositional semantic theory. We will return to this issue in more detail in Part II of the textbook.

Appendix:
Syntactic and semantic rules from Part I

1. Syntax

1.1. PS rules

```
CP → (XP) C'
C' → C IP
```

```
IP → NP I'
I' → I VP
```

```
VP → NP V'
V' → AdvP V'
V' → V' AdvP
V' → V' PP
V' → V (NP) (PP)
V' → V VP
V' → V CP
```

```
NP → (Det) N'
NP → NP's N'
N' → AP N'
N' → N' PP
N' → N (PP)
```

```
AP → (Deg) A'
A' → A PP
A' → Adv A'
A' → A (PP)
```

```
PP → (XP) P'
P' → P (NP)
```

1.2. The generalized X' schema

```
XP → (YP) X'
X' → ZP X'
X' → X' WP
X' → X (QP) (UP)
```

1.3. Transformations

Wh-movement
Move a wh-phrase to the nearest specifier of CP.

I-to-C movement
Move the content of I to C.

Verb Raising
Move an auxiliary verb to I.

Affix hopping
Move I onto the following main verb if they are not separated by *not*.

Do-support
Attach *do* to the I node.

Subject Movement
Move the subject from Spec-VP to Spec-IP.

2. Rules of composition

Subject-Predicate rule (SUBJPRED 1 & 2)
Part 1:
If $X = [_Y \text{ NP } Z]$ and Z denotes a set and NP is not a quantifier, then for any s:
$[[X]]^s = 1$ iff $[[NP]]^s \in [[Z]]^s$.
Part 2:
If $X = [_Y \text{ NP } Z]$ and Z denotes a set and NP is a quantifier, then for any s:
$[[X]]^s = 1$ iff $[[Z]]^s \in [[NP]]^s$.

Non branching trees (NONBR)
If $X = [_Y Z]$, then for any s: $[[X]]^s = [[Z]]^s$

Ignore traces (IT)
If $X = [_Z \text{ t } Y]$, then for any s: $[[X]]^s = [[Y]]^s$.

Ignore semantically vacuous elements (SEMVAC)
If $X = [_W \text{ y } Z]$ and y is a semantically vacuous element, then for any s: $[[X]]^s = [[Z]]^s$.

Predicate Modification (PM)
If $X = [_W Y Z]$ and both Y and Z denote sets, then for any s:
$[[X]]^s = [[Y]]^s \cap [[Z]]^s$

---

former
If $X = [_{N'} \textit{former } N']$ then for any s: $[[X]]^s = \{x: \text{there is an s' before s such that } x \in [[N']]^{s'}\}$

Objects of relations (OBJREL):
If $X = [_W Y Z]$, where Z denotes an individual and Y denotes a relation, then for any s: $[[X]]^s = \{v: <v, [[Z]]^s> \in [[Y]]^s\}$

> **the**
> If X = [$_{NP}$ *the* N'] then for any s: $[\![\textit{the } N']\!]^s$ is only defined if there is exactly one z such that $z \in [\![N']\!]^s$. Then, $[\![\textit{the } N']\!]^s$ is that z.

> **Quantified NPs** (QUANTNP)
> If X = [$_{NP}$ Det N'] and Det is a quantified determiner, then for any s:
> $[\![X]\!]^s = \{Q: <[\![N']\!]^s, Q> \in [\![Det]\!]^s\}$

> **not$_{sent}$**
> If X = [*not* Y] and Y denotes a truth value, then for any s: $[\![X]\!]^s = 1$ iff $[\![Y]\!]^s = 0$.

> **not$_{pred}$**
> If X = [*not* Y] and Y denotes a set, then for any s: $[\![X]\!]^s = D \backslash [\![Y]\!]^s = \{x: x \notin [\![Y]\!]^s\}$

Part II

Extending the Theory and Applying it to Crosslinguistic Differences

Chapter II-1
Introduction and roadmap to the second part

A person who never made a mistake never tried anything new.
(Albert Einstein)

This chapter situates the plot of Part II in the context of the book and gives a short preview of the topics to be discussed.

1. Aims and background

In this second part, we develop the syntactic and semantic analysis from Part I further and apply it to a series of phenomena at the syntax-semantics-interface. The phenomena chosen are quantifier scope, polarity, focus, ellipsis, and tense and aspect. On the one hand, these phenomena relate structure and meaning in an interesting way. On the other hand, they allow us to take a contrastive stance and compare English to other languages. A focus of our contrastive study is German. In preparation for our discussion of interface issues, we compare the clause structure of German to that of English. We have structured the presentation in such a way that readers who want to concentrate on English may largely skip the German-specific sections.

We have endeavored to keep this second part of the textbook fairly self-contained. Chapter II-2 provides a summary of the syntactic background introduced in Part I, and Chapter II-3 sketches the essentials of the set-theory-based semantics from Part I. We have usually taught the material in Part II as a second course building on a course teaching Part I. The necessary background may come from other introductions to syntax and semantics as well.

As in Part I, we keep technicalities to a minimum in order to get to a discussion of interesting data quickly. There is nothing novel about the individual analyses presented. The purpose of the text is to put existing theories together in a coherent way, and to present a consistent picture from a syntactic and a semantic perspective. We want to highlight what our field

152 *Introduction and roadmap to the second part*

is about and what it has accomplished in understanding language and grammar. Each thematic chapter closes with a references section. The sources of the analyses we present in the main text are listed there. We also point to further discussion in the literature and more in-depth theories of the phenomena we investigate. Just as in the first part, we aim to make the syntax-semantics interface quite accessible, so that students can get an understanding of central issues in the more technical literature, and perhaps also a first entry ticket to it.

We turn to short illustrations of what the next six chapters (clause structure, quantifiers and scope, negation and polarity, focus, ellipsis, tense and aspect) are about.

2. The topics ahead

2.1. Clause structure - English vs. German

The chapter on clausal structure reviews the building blocks that were introduced in Part I to tackle the structural analysis of English. A second purpose of this chapter is to go on to compare them to the syntactic properties of German. We only sketch one difference in the syntax of the two languages in this preview: the status of the modals and the I(nfl) projection.

Recall that modal auxiliaries have a special status in the grammar of English. English modals are conspicuously distinct from main verbs. They cannot co-occur with inflection either on a verb or on themselves, cf. (1), and we cannot find modals in non-finite forms, (2). Furthermore, only auxiliaries (not main verbs) can be inverted with the subject in interrogatives, as in (3). Accordingly, the syntactic analysis has modals occupy as their structural position the node that also hosts inflections, namely I(nfl).

(1) a. * *Robin musts/musted play the forward position.*
     b. * *Robin must plays/played the forward position.*

(2) * *Sally has may/might/must solve the problem.*

(3) a. *Can he help you?*   b. * *Helps he you?*

In German, such differences between verbs and modals do not arise. Modals have inflectional endings (e.g. *kannst*, 'can.2SG.PRESENT', *konntest*, 'can. 2SG.PAST' etc.) and non-finite modals are just fine; contrast the following with unavailable modal infinitives in English, e.g.**to can/to must*:

(4) *Sally hat die Aufgabe lösen können/müssen.*
     Sally has the problem solve can.INF/must.INF
     'Sally was able to / had to solve the problem.'

German modals do not stand out in terms of movement properties either. It's rather the case that *all* verbs are able to undergo inversion with the subject, and modals are just part of the class:

(5) a. *Kann er dir helfen?*   b. *Hilft er dir?*
         can he you.DAT help   helps he you.DAT
         'Can he help you?'   'Does he help you?'

Such facts indicate that there is no syntactic evidence for a specialized inflectional node in the structure of German, and hence, no IP. That is, the German clause consists of *just* VP and CP. The twist will be that a number of interesting phenomena are attested precisely in the VP and the CP in German. We discuss these additional structural possibilities (such as verb-second effects, or scrambling), in Chapter II-2. Interestingly, they are also intertwined with other topics, e.g. focus and scope. We turn to a brief preview of this latter area next.

2.2. Quantifiers and scope

In English, a sentence that contains two quantified noun phrases is frequently ambiguous. We illustrate this phenomenon with an example that has one quantified NP in subject position and the other as a direct object. Example (6) has the two interpretations paraphrased in (6a) and (6b).

(6) *A girl introduced every boy.*
     a. There is a girl who introduced every boy.
     b. Every boy was introduced by a (possibly different) girl.

Similarly, we see interaction of negation with a quantifier. English (7) is ambiguous between (7a) and (7b). It is interesting that the corresponding

154 *Introduction and roadmap to the second part*

German sentence in (7') is not; it is a (perhaps slightly suboptimal) way of saying that nobody saw the movie.

(7) *I discovered that everyone hadn't seen the movie.*
    a. My discovery: Not everyone had seen the movie.
    b. My discovery: Everyone had failed to see the movie.

(7') *Ich habe festgestellt, dass jeder den Film*
    I have discovered that everyone the.ACC movie.ACC
    nicht gesehen hatte.
    not seen had
    'I discovered that everyone hadn't seen the movie.'

The example in (7) had a subject NP and a negation – let's try the same with an object NP, (8):

(8) *I didn't invite one of her friends.*
    a. It is not the case that I invited a friend of hers.
    b. There is one friend of hers who I didn't invite.

The English example is ambiguous in a parallel way to (7). When we translate the example into German, the English ambiguity once more disappears. The two different word orders in (8') correspond to the readings (8a) and (8b) of the English example.

(8') a. *Ich habe keinen ihrer Freunde eingeladen.*
        I have Neg_one.ACC her.GEN friends invited
        'I invited none of her friends.'
    b. *Ich habe einen ihrer Freunde nicht eingeladen.*
        I have one.ACC her.GEN friends.GEN not invited
        'There is one friend of hers that I failed to invite.'

In Chapter II-3 we examine why the English and the German facts differ in this regard. Our answer involves the different structural possibilities the two languages offer.

2.3. Negation and polarity

The above examples show that there are circumstances in English in which quantifiers give rise to more interpretational possibilities than in German. Word order often disambiguates in German. However, English also has ways of reducing ambiguity. Compare (9b) and (9c) to the original example (9a) = (8). (9b) only has reading (8a) and (9c) only has reading (8b).

(9) a. *I didn't invite one of her friends.*
    b. *I didn't invite any of her friends.*
    c. *I didn't invite some of her friends.*

This is brought about by the change in the determiner. The determiner *any* is a so-called negative polarity item (NPI). It can occur in a negative sentence, and in various other environments, but not in an ordinary affirmative sentence.

(10) a. *I didn't invite any soccer players.*
     b. * *I invited any soccer players.*

Another example of an NPI is the expression *lift a finger*. The paradigm in (11) gives us a first impression of where NPIs can occur.

(11) a. *Joe didn't lift a finger to help with the move.*
     b. *Nobody lifted a finger to help with the move.*
     c. * *Everybody lifted a finger to help with the move.*
     d. * *Bill lifted a finger to help with the move.*

We examine in Chapter II-4 how the NPI status of *any* triggers the disambiguating effect we observe in (9).

2.4. Focus

We use the term focus to refer to the most prominent part of a linguistic expression. In the answer in (12b) below, the NP 'my cousin' replacing the wh-phrase *who* in (12a), is the focus. Interpretively, it is the 'new' and 'most important' part of the sentence. Phonologically, it is the most prominent part containing a pitch accent on *cousin*, indicated by capitalization.

(12) a. *Who did you invite?*   b. *I invited my COUsin.*

We investigate in Chapter II-5 how focus is interpreted semantically. The reader is introduced to a semantic analysis according to which focus introduces alternatives. In (12b), for example, you may find yourself contemplating alternatively that I invited my nephew, that I invited the landlord, that I invited Reinhold Messner and so on. Alternatives play a role in a number of phenomena. For example, take the interpretation of (13) below. (13a,b) differ in terms of stress, and they also differ in terms of interpretation.

(13)   a.   *Reinhold even climbed Mt TECHnical.*
            b.   *Reinhold even CLIMbed Mt Technical.*

There are some differences with respect to how focus behaves in English vs. German. One such difference concerns structural positions standardly available to focused constituents. Topicalized focus as in (14b) is degraded in English. German (15), on the other hand, is fine. German allows focused constituents to be fronted.

(14)   a.   *Who did you invite?*   b. $^{??}$ *My COUsin, I invited.*

(15)   a.   *Wen   hast   Du   eingeladen?*
                 who.ACC have   you   invited
                 'Who did you invite?'
            b.   *Meinen   COUsin   hab   ich   eingeladen.*
                 my.ACC   cousin. ACC   have   I   invited
                 'I invited my cousin.'

We use contrasts such as this one to show how the grammar of human languages must make reference to focus.

2.5. Ellipsis

Focus plays many roles in grammar and in particular it relates to the topic of Chapter II-6, ellipsis. Remember that English has the possibility of eliding a VP, as illustrated by the examples below.

(16)   *Lizzy will go to LA because Jane will.*

VP ellipsis can leave behind constituents, for example temporal adjuncts. Observe the difference between the well-formed (17a) and the strange (17b).

(17)   a.   *Lizzy will go to LA tomorrow because Jane will on Tuesday.*
            b.   # *Lizzy will go to LA tomorrow because Jane will tomorrow.*

Intuitively, you cannot strand material in the ellipsis clause if it is the same as material that already occurred in the antecedent clause. We relate this effect to focus. Informally speaking, you need to express a contrast between *tomorrow* and *Tuesday* in (17a), and you do this by focusing *on Tuesday*. You are unable to express such a contrast in (17b) and this makes the example odd.

Ellipsis also allows us to reexamine some important structural decisions we made in preceding chapters. For example, the ellipses in (18) confirm the movement operations we argue for in Chapters II-2 and II-3:

(18)   a.   *While Heidi likes fruit, I do _ chocolate.*
         b.   *Darcy will bring sweet potatoes, or perhaps purple kumara.*

The ellipsis chapter allows us to see how the theory introduced so far extends to cover a range of further data.

2.6. Tense and aspect

In Chapter II-7 we revise a simplification made up to this point: treating the inflectional morphology on a verbal stem as semantically vacuous. Intuitively, it makes a truth conditional difference whether we make a statement in the present tense or the past tense.

(19)   a.   *George W. Bush is president of the US.*
         b.   *George W. Bush was president of the US.*

In this chapter, we turn to temporal interpretation. The topic is closely related to its follow-up: aspect.

Linguists take tense to be the linguistic encoding of time. The tenses on which we will concentrate are the present and the past. The central question is how we can integrate tense with the syntactic and semantic objects in our repertoire. We follow the idea that an occurence of, say, a past tense as in Barbara Partee's famous example (20), refers to a particular time before now. For instance, in (20) you say that you did not turn off the stove at the time of you leaving the house 30 minutes ago.

(20)   *I didn't turn off the stove!*

In this view, tenses can be mapped quite directly to intervals on a timeline. This allows us to get the basic interpretation moving: The content of the Infl node is not vacuous, it is a time.

But recall from Part I that the VP describes situations. So, as things stand, we are sill missing something, since we have times on the one hand and situations on the other. We need to connect them. Aspect will help us make this connection, i.e. between situations and time intervals. But hold on - on the empirical/intuitive side, what is aspect?

Aspect is about the point of view the speaker takes on a situation or event. This type of aspect is hence also called viewpoint aspect. Aspectual properties will determine whether a situation is viewed as completed or ongoing. Let's consider the following pair:

(21) a. *Sue was preparing for her finals.*
b. *Sue prepared for her finals.*

While the tense contribution is identical - past - in the two sentences above, there is still a clear difference in the way we think about them. Sue's preparation event is described as in progress (at the relevant time interval in the past) in the first sentence, while it is viewed as completed in the second. The term for the incomplete type of viewpoint aspect is 'imperfective' while the second type of aspectual contribution, describing situations as finished, is called 'perfective'. We integrate aspect into structure and composition in Chapter II-7. We also discuss the English perfect (*have*+past participle), which turns out to be a special element in the tense/aspect domain. Finally, we point out a few crosslinguistic differences in this domain.

For quick overview, the thematic chapters of the second part are as follows:

Chapter II-2:   Clause structure – English vs. German
Chapter II-3:   Quantifiers and scope
Chapter II-4:   Negation and polarity
Chapter II-5:   Focus
Chapter II-6:   Ellipsis
Chapter II-7:   Tense and aspect

Chapter II-8 is our conclusion.

Chapter II-2
Clause structure - English and German

German books are easy enough to read when you hold them before the looking-glass or stand on your head – so as to reverse the construction [...]
(Mark Twain)

The first section of this chapter summarizes the syntactic system introduced for the analysis of English clauses in Part I of this textbook. The second section contrastively introduces a similar syntax framework for German. A short literature overview is provided in the third section.

1. Review of English clause structure

In the first section of this chapter, we review the key points of the syntactic analysis of English from Part I. This section should thus serve as a reminder to everyone who is already familiar with the structure of English from the first part of this book (or from equivalent sources) and as a brief introduction to the particular assumptions made here for everyone else. The discussion is set against a general background of an X' phrase structure and phrasal and head movement rules.

We use the following phrase structure (PS) rules to characterize clauses in English.

IP → NP I'
I' → I VP

CP → (XP) C'
C' → C IP

I and C are called functional categories as opposed to lexical catergories. The major lexical categories are N, V, A and P. The X' schema characterizes all phrase structure rules (cf. Chapter I-4 for more details).

> **The X' schema**
> XP → (YP) X'
> X' → ZP X'
> X' → X' WP
> X' → X (QP) (UP)

Let us remind ourselves of the motivation for the IP and CP rules above. We begin with IPs. The clearest case illustrating IPs in English is data like (1) with modal auxiliaries. One of the important characteristics of English clause structure is that it has a class of modals that are conspicuously distinct from main verbs as in (2):

(1)   *John might/can/must/will buy a turtle.*
(2)   *John bought a turtle.*

Remember that modal auxiliaries are in complementary distribution to tense and agreement morphology on the verb:

(3)   a. * *John might bought/buys a turtle.*
        b. * *John cans buy a turtle.*
        c. * *John musted buy a turtle.*

Also, in English, there can only be one modal per clause, same as only one agreement marking:

(4)   a. * *John has buys a turtle.*
        b. * *John can must buy a turtle.*

When we find items that are in complementary distribution, we account for this by putting them in the same structural position. This position is Inflection (Infl or I for short). It occurs between the subject NP and the VP. Modal auxiliaries, tense/agreement morphology and the infinitival marker *to* occur in I. (With this assumption, we make the silly prediction at the moment that *Mary walked home* should really sound like *Mary -ed walk home*. This is obviously false – we will fix it in a moment.)

Let's first address clauses that are slightly larger than the clauses that we have looked at so far:

Review of English clause structure 161

(5) a. *John believes* [CP *that* [IP *Mary bought a turtle*]]
 b. *John wonders* [CP *whether/if* [IP *Mary bought a turtle*]]

These clauses are the complements of the verbs *believe* and *wonder*. They contain a complementizer: *that, whether, if*. We propose that such clauses are CPs. This means that C (complementizer) is the head of the embedded clause CP, i.e. a big complementizer phrase. Is this plausible? Remember that heads select their complements. Hence, a verb that subcategorizes for a CP might select a CP headed by a particular C, if our rule is on the right track. This expectation is confirmed by (6):

(6) a. *I wondered* whether Mary had bought chocolate.
   * that Mary had bought chocolate.
 b. *I thought* that Mary had bought chocolate.
   * whether Mary had bought chocolate.
 c. *I know* that Mary had bought chocolate.
   whether Mary had bought chocolate.

(7) example subcategorization frame:
 thought: V, [_ CP(that)]

A particular C in turn selects a particular kind of IP. The C *whether* accepts an infinitival IP that contains *to*, while *if* doesn't. Similarly for *that* versus *for*:

(8) a. (*I wondered*) *whether to leave.*
 b. * (*I wondered*) *if to leave.*
(9) a. (*I want*) *for Bill to leave.*
 b. * (*I want*) *that Bill to leave.*

Since C selects I, we should view I as the head of the smaller clausal unit IP, as we have indeed done.

Notice that we haven't discussed the specifier of CP yet in this review section. We will come back to this in connection with transformations. So far we have only considered the phrase structure component of the syntax, without movement transformations. We turn to those next.

Transformations allow us to solve the puzzle with inflection and verbs. Remember that so far, we have generated *Mary -ed walk to school*. Let's examine verbs, auxiliaries and inflection more closely.

162   *Clause structure - English and German*

The auxiliaries *have* and *be* are particularly interesting:

(10)   a.   *Mary has eaten.*
       b.   *Mary was eaten.*
       c.   *Mary is eating.*
       d.   *Mary should eat.*
       e.   *Mary has been eating.*
       f.   *Mary should have been eaten.*

Clearly, when used as auxiliaries, *have* and *be* select a VP:

Have:	[_VP(PastPart)#]
Be:	[_VP(PastPart)#]
	[_VP(ing)#]

But how do *have* and *be* combine with the finite inflectional endings they bear? The position of negation gives us a useful indication. We first consider the position of negation in a sentence with a modal auxiliary verb:

(11)   *Mary should not be (*not) eating (*not) chocolate.*

The order is modal > negation > VP, i.e. I > negation > VP, since we identified the position of modals as I. So negation occurs between I and the VP:

(12)   [$_{IP}$ *Mary* [$_{I'}$ *should* [*not* [$_{VP}$ [$_{V'}$ *be* [$_{VP}$ [$_{V'}$ *eating chocolate*]]]]]]

Now that we know where negation is located in the clause structure, consider the position of negation in sentences with *have* and *be* (and without modal auxiliaries):

(13)   a.   *Mary (*not) is not eating (*not) chocolate.*
       b.   *Mary (*not) has not (*not) eaten chocolate.*
       c.   *Mary (*not) has not been (*not) eating (*not) chocolate.*

The key observation is that the negation *not* occurs after the first auxiliary verb – that is the auxiliary verb that bears the inflection features. If *not* is between I and VP, then here is a way to combine a verb with inflectional morphology that accounts for this: The finite auxiliary verb moves to I.

> **Verb raising** (V-to-I movement)
> Move an auxiliary verb to I.

Notice how this rule is indeed restricted to auxiliary verbs, that is, *have* and *be*. What happens with main verbs? They do not seem to raise to I:

(14) a. *Mary likes not chocolate.
     b. *Sam went not to the store.

Since the verb does not seem to raise, we assume instead that the affix in I moves down to the verb. This is called affix hopping.

> **Affix hopping**
> Move I onto the following main verb if they are not separated by *not*.

This rule allows us to combine inflection with main verbs, unless there is negation. What about negated main verbs? The presence of negation interferes with affix hopping:

(15) a. *Mary not likes chocolate.
     b. *Sam not goes to the store.

Recall that a semantically empty verb *do* is inserted to bear the inflectional morphology. The rule of do-support captures this.

(16) a. *Mary does not like chocolate.*
     b. *Sam did not go to the store.*

> **Do-support**
> Attach *do* to I.

This rule only applies if all else fails, i.e. if we can have neither affix hopping nor verb raising. In cases in which we can have verb movement (with an auxiliary verb) past negation, the insertion of *do* is not warranted.

(17) a. *Mary has not eaten.*
     b. * *Mary does not have eaten.*

Something must force an affix to combine with a verb, or else we would get *Mary -ed like chocolate*. Intuitively, it's the unattached morpheme *-ed* sitting in I that causes the problem. Based on this intuition, we suggest the following filter:

> **Stray Affix filter:**
> A bound morpheme must be attached to a stem at S-structure.

Next, let's recap question formation in English. We first review the syntax of yes/no-questions. Consider (18)–(20):

(18) a. *Mary should eat chocolate.*
 b. *Should Mary eat chocolate?*
(19) a. *Bill has eaten spinach.*
 b. *Has Bill eaten spinach?*
(20) a. *Mary is eating Reeses.*
 b. *Is Mary eating Reeses?*

This is traditionally called Subject-Auxiliary Inversion (SAI): the auxiliary verb and the subject are in reverse order in yes-no questions. In our terms, it looks like the content of I has moved across the subject.

This is supported by the fact that main verbs cannot undergo this movement in present day English:

(21) a. * *Ate Mary chocolate?*
 b. * *Went Sam to the store?*

Well, we wouldn't expect them to, because they are not in I, they remained under V (and were joined by the affix). What actually happens is that do-support is once more involved:

(22) a. *Did Mary eat chocolate?*
 b. *Did Sam go to the store?*

This fits quite well with what we have said so far: The content of I moves across the subject. Perhaps, the distance between verb and inflection is then too great for affix hopping to apply. Remember that that is a sensitive process that wants things close together (cf. negation). The only thing that can rescue us from the Stray Affix filter is do-support.

So where does the content of I move to? The only thing to the left of the subject that we have encountered so far is C. Now notice that when there is a complementizer, SAI cannot apply:

(23) a. *I wondered whether Mary has eaten the chocolate.*
 b. **I wondered whether has Mary eaten the chocolate.*

A moved auxiliary and a complementizer are in complementary distribution. Hence we suggest that SAI amounts to the following movement transformation:

I-to-C Movement
Move the content of I to C.

V-to-I and I-to-C movement are called head movement (because it is the head of a phrase that moves). When we remove a category from a place in the tree, we leave *t* as shorthand for trace. This element is silent. In the tree representation in (24) below, the auxiliary verb *has* moves first from V to I and then from I to C:

(24)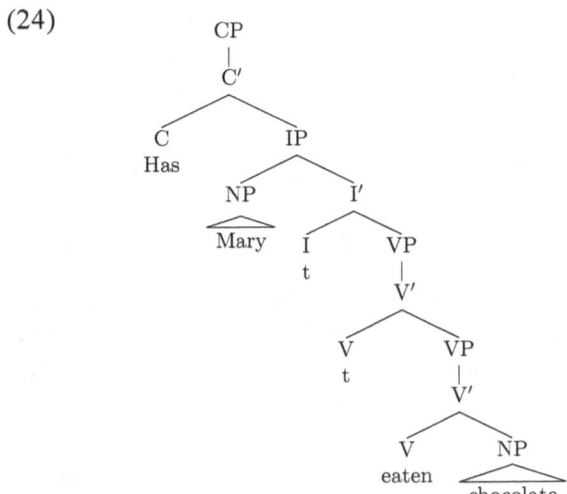

Next we look at so-called information questions or slightly more technically: wh-questions. This reminds us of another transformation – wh-movement. Consider the interrogative sentence in (25).

(25)   What will Sue buy?

Notice that I-to-C movement has applied here, just like in yes-no questions like (26). (*Sue* is the subject. The auxiliary *will* occurs to the left of the subject, hence it must have undergone I-to-C movement.)

(26)   Will Sue buy ice cream?

But what's more, in (25), *what* occurs in the very beginning of the sentence. *What* is to the left of the fronted auxiliary, and hence to the left of C. Now *what* is a (short) wh-phrase (note that wh-phrases can contain more material, e.g. *which organic ice cream from the store on Victoria St*). Our CP rule repeated below includes a specifier of CP. That gives us a slot for the wh-phrase.

CP → (XP) C'
C' → C IP

So the word *what* is sitting in the specifier position of the CP at Surface Structure (S-Structure for short), the structure we see or hear. Movement allows us to reconcile two things: (i) the complement status of the wh-phrase, which requires it to occur in the position following *buy*; (ii) the linear order we observe, in which *what* gets fronted all the way up. We assume the following rule to model the phenomenon:

Wh-movement:
Move a wh-phrase to the specifier of CP.

This rule moves a phrase, not a head. It is therefore an instance of phrasal movement. Note that generating *What will Sue buy?* involves two transformations, as shown in (27). We call this a derivation of the sentence (a series of tree structures). There is an intermediate step between D-Structure and S-Structure.

(27)   [$_{CP}$ [$_{C'}$ [$_{IP}$ Sue will [$_{VP}$ buy what]]]]
       [$_{CP}$ [$_{C'}$ **will** [$_{IP}$ Sue _ [$_{VP}$ buy what]]]]
       [$_{CP}$ **what** [$_{C'}$ will [$_{IP}$ Sue _ [$_{VP}$ buy _]]]]

We put a *t* for "trace" in the place where a constituent started out a movement (just like in the case of the moved auxiliary verb *have* above). Since more than one element might move, we put an index on a trace (t_1, t_2 etc.) and the same index next to the corresponding moved constituent to indicate which traces and displaced elements belong together; cf. (28):

(28)   [$_{CP}$ *what* [2 [$_{C'}$ *will*$_1$ [$_{IP}$ *Sue* t_1 [$_{VP}$ *buy* t_2]]]]]

One more remark on the notation in (28): We have bracketed the movement index of *what* with the sister of *what*. This is the notation used in Heim & Kratzer (1998). Its motivation comes from interpretation: the movement index triggers an interpretation rule called predicate abstraction, which creates sets (in the example at hand, this rule yields {x: Sue will buy x}). We will discuss this in detail in Chapter II-3. We have not bracketed the index on *will* with the sister of *will*, however (it only shows up as a subscript). This is because we do not want to apply the rule predicate abstraction here (it would not yield a useful result). In this textbook, we assume that phrasal movement yields structures in keeping with Heim and Kratzer, while head movement does not. It is quite possible that this assumption is not ultimately correct, but it does produce the correct results for the data we analyze.

Above, we have chosen an example with an auxiliary. Note that if we choose one without an auxiliary, SAI in wh-questions behaves in exactly the same way as in yes-no questions. Do-support is used:

(29)   *What did Sue buy?*

☻ **Exercise.**[1] *Further applications of the movement rules introduced: Negative preposing and fronting with* only. Give the structural representations (i.e. syntactic tree structures) for each of the sentences below:

(E1)   a.   *Under no circumstances could she accept the offer.*
        b.   *Not once has he hesitated.* (National Geographic 5/2011: 102)
        c.   *No way is this happening!* (Alanis Morissette is back!! iTunes customer review, 5/12/2012)

---

[1] A reminder on notation from Part I: we distinguish between exercises that consist in relatively routine transfer of maintext discussions (☻) vs. exercises we consider theoretically challenging (♛).

(E2)   a.   *Only after many attempts did the penny drop.* (After comment on http://www.bbc.co.uk/blogs/haveyoursay/2010/04/...)
       b.   *Only then has he planned some "down time" for debate preparation.* (http://thecaucus.blogs.nytimes.com/...)

Hints: The auxiliary is to the left of the subject. This lets you establish its Surface Structure position. What you still have to do is establish whether it arrived there due to just one step of head-movement (from I-to-C) or two (a preceding step of V-to-I). This will depend on the auxiliaries. Next, what about the fronted phrase that contains a negative word and *only* respectively? To complete the tree, transfer the phrasal type of movement you have encountered in questions.   □

We consider one final transformation, which – like wh-movement – is movement affecting a phrase but which does not displace the phrase all the way to Spec-CP. Syntacticians have proposed that Spec-IP, where we find the subject at Surface Structure in English, is not really the place where the subject first starts out. Instead, at Deep Structure, the subject is in Spec-VP. This is called the VP internal subject hypothesis. (Notice that this analysis is attractive in that VPs are able to have a specifier like all other categories.) What is the motivation for this?

One bit of evidence is that sometimes, we seem to be able to see the subject in Spec-VP in embedded contexts such as (30):

(30)   *I saw* [$_{VP}$ *Bill run*]

In an intuitive sense, *Bill* is the subject of the embedded verb *run*. And since there is no evidence for a category I (no modal or inflection in the bracketed consitutent above), *Bill run* could very well be a VP.

Another bit of evidence is that sometimes, it looks like parts of the subject get left behind in Spec-VP when the subject moves to Spec-IP:

(31)   a.   *The students must all leave.* = *All the students must leave.*
       b.   [$_{IP}$ [$_{NP}$ *the students*] [1[$_{I'}$ *must* [$_{VP}$ **all** t_1 *leave*]]]

It looks as if *all* really belongs to the subject. But it can occur after the material in I. This can be explained by saying that the subject is in Spec-VP at Deep Structure and moves to Spec-IP on the way to Surface Structure. It may leave behind elements like *all* (which are called floated quantifiers). The following movement transformation incorporates this suggestion.

Subject movement
Move the subject from the specifier of VP to the specifier of IP.

---

(32) is a derivation of a simple example incorporating movement of the subject from Spec-VP to Spec-IP:

(32)   *Bill snores.*
       D-Structure: [IP _ [I' -s [VP *Bill snore*]]]
       S-Structure: [IP *Bill* [1[I' _ [VP t_1 *snore+s*]]]]

☞ THE BASICS BOX: ***English clause structure*** *(Recap from Part I)*
   ✓ The X' schema characterizes all phrases.
   ✓ English clauses have a CP and an IP layer.
   ✓ Transformations modify PS trees. Sentences are analyzed by derivations, which link Deep Structure to Surface Structure.
   ✓ Movement transformations in English include V-to-I movement, I-to-C movement and wh-movement.
   ✓ Subjects in English originate in Spec-VP, then move to Spec-IP.

---

2. German clause structure

Let us compare the standard phrase structural analysis of English clauses from the previous section to the syntax of a language that, though related, is still different in interesting ways – German.

In German, there is much less reason to think that there is a category I. German modal verbs behave like main verbs. In contrast to English modals, they inflect quite productively (see the example below). Thus they are not in complementary distribution with inflection. This is a first indication that German modal verbs belong to the lexical category V instead of constituting their own category I.

(33)   können 'can':
       a.   (ich) kann   '(I) can'   can.1SG.PRESENT
            (du) kannst   '(you) can'   can.2SG.PRESENT
            (sie) kann   '(she) can'   can.3SG.PRESENT

	(wir) können	'(we) can'	can.1PL.PRESENT
	(ihr) könnt	'(you) can'	can.2PL.PRESENT
	(sie) können	'(they) can'	can.3PL.PRESENT
b.	(ich) konnte	'(I) could'	can.1SG.PAST
	(du) konntest	'(you) could'	can.2SG.PAST
	(sie) konnte	'(she) could'	can.3SG.PAST
	(wir) konnten	'(we) could'	can.1PL.PAST
	(ihr) konntet	'(you) could'	can.2PL.PAST
	(sie) konnten	'(they) could'	can.3PL.PAST

German modal verbs select for a VP headed by a verb bearing an overt infinitival inflection -*en*.

(34)   Ich   kann   schwimm***en***.
       I   can.1SG.PRES   swim.INFIN
       'I can swim.'

(35)   *können* 'can': V, [VP(-*en*) _]

Furthermore, modals can appear in non-finite forms and can be iterated. There is no reason to think that they occupy a unique position in the clause (like I in English). Assigning them category V fits the facts much better, because we know that verbs can embed VPs (e.g. *have* and *be* above).

(36)   a. * *Lisa has must solve the problem.*
       b. * *She must can solve the problem.*

(37)   a.   Lisa   hat   die   Aufgabe   lösen   **müssen.**
            Lisa   has   the.ACC   problem.ACC   solve   must
            'Lisa had to solve the problem.'
       b.   *(Ich glaube,)*   dass sie   die   Aufgabe
            (I believe)   that she   the.ACC   problem.ACC
            lösen **können**   ***muss***.
            solve can   must
            '(I believe) that she has to be able to solve the problem.'

English modals are also distinguished from main verbs in that that they can undergo SAI in questions, while main verbs cannot. We have modeled this in terms of different structural positions for main vs. auxiliary verbs, of which I-to-C movement targets only the position of auxiliaries. German modals don't stand out in this way, since modal and other verbs alike invert in questions:

(38) a. *Can she help you?* b. **Helps she you?*

(39) a. *Kann sie dir helfen?* b. *Hilft sie dir?*
    can she you.DAT help   helps she you.DAT
    'Can she help you?'   'Does she help you?'

So here, also, the motivation for structurally distinguishing modals from other verbal elements in English is lacking in German. (39b) also shows that German does not have a rule of do-support that is enforced systematically in questions, negation, or VP-ellipsis in English, where we can see inflection information occuring separately from the verb (see Chapter II-6 for ellipsis).

Exercise. *Status of other I-candidates: to/zu.* Strengthen the case that German does not have empirically solid representatives for a specialized auxiliary-type category like I, by using the data below. Compare *zu* and *to*.

(E3) a. **Peter hat sich vorgenommen zu* [VP *Muffins backen*]
        Peter has REFL planned to muffins bake
    b. **Peter hat sich vorgenommen* [VP *Muffins backen*] *zu.*
        Peter has REFL planned muffins bake to
    c. *Peter hat sich vorgenommen, Muffins zu backen.*
        Peter has REFL planned muffins.ACC to bake
        'Peter has planned to bake muffins.' ☐

To sum up our discussion of the lack of evidence for the I-domain in German, we do not encounter the same complex theoretical problem of combining inflectional morphology with verbs (modals vs. auxiliaries vs. main verbs, negation and do-support) that motivated the English rule system. German inflection does not ever appear to occur in a structural position separate from the verb. We therefore make the parsimonious assumption that German clause structure is simpler in having only one projection above VP, namely CP. We further assume that German verbs are born into the syntax fully inflected.

However, while lacking syntactic evidence for I and the IP projection, German clause structure is interestingly more complex in other ways. For starters, we have to distinguish embedded clauses from matrix clauses. In English, these two types of clauses look essentially the same structurally. In German, as in many other Germanic languages, they don't. Let's first look at embedded clauses:

(40) *(Hans sagt)* dass der Hund den Knochen
 (Hans says) that the dog the.ACC bone.ACC
 frisst.
 eats
 '(Hans says) that the dog eats the bone.'

We assume the following structure for the embedded clause (given here both as labeled bracketing and the equivalent tree structure):

(41) a. [$_{CP}$ [$_{C'}$ *dass* [$_{VP}$ [$_{NP}$ *der Hund*] [$_{V'}$ [$_{NP}$ *den Knochen*] *frisst*]]]]
 b.

```
              CP
              |
              C'
             / \
            C   VP
          dass  / \
              NP   V'
             /  \  / \
           Det  N' NP  V
           der  |  / \ frisst
                N Det N'
              Hund den |
                       N
                    Knochen
```

That, in turn, suggests the following set of PS rules, in which notably the C head is a sister directly to the VP:

CP → (XP) C'
C' → C VP

VP → NP V'
V' → (NP) (PP) V

A few more comments: While Spec-CP is empty in the example just considered, there may be a phrase in there. This happens in questions and in relative clauses. In this respect, German is just like English (example given in (a), structural analysis in (b)):

(42) a. ..., *welchen   Knochen   der   Hund frisst*
             which.ACC   bone.ACC   the   dog   eats
         '..., which bone the dog eats.'
     b. [CP [*welchen Knochen*] 1 [C' [VP [NP *der Hund*] [V' t₁ *frisst*]]]]

(43) a. ..., *den   der   Hund frisst*
             which   the   dog   eats
         '..., which the dog eats.'
     b. [CP *den*₁ [C' [VP [NP *der Hund*] [V' t₁ *frisst*]]]]

Interestingly, in standard German, we cannot have both an element filling Spec-CP and an element filling C in embedded clauses (again similar to English). And just like in English dialects are less restrictive. In some Southern German dialects, the following structures are possible:

(44) ..., *der   wo   mir   das   Buch   geschenkt hat.*
          which   COMPL   me.DAT   the.ACC   book.ACC   given   has
      '... who gave me the book.'

(45) ..., *wen   dass   der   Hund   begrüsst.*
          who.ACC   that   the   dog   greets
      '... whom the dog greets.'

Note in the set of PS rules above that the subject is in Spec-VP. Without the VP internal subject hypothesis, we might have been mislead into assuming that there is an IP motivated solely by its specifier (the subject) – most displeasing! (And in fact, even the displeasing option wouldn't appear as a viable one, when you have done the exercise below.)

☕ **Exercise.** *Is a special* **Spec**-*IP position like in English warranted?* Or are the already required Spec-VP and Spec-CP sufficient? Use the data below constrastively to make a case as to why Spec-IP may (not) appear as necessary in German.

(E4) a. *Was würde [_ mit ihm zu*
what would with him.DAT to
besprechen] sich noch lohnen?
discuss REFL still be_worthwhile
'What would it be worthwhile to discuss with him?'
b. *Was haben den Fritz [_ für Bücher]*
what have the.ACC Fritz.ACC for books
beeindruckt?
impressed
'What kinds of books impressed Fritz?'

(E5) a. *Es schneit auf der Alb.*
it snows on the.DAT Alb.DAT
'It is snowing on the Alb.'
b. *Auf der Alb schneit es.*
on the.DAT Alb.DAT snows it
'It is snowing on the Alb.'

(E6) a. *Es wurde meistens nur geredet.*
it was mostly only talked
'There was mostly just talk.'
b. *Meistens wurde (*es) nur geredet.*
mostly was (*it) only talked
'There was mostly only talk.'
c. *Es wachsen hier viele Buchen.*
it grow here many beeches
'Many beech trees grow here.'

Hints: An English-style Spec-IP shows its signature in partiular in: (i) barring extraction, (ii) the appeareance of expletives (*there/it*). Interpret the facts illustrated in (E4)-(E6) for German. Note that expletives in German may be generated in Spec-CP (E6c). (E6a,b) are passive constructions. □

The examples also show that, unlike in English, the verbal head follows its complements in German. We have called this the headedness parameter in Part I. Some languages are consistently head initial (English), others are consistently head final (Japanese) and yet others seem to vary (German). For instance, while the CP in German is head-initial, the VP is head-final.

Below are a couple more examples of embedded, verb-final clauses. They use a modal verb and the auxiliary verb *haben* 'have' respectively. The different verb types, so important in English, make no difference for syntax (though note that the data provide more evidence for VP being head final in German since all verbs follow their complements). Subcategorization frames for the verbs are also given.

(46) ..., *weil der Hund den Knochen gefressen hat.*
because the dog the.ACC bone.ACC eaten has
'..., because the dog has eaten the bone.'

(47) ..., *weil der Hund den Knochen fressen kann.*
because the dog the.ACC bone.ACC eat can
'..., because the dog can eat the bone.'

(48) [CP [C' *weil* [VP [V' [VP *der Hund* [V' *den Knochen fressen*]] *kann*]]]]

(49) a. *haben* 'have': V, [VP(PastPpl) _]
b. *können* 'can': V, [VP(inf) _]

Next, we consider German matrix clauses. Here we encounter a phenomenon called verb-second (V2): in an ordinary main clause in German, exactly one constituent precedes the finite verb (which as a consequence is in second position, hence the term V2). This can be almost any constituent, cf. (50) (although appropriateness of a particular choice for the constituent preceding the verb depends on further factors like intonation or context). The sentence position of this first constituent is called the **prefield**.

(50) a. *Der Hund frisst den Knochen.*
the dog eats the.ACC bone.ACC
'The dog eats the bone.'
b. *Den Knochen frisst der Hund.*
the.ACC bone.ACC eats the dog
'The dog eats the bone.'
c. *Gestern hat der Hund den Knochen gefressen.*
yesterday has the dog the.ACC bone.ACC eaten
'The dog ate the bone yesterday.'
d. *Es hat gestern der Hund den Knochen gefressen.*
EXPL has yesterday the dog the.ACC bone.ACC eaten
'The dog ate the bone yesterday.'

e. *Welchen Knochen hat gestern der Hund gefressen?*
which.ACC bone.ACC has yesterday the dog eaten
'Which bone did the dog eat yesterday?'

f. *Welcher Hund hat gestern den Knochen*
which dog has yesterday the.ACC bone.ACC
gefressen?
eaten
'Which dog ate the bone yesterday?'

We take matrix clauses to be CPs. The constituent preceding the finite verb is in Spec-CP and the finite verb is in C. Both are moved into their respective positions. The movement of the finite verb is similar to the movement of auxiliaries to C in English. The movement of the constituent into the prefield is similar to wh-movement (in that it targets Spec-CP), and indeed it *is* wh-movement in interrogatives.

(51)　*Welchen Knochen frisst der Hund?*

(52)

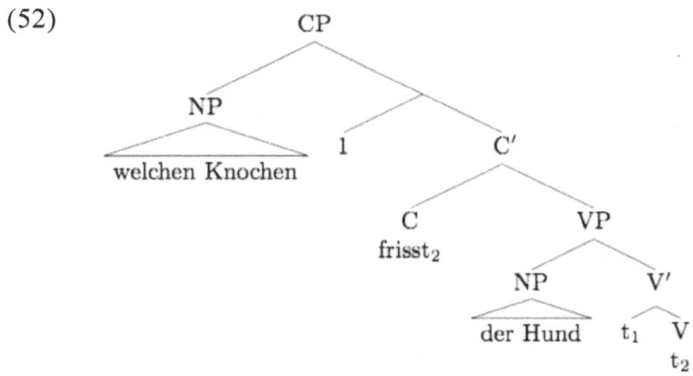

While both German and English make use of their CP layer in questions, V2 clause structure in German really stands out in declaratives. Here, too, the finite verb is in C, following the constituent fronted to Spec-CP. The structure of German matrix declaratives is just like that of questions:

(53)　*Den Knochen frisst der Hund.*
　　　the.ACC bone.ACC eats the dog
　　　'The dog is eating the bone.'

(54)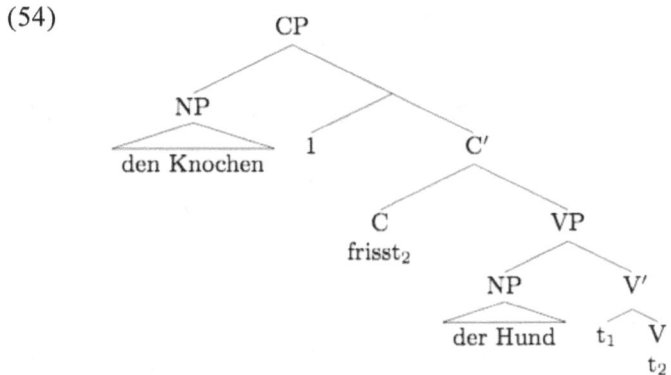

Here is some additional evidence that the verb moves in V2 clauses. Consider (55). The particle *ab* belongs to the verb *abholen* 'fetch/pick up' and in the embedded clause occurs together with the verb in the final position (also: *anrufen* 'call', *auffangen* 'catch' and many more). In a main clause, the verb occurs in second position as expected, but the particle is still in the final position. This is amenable to an analysis in which the verb moves to the C position, but the particle is left behind in the original position. In (56), we see an especially interesting case: a so-called inseperable verb *bausparen* 'save money towards a mortgage' (also: *uraufführen* 'premiere', *notlanden* 'emergency land'). In such cases, interestingly, the V2 structure is blocked. The C position has to be occupied, but neither the whole complex verb nor just its verbal part without the "particle" seems to be able to move there. Both V2 alternatives are thus degraded. This suggests that there is something marked about the V2 position of the verb while the final position is basic.

(55) a. *..., dass Hans das Kind **abholt**.*
           that Hans the.ACC child.ACC picks up
           '..., that Hans picks up the child.'
     b. *Hans **holt** das Kind **ab**.*
           Hans picks the.ACC child.ACC up
           'Hans picks up the child.'

(56) a. *..., dass wir seit letztem Monat **bausparen**.*
           that we since last month save_money_towards _mortgage
           '..., that we started to save money last month.'

b. *?? Wir **sparen** seit letztem Monat bau.*
*?? Wir **bausparen** seit letztem Monat.*

Further intuitive support for movement may be drawn from negation, which occurs rather late in the sentence and low in the structure:

(57) Den   Knochen frisst er nicht.
      the.ACC bone.ACC eats   he not
      'He doesn't eat the bone.'

Since negation semantically needs to operate on a truth value denoting category, a good place to interpret it is adjoined to VP, where the verb has combined with all its arguments (see Part I). (57) can be understood more easily if the verb plus arguments occur in a higher position at S-Structure than their D-Structure position.

☕ **Exercise.** Provide a derivation of (57). Then compositionally interpret the Deep Structure. (*Hint:* the easiest option for interpretation involves movement of the verb, the subject and the object. For a way to model movement of the subject, read this section to the end first.) □

As for strengthening evidence regarding the position to which the verb moves (the C position), we can consider data from sentence embedding verbs.

(58) a. *Stefan sagt, [dass er das   Buck   gelesen hat].*
         Stefan says that he the.ACC book.ACC read   has
         'Stefan says that he has read the book.'
      b. *Stefan sagt, [das   Buch   hat er gelesen].*
         Stefan says the.ACC book.ACC has he read
         'Stefan says that he has read the book.'
      c. * *Stefan   sagt, [dass das Buch hat er gelesen].*
           Stefan says that the book has he read

(58) shows that in the complement clause of some verbs, e.g. *sagen* 'say', we can have a complementizer or V2 but not both. The two options seem to exclude each other, i.e. we find the usual type of syntactic evidence when two elements compete for the same position. Therfore, what the V2 effect targets in German is really the C domain.

This almost concludes our overview of the most important aspects of German clause structure. One further phenomenon will be important below and is briefly discussed here. The word order in the area after the C position (that is, the area after the complementizer in embedded clauses, and after the finite verb in main clauses) is quite flexible (this area is often called the **middle field**). For example, the linear order of subject and object can be reversed. And if we have more than one object, their relative position is quite flexible, too:

(59) a. ..., dass der Hund den Knochen frisst.
        that the dog the.ACC bone.ACC eats
    b. ..., dass den Knochen der Hund frisst.
        that the.ACC bone.ACC the dog eats
        '..., that the dog eats the bone.'

(60) a. Gestern hat der Mann dem Kind das
        yesterday has the man the.DAT child.DAT the.ACC
        Buch gezeigt.
        book.ACC shown
    b. Gestern hat dem Kind der Mann das
        yesterday has the.DAT child.DAT the man the.ACC
        Buch gezeigt.
        book.ACC shown
    c. Gestern hat das Buch der Mann dem
        yesterday has the.ACC book.ACC the man the.DAT
        Kind gezeigt.
        child.DAT shown
        'Yesterday, the man showed the book to the child.'

We should note that availability and appropriateness of these reordering possibilities (similar to movement to the prefield) depend on other factors such as intonation and context. We come back to this point in Chapter II-5. At any rate, the data suggest that another movement transformation can take place in German. That is, (59b) is the result of movement applying to an underlying structure like (59a) and similarly for (60). What is this movement?

Suppose that an adverb like *gestern* 'yesterday' can be adjoined to the VP. Then the position of *gestern* relative to the object NP in (61) reveals that the NP is moved out of the VP. The landing site of the movement is

180   *Clause structure - English and German*

below C, so this is a fairly short movement. We take it that the moved constituent is adjoined to VP.

(61) a. ..., *weil   gestern   der Hund   den   Rollbraten*
          because yesterday the dog   the.ACC   roast.ACC
          gefressen hat.
          eaten   has
      b. ..., *weil   den   Rollbraten gestern   der Hund*
          because the.ACC   roast.ACC   yesterday the dog
          gefressen hat.
          eaten   has
      '..., because yesterday the dog ate the roast.'

The movement is called scrambling and it can be modeled quite straightforwardly by the movement transformation below.

Scrambling
Adjoin a phrase to VP.

The structural representation of (59b), for instance, looks like (62) below:

(62)

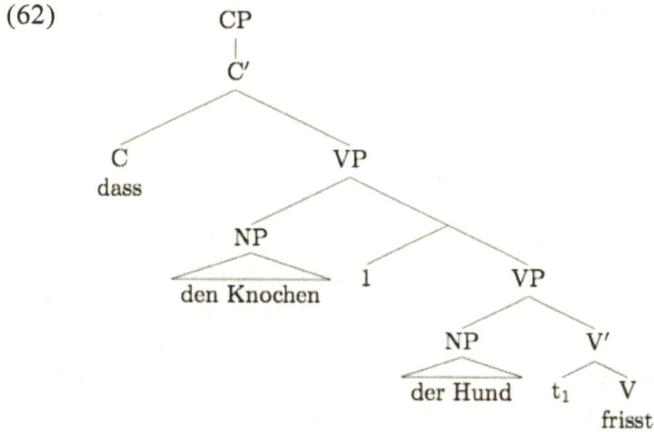

Such free word order is, of course, quite impossible in English, and correspondingly, English is said not to have this transformation. Scrambling will play an interesting role when we will get to compare interpretive possibilities in German vs. English in the following chapter.

⊕ **Exercise.** Speculate informally why word order in German is less restricted than in English. ☐

⛛ **Exercise.** Develop arguments for your intuition from the preceding exercise. (*Hint*: we suggest that you take a historical perspective. Find out how earlier stages of English behaved with respect to some of the reordering possibilities German has. When did such possibilities decline? (Cf. the third section below for some literature on the topic.)) ☐

A lot more can be said about German clause structure, but this should suffice for the beginning.

☞ THE BASICS BOX: *German clause structure*
- ✓ German clauses have a CP layer right above VP, no IP layer.
- ✓ The instantiation of the X' schema in German is not consistently head-initial or head final.
- ✓ Main clauses look different from embedded clauses because transformations apply that yield V2 structures.
- ✓ Movement transformations in German include V-to-C movement and movement to the prefield, Spec-CP.
- ✓ Scrambling, re-ordering of arguments in the middle field, is adjunction to VP.

---

3. Selected references

References for the standard syntactic analysis summarized in the first section of this chapter can be found in Part I of this book. We think that a good summary is provided in particular by Haegeman and Guéron (1999).

The discussion of German clause structure is ongoing. Our presentation relies in particular on work found in Haider (1993), Reis (2001) and Sternefeld (2006). Cf. von Stechow and Sternefeld (1988) for an IP/CP analysis.

It is interesting to relate English modals diachronically to today's German. According to Roberts and Roussou (2003), the loss of the infinitival ending (*-en*; compare *müssen* 'must.INFIN' in German) was crucial as to why the English modals developed into a categorial class of their own. There is a large literature on the history of English auxiliaries; cf. Roberts (1993), Warner (1993), Denison (1993), Gergel (2009), among others.

A historical perspective on the rigidification of English word order more generally – possibly being caused by the loss of morphology – is also interesting. See Roberts (1993) on head movement and Speyer (2010) on phrasal movement, together with the references cited there.

The particular type of co-occurrence restriction between finite verbs in embedded V2 clauses and complementizers in V-final clauses goes back to the work of den Besten (1977). There is a significant body of work on the V2 phenomenon and embedded vs. main clauses; see e.g. Diesing (1990), Santorini (1995), Vikner (1995), Fischer et al. (2000), Kroch et al. (2000), Hegarty (2005), Truckenbrodt (2006), Reis (2013) – the latter on the widely discussed topic of why *weil* 'because' clauses can obviate V2 effects in colloquial German.

The terms prefield and middle field come from a descriptive linguistic tradition of dividing clauses in German and other Germanic languages into so-called topological fields. An early reference is Drach (1937); cf. Reis (1980); Höhle (1986); Bußmann (2002); Pafel (2009) for discussion.

For particle verbs as an argument for movement, see (cf. Höhle (1991b), reply to Frey and Tappe for further discussion), Haider (1993), Sternefeld (2006), among others.

Lenerz (1977) is an important early contribution to analysing the reordering of constituents in German. There is a host of references regarding scrambling, including Diesing (1990a) for the position of adverbs; and see especially the papers in Grewendorf and Sternefeld (1990). Compare Johnson and Tomioka (1997) as well as Haider and Rosengren (2003) for recent discussion. Scrambling not only exists in Germanic; cf. e.g. Sauerland (1999) for a comparison with Japanese (and the references cited there). The fact that a language like Japanese has scrambling meshes well with a claim in the literature (e.g. Haider and Rosengren 2003) that the operation only appears in head-final languages (both Japanese and German are head-final in the VP). For a suggestion why scrambling might have died out in English, see Speyer (2010).

Chapter II-3
Quantifiers and scope

> *[E]very man was not born with a silver spoon in his mouth.*
> (Sancho Panza in Miguel de Cervantes' *Don Quixote*)

This chapter gives an introduction to a compositional semantics for natural language quantifiers and scope ambiguity phenomena.

Section 1 recapitulates the interpretation of referential vs. quantificational NPs from Part I. Readers who have worked their way through the first part of the book can skim through this section reminding themselves of the semantic denotations of different kinds of NPs. For readers who did not have exposure to the syntax and semantics of Part I (or some similar background), the section introduces the basic set theoretic interpretation of quantifiers. Section 2 of the chapter discusses ambiguities involving quantified NPs. The notion of scope is introduced. Section 3 deals with some prominent facts about quantifiers and scope in German. It contrasts the behavior of those elements to English as discussed in section 2, building on the structural analysis of the German clause introduced in Chapter II-2. Finally, section 4 provides references.

1. Interpreting referential vs. quantified noun phrases

1.1. Referential NPs

Quantifiers offer a good perspective on how the meaning of complex natural language expressions is put together from the meanings of their parts. In the case of quantified noun phrases, composition is more complex than in the case of referential NPs, even if their syntactic structure may look similar (e.g. *every cat* vs. *the cat*). Let us first recall what we know about referential noun phrases. Many NPs refer to an individual. That is, the meaning of that NP is a particular thing (a person, an object, a place). Here are some examples:

(1) a. *Sir Edmund Hillary*
b. *the chancellor of this country*
c. *the new book by Rowling*
d. *this mountain*
e. *she*

These are called **referential NPs**. Remember that we write [[X]] for the intension of a linguistic expression X, and $[[X]]^s$ for the extension of X, i.e. the meaning of X in situation s. Example (2) illustrates this:

(2) $[[\textit{the chancellor of this country}]]^s$ = Angela Merkel
(if *this country* refers to Germany and s is in 2013)

The NP in (1b) refers to the individual Angela Merkel if *this country* is Germany and the time of s is e.g. in 2013 (it would be Gerhard Schröder if the situation talked about were in 2004, it could be Werner Faymann if *this country* referred to Austria, etc.). The denotation of a referential NP is an individual.

The meaning of a clause containing a referential NP as a subject comes about by combining the meaning of the NP with the meaning of a **predicate**. Examples for predicates are: *is present, is wearing a hat, smokes, likes dogs*. We assume (with the semantic system introduced in Part I) that all these denote sets:

(3) a. $[[\textit{is present}]]^s$ = {x: x is present in s}
b. $[[\textit{likes dogs}]]^s$ = {x: x likes dogs in s}

That is, a predicate, or property, is the set of all those things that have the property. (We sometimes omit "in s" in the presentation; e.g we may simplify (3b) to {x: x likes dogs}. This is still intended to be the meaning of a predicate in a given situation). In a clause like (4a), the property denoted by the predicate is attributed to the subject. The mode of combination of a referential NP with a predicate is illustrated in (4) below (remember that *iff* stands for "if and only if"):

(4) a. $[[\textit{The chancellor of this country is present}]]^s = 1$
iff $[[\textit{the chancellor of this country}]]^s \in [[\textit{is present}]]^s$
iff Angela Merkel ∈ {x: x is present in s}

b. *The chancellor of this country is present* is true in a situation s iff Angela Merkel is present in s.

Let us stress two important points about this sample analysis. The first is our idea of sentence meanings. The meaning of a sentence in a situation is a truth value (either true or false). Semanticists take this to be the most important intuition about sentence meanings: we know the meaning of a sentence if we know when it would be true and when it would be false. Putting it differently: we know which situations would be described by the sentence. The second thing is our idea about how semantics works. We assume that we are able to predict the meaning of a complex expression, e.g. a sentence, if we know the meanings of its parts – that is, its constituent parts. This is the Fregean **principle of compositionality**. Our semantics is a system of rules of composition that allow us to combine the meanings of syntactic parts of a sentence to the meaning of the whole. Here is the first such rule, requiring that for an IP to be true, the individual denoted by the NP daughter must be a member of the predicate denotation:

Subject-Predicate rule (to be extended)
If $X = [_{IP} \text{ NP I'}]$, then for any s:
$[[X]]^s = 1$ iff $[[NP]]^s \in [[I']]^s$.

1.2. Quantifiers: non-referential NPs

In contrast to definites and names, noun phrases like *nothing, every boy* etc. do not refer to any individual. They are quantificational NPs. Remember from Part I the example set in (5):

(5) a. *Every turtle has back problems.*
     b. *No turtle has back problems.*
     c. *Some turtle has back problems.*
     d. *Exactly 5 turtles have back problems.*
     e. *Most turtles have back problems.*

We know about the denotations of $[[turtle]]^s$ and $[[has\ back\ problems]]^s$. Those are sets, namely {x: x is is a turtle in s} and {x: x has back problems in s}. How can the claims made in (5) be described in terms of those sets? After having taken a minute to think about this, consider (5') below. (5') expresses the claim each sentence in (5) makes in terms of a relation between the two sets.

(5') a. $[[turtle]]^s \subseteq [[has\ back\ problems]]^s$
      b. $[[turtle]]^s \cap [[has\ back\ problems]]^s = \emptyset$
      c. $[[turtle]]^s \cap [[has\ back\ problems]]^s \neq \emptyset$
      d. $card([[turtle]]^s \cap [[has\ back\ problems]]^s) = 5$
      e. $card([[turtle]]^s \cap [[has\ back\ problems]]^s) > 0.5 \times card([[turtle]]^s)$

Having an understanding of the truth conditions of the sentences, we can work our way towards finding out the contribution of the quantified NPs and then the quantified determiners. As a first step, compare the sentences in (5) to those in (6).

(6) a. *Nothing is dusty.*
     b. *Everything is dusty.*
     c. *Something is dusty.*

The meaning of the morpheme *-thing* attaching to *no, every* etc. here seems to be the domain of discourse D, by which semanticists mean the set of all relevant individuals. Now, we can identify the contribution of the quantified NP:

(6') a. For any situation s: $[[nothing]]^s = \{P: P \cap D = \emptyset\}$
         For any situation s, the meaning of *nothing* in s is the set of all those sets whose intersection with D is empty; i.e. the set of properties that no relevant entity has.
      b. For any situation s: $[[everything]]^s = \{P: D \subseteq P\}$

This intermediate step helps us to find out what the meaning of the quantified NP *no turtle* is. Just like *nothing* denotes the set of all properties that no entity has, *no turtle* denotes the set of all properties that no turtle has. That is the set of all sets whose intersection with the turtles is empty. The quantified NP *every turtle* denotes the set of properties that every turtle has (and similarly for the other quantified NPs):

(7) a. $[[no\ turtle]]^s = \{P: P \cap [[turtle]]^s = \emptyset\}$
     b. $[[every\ turtle]]^s = \{P: [[turtle]]^s \subseteq P\}$

Recall that a property is a set. A quantified NP thus denotes a set of sets. (Interestingly, this is quite a different kind of interpretation than a referential NP has; see Part I for more discussion.). We need to combine such denotations for quantified NPs with the predicate. Our Subject-Predicate rule needs to be revised. The rule we have so far, which requires that the subject NP be a member of the set denoted by the predicate, is not appropriate for quantified NP subjects. A set of sets (the quantified NP) cannot be a member of a set of individuals. In the case of quantifiers, it's the predicate that needs to be a member of the subject denotation, not vice versa. We therefore revise the rule by specifying in the old first part the condition of application "if NP is not a quantifier" and adding the second part for quantifiers.

Subject-Predicate Rule (SUBJPRED 1 and 2, respectively)
Part 1:
If $X = [_{IP} \text{ NP I'}]$ and NP is not a quantifier, then for any s:
$[[X]]^s = 1$ iff $[[NP]]^s \in [[I']]^s$.
Part 2:
If $X = [_{IP} \text{ NP I'}]$ and NP is a quantifier, then for any s:
$[[X]]^s = 1$ iff $[[I']]^s \in [[NP]]^s$.

Now that we know what the meaning of a quantified NP is, we can ask what the meaning of a quantified determiner is. The determiner combines with its N' sister constituent in the syntactic structure to give us the meaning of the NP (following the principle of compositionality). The N' sister denotes a set (e.g. *turtle* in (5), but note that the N' can include more material, e.g. *middle-aged green turtle*). Such sets introduced by the sister constituent of the quantified determiner need to play the same role that D, the universe of discourse, in the case of *nothing* or *everything*. But while *-thing* denotes the entire universe of discourse, this first set restricts the claim made by the quantifier; e.g. to the set of turtles (or middle-aged green turtles), rather than the set of all entities. This first argument of the quantified determiner is therefore sometimes called the restrictor (or restriction) of the quantifier. The other set, usually expressed through the verbal predicate, is the second argument of the quantified determiner (it is sometimes called the nuclear scope). The quantified determiner establishes a relationship between these two sets. Which relationship this is depends on the determiner. *Every* requires that there be a subset relation between the two sets; *no* requires that they be disjoint etc. We can give the following lexical entries for the quantified determiners in (5):

(8) a. For any s: $[[every]]^s = \{<P, Q>: P \subseteq Q\}$
b. For any s: $[[no]]^s = \{<P, Q>: P \cap Q = \emptyset\}$
c. For any s: $[[some]]^s = \{<P, Q>: P \cap Q \neq \emptyset\}$
d. For any s: $[[exactly\ 5]]^s = \{<P, Q>: card(P \cap Q) = 5\}$
e. For any s: $[[most]]^s = \{<P, Q>: card(P \cap Q) > 0.5 \times card(P)\}$

Thus quantified determiners denote relations – relations between sets, not individuals.

Exercise. *Further quantified determiners.* Offer lexical entries for the quantifiers in (E1a–c). Then think about the semantic contribution of (E1d).

(E1) a. *exactly seven*
b. *less than four*
c. *many*
d. *neither*

Hints: For *many*, consider the intersection of the two arguments P and Q and impose a requirement on its cardinality, by taking the role of context into account. Give concrete examples of what you would take to be a suitable requirement for *many* in particular contexts. Provide a semantics for *neither* by considering *no* and establishing what *neither* additionally requires. Remembering the semantics of *the* and presuppositions will help you.

□

Exercise. *Fieldwork on quantifiers.* Imagine that you are a linguist investigating a language that nobody has ever documented and analyzed before. You have elicited three lexical items you suspect are quantified determiners (let's call them *quant1, quant2* and *quant3*), because they occur with expressions that you are pretty sure are nouns and verbal predicates. That is, you have elicited sentences that we can represent as in (E2). Design a way of eliciting data that will allow you to establish the meanings of *quant1, quant2* and *quant3*.

(E2) a. *quant1 birds sang.*
b. *quant2 birds sang.*
c. *quant3 birds sang.*
d. *quant1 trees died.*
e. *quant2 women invited Kim.*
...

Hints: Would you have been able to say which set theoretic relation the word for *every* in your language expresses? Probably not. Assume that your imaginary consultants will not be able to directly access their linguistic knowledge in this way either. Like yourself, they can tell whether or not a sentence is true in a certain situation. This means that you have to come up with ways of presenting them with situations. You can then ask them about the truth or falsity of each sentence in the situation. Formulate some ideas. *Further suggestion*: If you can work in a group, ask a member of the group to decide on set theoretic meanings for *quant1, quant2* and *quant3*. This group member writes down the meanings s/he has decided on without showing the rest of the group. S/he is your language consultant - try out the method(s) you have devised. ☐

While we have now (re-)ascertained the meanings of quantified NPs and quantified determiners, we still need to pin down how a quantified determiner combines with its first argument to yield the meaning of the corresponding NP. Note that we want to specify how a relation is to be combined with a semantic object that fills one of the argument slots of the relation. This should remind you of transitive verbs and their combination with their syntactic objects: transitive verbs denote relations between individuals and the object NP fills one argument slot. The relevant rule is Verb-Object (see Part I). While transitive verbs (which are relations between individuals) yield sets of individuals after combining with an object, quantified determiners (which are relations between sets) yield sets *of sets* after combining with their restrictor. Composition is modeled by the following rule:

Quantified NPs (QUANTNP)
If $X = [_{NP} \text{Det } N']$ and Det is a quantified determiner, then for any s:
$[[X]]^s = \{Q: <[[N']]^s, Q> \in [[\text{Det}]]^s\}$.

We are now able to go through a calculation of the truth conditions predicted for our examples above and similar data. We do this in (9). At each step we derive the meaning of the larger structure from the meanings of its parts, using a rule of composition. (For example, starting with the entire sentence, the IP, we use the Subject-predicate rule to combine the meanings of the subject NP and its sister constituent, I'.) The appendix of Part I of the book spells out all relevant semantic rules. (We may not always indicate all rules that come into use, for the sake of perspicuity.)

(9)   [[[$_{IP}$ [$_{NP}$ *every student*] [$_{I'}$ *passed*]]]]^s = 1 iff   (SUBJPRED 2)
[[[$_{I'}$ *passed*]]]^s ∈ [[[$_{NP}$ *every student*]]]^s iff   (NONBR, LEX)
{x: x passed in s} ∈ [[[$_{NP}$ *every student*]]]^s iff   (QUANTNP)
{x: x passed in s} ∈ {Q: <[[[$_{N'}$ *student*]]]^s, Q> ∈ [[*every*]]^s } iff
                                                                            (SIMPL)
<[[[$_{N'}$ *student*]]]^s, {x: x passed in s}> ∈ [[*every*]]^s iff   (LEX)
<[[[$_{N'}$ *student*]]]^s, {x: x passed in s}> ∈ {<P, Q>: P ⊆ Q} iff (SIMPL)
[[[$_{N'}$ *student*]]]^s ⊆ {x: x passed in s} iff   (LEX)
{x: x is a student in s} ⊆ {x: x passed in s}

Remember: the point of this is to show that we have developed an interpretation component for our grammar (with lexical entries for the quantifiers and other items, and rules of composition that follow the syntactic structure) which is suitable to account for the intuitive truth conditions that these examples have.

🕒 **Exercise.** *Practicing compositional calculation.* Calculate truth conditions for sentence (E3a-c) in a step-by-step fashion. Make sure you analyze correctly what happens when the restrictor is more complex as in (E3b,c). *Hint:* Remember Predicate Modification, and assume that the relative clause denotes the following set: {x: Jones picked x in s}.

(E3)   a.   *Exactly seven jurors voted.*
         b.   *Exactly seven female jurors voted.*
         c.   *Exactly seven jurors who Jones picked voted.*   ☐

☞ **THE BASICS BOX:** *Referential NPs vs. quantifiers*

✓ Referential NPs denote individuals, predicates denote sets; simple sentences with referential subjects state that the individual denoted by the subject is an element of the set denoted by the predicate.

✓ Quantified NPs denote sets of sets of individuals. Simple sentences with a quantified subject state that the predicate is an element of the set denoted by the quantified NP.

✓ Quantified determiners denote relations between sets of individuals; e.g. *every* requires that the first set should be a subset of the second; *some* that the intersection of the two sets involved should not be empty; etc.

1.3. Paraphrases

Let us make a small practical point next, before turning to the issue of ambiguities. We have a neat, pretty precise understanding of the semantic contribution of a quantified NP now. When examples become more complex, it will be convenient to relate the set theoretic description of the meanings of sentences with quantifiers to verbal paraphrases. Here are some examples (sentence in (a), set theoretic meaning in (b) and paraphrase in (c)):

(10) a. *Every student snores.*
 b. {x: x is a student} $\subseteq$ {x: x snores}
 c. For every x such that x is a student: x snores.

(11) a. *No student smokes.*
 b. {x: x is a student} $\cap$ {x: x smokes} = $\varnothing$
 c. There is no x such that x is a student and x smokes.

Note that what is offered as a paraphrase is a verbal rendering of the mathematics of the meaning as given by the set theoretic semantics. A useful paraphrase should share its precision with the semantics while being fairly easily comprehensible. The usefulness of this will hopefully become clearer as we proceed.

2. Ambiguities

We are now ready to return to an observation from the introduction to Part II (Chapter II-1): sentences with quantifiers can give rise to more than one possible interpretation. We organize the discussion according to the structural positions involved in the ambiguous examples.

2.1. Ambiguities between quantified subject NPs and elements in the I-domain

The instance of this phenomenon that we consider first is the following:

(12) *Many bottles didn't arrive.*

192 *Quantifiers and scope*

This can mean either that the cardinality of the non-arriving bottles is large or that it is not the case that the cardinality of the arriving bottles is large:

(13)   a.   card({x: x is a bottle and x did not arrive}) is large
            'There are many bottles that failed to arrive.'
       b.   card({x: x is a bottle and x arrived}) is not large
            'It is not the case that many bottles arrived.'

Note how the paraphrases mirror the set theoretic description of the two meanings in removing the ambiguity. We stick here to a somewhat informal characterization of the meaning of *many*, for simplicity: we require the cardinality of the intersection of P and Q to be large (your own suggestion from the earlier exercise (E1) may well be more sophisticated. For additional practice, you can use your semantics for (12) and the following discussion; do you capture the ambiguity?).

The two interpretations in (13) are true in different scenarios. Let us suppose that we are talking about a particular set of bottles, ten in all, that a party put into a river upstream to be picked up again further downstream (a "message in a bottle" type game). Let us further suppose that anything more than 4 counts as many in this scenario. Here is a relevant situation (the bottles are numbered and a * underneath a bottle means that this object has the property in question, i.e. it has arrived):

(14)   sit1:   bottles: 1 2 3 4 5 6 7 8 9 10
               arrive: * * *   * *   (13a) true, (13b) false

Conversely, suppose that the overall number of bottles is seven. Then here is a second situation in which the first reading is false but the second reading is true:

(14') sit2:   bottles: 1 2 3 4 5 6 7
               arrive: * * *   *   (13a) false, (13b) true

We have found a situation in which one reading is true while the other one false for both readings. This means the two readings are genuinely distinct.

To hone in our intuitions about this kind of ambiguity a little more, we informally consider the following example:

(15)   *It didn't rain on more than 3 of these days.*
   a.   'It is not the case that it rained on more than 3 days.'
   b.   'There were more than 3 days on which it didn't rain.'

The difference can be illustrated by looking e.g. at the following situations:

(16)   sit1:   1 2 3 4 5 6 7 8 9
               * * * *   (15a) false, (15b) true
       sit2:   1 2 3 4 5
               * * *   (15a) true, (15b) false

In order to detect ambiguity with quantifiers like the ones above, you can convince yourself of the existence of distinct readings by finding situations in which one reading is true and the other false. If you do, this means that the putative readings indeed yield different truth conditions.

The phenomenon illustrated by (12) and (15) is very interesting to semanticists because the source of the ambiguity is not immediately clear. One source of ambiguity we have come across is lexical ambiguity (*the inspector took a picture of the bank*), another is structural ambiguity (*the woman hit the man with the stick*). Clearly, our examples are not a case of lexical ambiguity – none of the words assumes two different interpretations. Hence it would be attractive to find a structural ambiguity in these examples. It is, however, not immediately obvious how they are to be reduced to structural ambiguity either. In contrast to *the woman hit the man with the stick* and the like, there is exactly one S-Structure for our data.

A standard analysis manages to find two different structures to interpret in the following way. One structure is the S-Structure, the other the D-Structure. In the case of (12), interpreting the S-Structure (17) gives rise to the meaning in (13a) above. Assume for now that the predicate, the node I', denotes the set {x: x did not arrive} – we will investigate below the details of interpreting the I'. (17') below offers the crucial steps in the interpretation of (17).

(17) *Many bottles didn't arrive.*   [Surface Structure]

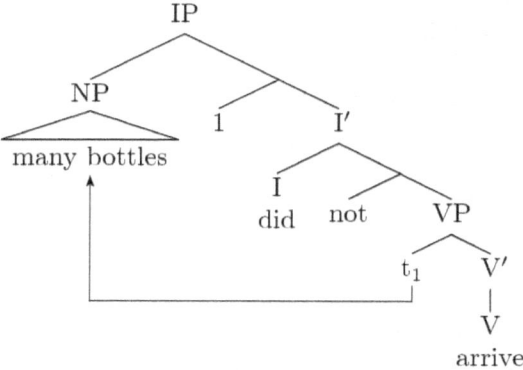

(17') a. $[\![many]\!]^s = \{<P, Q>: \text{card}(P \cap Q) \text{ is large}\}$
b. $[\![many\ bottles]\!]^s = \{Q: <[\![[_{N'}\ bottle]\ ]\!]^s, Q> \in [\![many]\!]^s\}$
$= \{Q: \text{card}(\{x: x \text{ is a bottle in } s\} \cap Q) \text{ is large}\}$
c. $[\![\ [1[\ didn't\ t_1\ arrive]\!]\ ]\!]^s = \{x: x \text{ did not arrive in } s\}$
d. $[\![many\ bottles\ didn't\ arrive]\!]^s = 1$ iff   (SUBJPRED 2)
$\{x: x \text{ did not arrive in } s\} \in [\![many\ bottles]\!]^s$ iff
$\text{card}(\{x: x \text{ is a bottle in } s\} \cap \{x: x \text{ did not arrive in } s\})$ is large

In (17), the index 1 is the movement index of the NP *many bottles*. This is the same as the index on the trace t_1 in Spec-VP, the original position, to indicate the movement relationship. Remember that we derive the S-Structure from a structure like (18):

(18) *Many bottles didn't arrive.*   [Deep Structure]

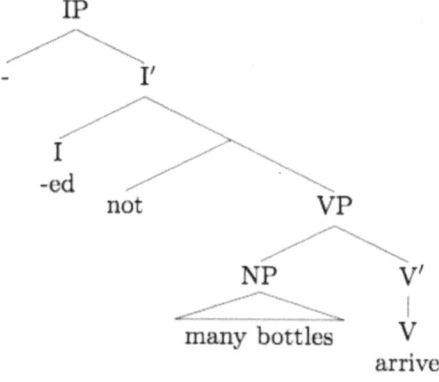

Interpreting the VP in (18) results in (19):

(19)   card({x: x is a bottle and x arrived}) is large

It seems reasonable to suppose that negation will have the effect of reversing the truth conditions (we will repeat below the rule for negation from Part I that derives this supposition). This yields (19') below. Thus we derive the desired truth conditions, the second interpretation (13b). The second possible reading of the example can be accounted for if we interpret the subject NP in its D-Structure position (this is often called reconstruction).

(19')   card({x: x is a bottle and x arrived}) is *not* large

The analysis provided for the *bottles* example amounts to the claim that indeed the sentence provides two different structures which we may interpret – the Surface Structure and some other structure that is derivationally related to it. A note before we proceed with technicalities: the phenomenon is quite general. We have considered negation, just outside VP, and how it interacts with quantifiers. But other elements in the I-area, such as modals, also give rise to an ambiguity along similar lines. In (20), there are some more examples that motivate our analysis (we do not formally analyze the examples with modals because we would need to talk in much more detail about the modal itself in order to do so; we limit ourselves to considering our intuitions).

(20)   a. *One of my friends must be present.*
       Paraphrase 1: 'There is one friend of mine such that s/he must be present.'
       Paraphrase 2: 'It must be the case that some friend of mine or other be present.'
   b. *Everyone can win the lottery.*
   c. *Three people should not be nominated.*

☺ **Exercise.** *Modals and quantifiers.* Give unambiguous paraphrases for the sentences in (20b, c) above.   □

To sum up: ambiguities between a quantified subject and elements in the I-area show that the subject may be interpreted underneath negation and modals or stay above.

Let us now make the formal details precise. We introduce two rules of interpretation whose impact we have discussed in intuitive terms above. The first rule targets the interpretation of nodes that contain an index as one of their daughters:

Predicate Abstraction Rule (PREDABS)
If $X = [\ i\ Y]$ and i is a numerical index, then for any s:
$[[X]]^s = \{x: [[Y]]^s_{[x/i]} = 1\}$, where $[[Y]]^s_{[x/i]}$ is the interpretation of Y in s, except that we replace every trace t_i in the structure with x in the interpretation.

The introduction of x into the computation explains how we obtain the set in (17'c) above. It is the job of the Predicate Abstraction rule to create a set. (Note that Predicate Abstraction is a genuine revision of assumptions from Part I, where we basically ignored movement and traces, treating them as semantically vacuous. This is not generally tenable).

🕒 **Exercise.** *Relative clauses.* Let's come back to the relative clause from (E3c), repeated below.

(E4) c. *Exactly seven jurors who Jones picked voted.*

We have assumed above that the meaning of the relative clause is {x: Jones picked x in s}. Draw a syntactic structure for the relative clause and compositionally interpret it step by step using Predicate Abstraction. Show that the result of your calculation is precisely what we had assumed. ☐

Next, let us recall that the contribution of negation. The semantic effect of sentence negation is to reverse truth values: if the sister constituent is true in a situation, then the result after applying negation is false in that situation, and vice versa:

Negation (NEG)
If $X = [\textit{not}\ Y]$ and Y denotes a truth value, then for any s:
$[[X]]^s = 1$ iff $[[Y]]^s = 0$.

Ambiguities 197

In order for this rule for negation to apply e.g. in (18), the subject NP must originate in Spec-VP (or else there would be no truth-value denoting constituent Y as the sister of negation).

The rules given allow the step by step compositional interpretation of the trees we have considered in this section. Let us calculate here the truth conditions for (17), which allows us to illustrate the workings of both the Predicate Abstraction rule and the Negation rule:

(21) $[\![\, [_{IP} \, [_{NP} \, \textit{many bottles}] \, [1 [_{I'} \, \textit{did} \, [\textit{not} \, [_{VP} \, t_1 \, \textit{arrive}]]]] \,]\!]^s = 1$ iff

(SUBJPRED 2)

$[\![\, [1 [_{I'} \, \textit{did} \, [\textit{not} \, [_{VP} \, t_1 \, \textit{arrive}]]]] \,]\!]^s \in [\![\, [_{NP} \, \textit{many bottles}] \,]\!]^s$ iff

(PREDABS)

$\{x: [\![\, [_{I'} \, \textit{did} \, [\textit{not} \, [_{VP} \, t_1 \, \textit{arrive}]]] \,]\!]^s_{[x/1]} \} \in [\![\, [_{NP} \, \textit{many bottles}] \,]\!]^s$ iff

(SEMVAC)

$\{x: [\![\, [\textit{not} \, [_{VP} \, t_1 \, \textit{arrive}]] \,]\!]^s_{[x/1]} \} \in [\![\, [_{NP} \, \textit{many bottles}] \,]\!]^s$ iff

(NEG; SUBJPRED 1)

$\{x: [\![[t_1]]\!]^s_{[x/1]} \notin [\![\textit{arrive}]\!]^s_{[x/1]} \} \in [\![\, [_{NP} \, \textit{many bottles}] \,]\!]^s$ iff

(SIMPL)

$\{x: x \notin [\![\textit{arrive}]\!]^s \} \in [\![\, [_{NP} \, \textit{many bottles}] \,]\!]^s$ iff

(LEX)

$\{x: x \notin \{z: z \text{ arrives in } s\}\} \in [\![\, [_{NP} \, \textit{many bottles}] \,]\!]^s$ iff

(SIMPL)

$\{x: x \text{ did not arrive in } s\} \in [\![\, [_{NP} \, \textit{many bottles}] \,]\!]^s$ iff

(QUANTNP)

$\{x: x \text{ did not arrive in } s\} \in \{Q: < [\![_{N'} \, \textit{bottles}]]\!]^s, Q> \in [\![\textit{many}]\!]^s \}$ iff

(SIMPL)

$<[\![_{N'} \, \textit{bottles}]\!]^s, \{x: x \text{ did not arrive in } s\}> \in [\![\textit{many}]\!]^s$ iff

(LEX)

$<[\![_{N'} \, \textit{bottles}]\!]^s, \{x: x \text{ did not arrive in } s\}> \in \{<P, Q>: \text{card}(P \cap Q) \text{ is large}\}$ iff

(SIMPL)

card $([\![_{N'} \, \textit{bottles}]\!]^s \cap \{x: x \text{ did not arrive in } s\})$ is large iff

(LEX)

card $(\{x: x \text{ is a bottle in } s\} \cap \{x: x \text{ did not arrive in } s\})$ is large iff

(SIMPL)

card $(\{x: x \text{ is a bottle in } s \text{ and } x \text{ did not arrive in } s\})$ is large

198 *Quantifiers and scope*

Next comes a very important terminological definition at the syntax-semantics interface. The tree in (22) subsequently illustrates the relevant configuration.

Scope
The scope of an expression is that expression's sister in the structure that we interpret.

---

(22) Schematic illustration of the notion of scope

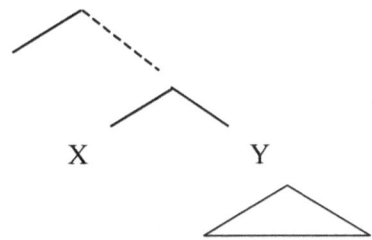

This abstract tree contains an expression X and a constituent Y, which is X's sister. Hence Y is X's scope in this tree. Any expression dominated by Y is said to be **in the scope** of X. Equivalently, we say that X **has scope over** Y and everything dominated by Y. In the previous example (17), *many bottles* has scope over its I' sister and everything dominated by this I' node. Sometimes we are interested in matters of scope concerning two expressions and want to relate them to each other – for example, the quantified NP *many bottles* and the negation in (17). We say that the NP *many bottles* **has scope over** negation in (17) (or equivalently: that the NP **has wide scope relative to** negation; that negation **has narrow scope relative to** the NP). This means that negation is in the NP's scope.

🕒 **Exercise.** *Terminology.* Apply this new terminology to (18) above. ☐

Scope as defined above is a structural notion. We can read it off the syntactic tree that is the input to interpretation. But notice that the scope of an expression determines what the truth conditions are. When negation has wide scope, we get an interpretation paraphrasable as "it is not the case that...". And when a quantifier like *many N* has wide scope, we get an interpretation paraphrasable as "there are many N such that ...". We will rely on this connection between scope and paraphrase when we relate trees to interpretations.

When you compare (17) to (18), you see that the two trees differ in terms of the scope of negation relative to the NP *many bottles*. The ambiguity is a scope ambiguity, as will be the further ambiguities discussed in this chapter. We analyze scope ambiguities as a special instance of structural ambiguity.

2.2. Digression: Pronouns, variables

We leave our main topic – quantifier scope – for the space of this digression and pursue an issue opened up by our rule of Predicate Abstraction: the issue of variables in natural language. (This section can be skipped for the purpose of understanding the rest of this chapter. It is a good preparation for the analysis of tense in Chapter II-7, though.)

Traces are variables. This means that while they occupy an argument slot like a referential NP, they do not refer to any one particular individual. Suppose a constituent Y contains a trace:

(D1)   [$_Y$... t_i ...]

and suppose that Y is in the scope of a numerical index i interpreted by the rule Predicate Abstraction repeated below.

Predicate Abstraction Rule (PREDABS)
If X = [i Y] and i is a numerical index, then for any s:
$[[X]]^s = \{x: [[Y]]^s_{[x/i]} = 1\}$,
where $[[Y]]^s_{[x/i]}$ is the interpretation of Y in s, except that we replace every trace t_i in the structure with x in the interpretation.

Then the meaning of t_i is whatever meta-language variable we chose in the application of the rule. In (D2a), for example, the trace occupies the position of the subject of *enjoy* but it does not refer to any individual. Instead, together with Predicate Abstraction, it helps create the set {x: x enjoys gardening}.

(D2)   a.   *No woman who enjoys gardening plants cotoneaster.*
            [$_{NP}$ *no* [$_{N'}$ *woman* [$_{CP}$ *who$_i$* [*t$_i$ enjoys gardening*]]]]
       b.   *No woman such that she enjoys gardening plants cotoneaster.*
            [$_{NP}$ *no* [$_{N'}$ *woman* [$_{CP}$ *such$_i$* [*that* [*she$_i$ enjoys gardening*]]]]]

Interestingly, it is possible to do the same thing employing a pronoun as in (D2b), which (although clunky) is equivalent to (D2a). This indicates that pronouns in natural language are also variables. The idea is supported by the (less clunky) (D3). (D3a) has the meaning in (D3c). The NP is analyzed in (D3b). The contribution of the N' has to be as in (D3d).

(D3) a. *No woman who likes her garden plants cotoneaster.*
      b. [$_{NP}$ *no* [$_{N'}$ *woman* [$_{CP}$ *who$_i$* [*t$_i$ likes her$_i$ garden*]]]]
      c. {x: x is a woman and x likes x's garden}
         ∩ {x: x plants cotoneaster} = ∅
      d. [[[$_{N'}$ *woman* [$_{CP}$ *who$_i$* [*t$_i$ likes her$_i$ garden*]]]]]^s =
         {x: x is a woman and x likes x's garden}

This in turn means that not only do we have to use Predicate Abstraction to interpret the relative clause, but also that it affects the trace and the pronoun in a parallel way. We revise the rule slightly to incorporate this insight.

Predicate Abstraction Rule (PREDABS)
If X = [i Y] and i is a numerical index or a relative pronoun with index i, then for any s:
[[X]]^s = {x: [[Y]]$^s_{[x/i]}$ = 1},
where [[Y]]$^s_{[x/i]}$ is the interpretation of Y in s, except that we replace every trace t$_i$ and every pronoun pro$_i$ in the structure with x in the interpretation.

🕒 **Exercise.** *Practice Predicate Abstraction.* Interpret (D3a) step by step. □

But now, we seem to have maneuvered ourselves into a slightly odd position. While it makes sense to see the pronoun in (D3) as a variable whose semantic role is dictated by Predicate Abstraction, we had decided earlier, when we talked about referential NPs, that pronouns were, in fact, referential. Some relevant examples are given below.

(D4) a. *Her cat is ill.*
      b. *She left Akaroa.*
      c. *Sandy likes her.*
      d. *Sandy likes him (them/us/you).*

There is no indication that Predicate Abstraction is involved in such cases. We will continue to view these pronouns as referential. Suppose for example that (D4a) is preceded by *How is Lucy doing?*. You will take *her* to refer to Lucy and the sentence is true iff Lucy's cat is ill.

Note, however, that this depends on the context. If the context was such that we were talking about Karen instead, the pronoun would refer to Karen. It is, in other words, variable what the referent of these pronouns is. We assume that when a pronoun is not interpreted via Predicate Abstraction, we interpret it relative to context. Context has to furnish an appropriate referent. We will not introduce a sophisticated analysis here. For simplicity, we model the presence of contextual information on pronouns by the same subscript already in use in the Predicate Abstraction rule. We generalize the interpretation of pronouns as follows:

(D5)   Pronouns
       For any s, $[[pro_i]]^s_{[x/i]} = x$

The subscript says that the pronoun is assigned this semantic value. Here are some examples in which the semantic value, we assume, comes from the context:

(D6)   a. $[[she_1]]^s_{[Lucy/1]}$ = Lucy
       b. $[[Sandy\ likes\ her_2]]^s_{[Karen/2]}$ = 1 iff Sandy likes Karen in s.

In sum, pronouns are variables and have to be interpreted relative to a value assignment. The value assignment may come from Predicate Abstraction or from the context.

🕒 **Exercise.** *Pronouns and quantifiers.* Consider the example below:

(D7)   *No woman phoned her mother.*

Paraphrase two different possible interpretations of the example, one in which the meaning of *her* depends on the context and one in which it doesn't. Draw the corresponding syntactic structures. How are they different? (*Hint:* Pay attention to the index on the pronoun, to movement and the movement index.)   ☐

It seems we have still left out something important concerning our pronoun examples. Compare (D4c) to (D4d). The version with *her* is only appropriate in a context that provides a relevant female referent, while it needs to be a male referent in the version with *him*. We say nothing about this so far, but in order to be realistic, we should take into account the form of the pronoun. Semanticists have suggested that the gender information included in the form of the pronoun is a presupposition. This is incorporated in the more detailed semantics below:

(D5')   Pronouns
   For any s, $[[she_i]]^s_{[x/i]}$ is only defined if x is female.
         Then, $[[she_i]]^s_{[x/i]} = x$
   For any s, $[[he_i]]^s_{[x/i]}$ is only defined if x is male.
         Then, $[[he_i]]^s_{[x/i]} = x$

⊕ **Exercise.** *More pronouns.* Extend the list of pronoun interpretations to include *I, you, it, they* and *we*. (*Hint:* You want to think not only about gender, but also number and person features.) ☐

⚖ **Exercise.** *Contrasting special pronouns across languages.* First, describe different meanings of the pronoun *you* as precisely as you can. Can you find examples in which it is not strictly second person? Second, describe the meaning of one of the following pronouns: French *on*, English *one*, German *man*. (*Hint*: Collect examples containing the pronoun of your choice and state which person and number are presupposed in the examples you have collected.) ☐

2.3. Ambiguities between quantified objects and elements in the I-domain

Having understood ambiguities with negation and subjects in subsection 2.1, it is easy to see that parallel ambiguities exist when we consider an object quantifier.

(23)   *Bill didn't answer many questions.*

(23')   a.   card({x: x is a question and Bill did not answer x}) is large
         'There are many questions that Bill failed to answer.'
      b.   card({x: x is a question and Bill answered x}) is not large
         "It is not the case that Bill answered many questions."

We recognize this as an ambiguity of scope: either the negation can take wide scope as in (23'b) or the quantifier *many* can take wide scope, (23'a). What remains for us to do is to determine two different syntactic structures for (23) that reflect these relative scopes. The surprising reading in this regard is (23'a), because the Surface Structure is not one in which the quantifier takes wide scope. Linguists have suggested that we can associate with our example yet another structure which differs from the Surface Structure in that the object is raised above the I domain and negation:

(24)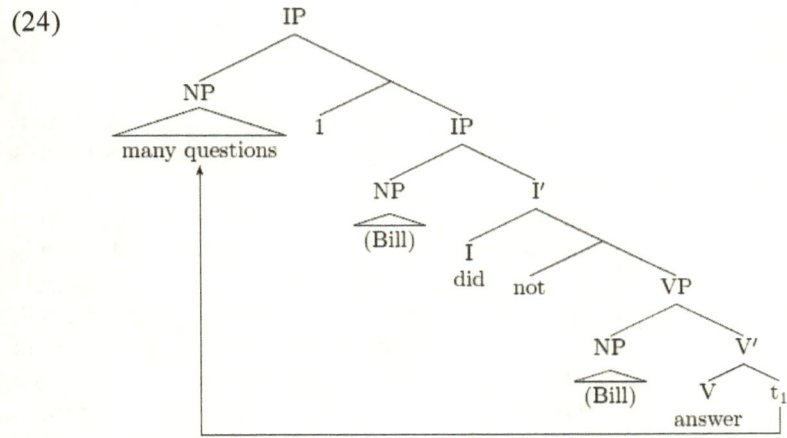

The subject, as we now know, can be interpreted in Spec-VP or Spec-IP. In this case, both calculations will lead to the same result, since we are dealing with a referential subject, not a quantified subject.

⊕ **Exercise.** *Interpreting referential NPs in different positions.* Prove that the two positions for a referential NP lead to the same result by compositionally interpreting both versions of the tree in (24). □

Suppose that the sister of *many questions* contributes the set {x: Bill did not answer x in s}. Then we get the desired reading from this structure, (23'a). In (24'), we present some crucial steps in the calculation (computing the full calculation is part of the exercise above).

(24') $[\![\ [_{IP} \ [many \ questions] \ [1 [_{IP} \ \_ \ [_{I'} \ did \ [not \ [_{VP} \ Bill \ answer \ t_1]]]]]] \ ]\!]^s =$ 1 iff (SUBJPRED 2)
$[\![\ [1 [_{I'} \ did \ [not \ [_{VP} \ Bill \ answer \ t_1]]]] \ ]\!]^s \in [\![\ [_{NP} \ many \ questions] \ ]\!]^s$ iff (PREDABS)
{x: $[\![\ [_{I'} \ did \ [not \ [_{VP} \ Bill \ answer \ t_1]]] \ ]\!]^s_{[x/1]}=1$} $\in [\![\ [_{NP} \ many \ questions] \ ]\!]^s$ iff (Various rules, including: NEG; SUBJPRED 1; V- OBJ)
{x: Bill did not answer x in s} $\in [\![\ [_{NP} \ many \ questions] \ ]\!]^s$ iff

(Various rules, including: QUANTNP)
card ({x: x is a question in s and Bill did not answer x in s}) is large

The calculation in (24') convinces us that the PS tree in (24) is useful: it explains the interpretation (23'a) of our example. But how is it derived? The structure in (24) is called a **Logical Form** (LF) of the sentence. A Logical Form is derived from a S-Structure by movement transformations, just like S-Structure is derived from D-Structure by movement transformations. We assume that the S-Structure tree represents the sequence of words that we pronounce. So what happens at LF is not audible or visible. (It is for this reason that we have not encountered LF earlier.)

It may seem rather ad hoc to assume that there is such a structure, which we cannot see or hear, just to generate the reading in question. Indeed, this is not without contention among linguists. But there are several arguments in favor of this solution, some of which we will return to when we talk about ellipsis. For the moment, we will suppose that there is a movement called **Quantifier Raising** (QR), which takes a quantifier and moves it to a position adjoined to a truth-value denoting category. You see this movement illustrated in (24), where the NP *many questions* is adjoined to IP. The movement happens on the way to Logical Form. It is interpreted via our Predicate Abstraction Rule and it helps us derive scope ambiguity.

> **Quantifier Raising** (QR)
> Adjoin an NP to a truth value denoting category.

Let us also address how to derive the other reading (23'b) of (23). We basically need to negate *Bill answered many questions*. Thus there needs to be a constituent to give us the meaning in (25):

(25)   card({x: x is a question and Bill answered x}) is large

What is not entirely clear, perhaps, is how we find the second set that *many* wants to combine with, namely {x: Bill answered x}.

The following structure will serve:

(26)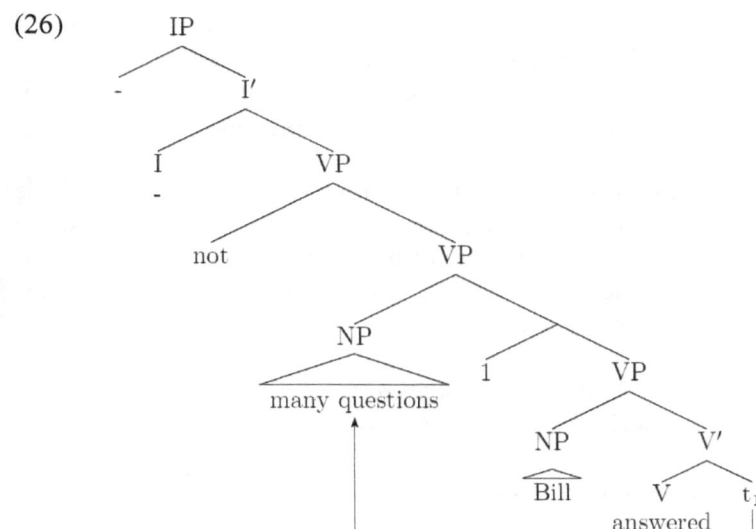

This is a structure in which the object has raised a very short way to adjoin to VP. The VP it adjoins to denotes the desired set. Notice, incidentally, that this short movement of the object looks just like scrambling syntactically: it is adjunction to VP (compare (62) from Chapter II-2 to (26) above). We will come back to the connection between scrambling and QR later. Below are some crucial steps in the interpretation of (26) to illustrate that it gives rise to the desired reading, (23'b).

(26')   a. [[[1 [$_{VP}$ *Bill answer t_1*]]]]^s = {x: Bill answered x in s}
                                                        (by P<small>RED</small>A<small>BS</small> etc.)
        b. [[[$_{VP}$ [*many questions*] [1 [$_{VP}$ *Bill answered t_1*]]]]]^s = 1 iff
            card({x: x is a question in s and Bill answered x in s}) is large
        c. [[[$_{IP}$ [$_{VP}$ *not* [$_{VP}$[*many questions*] [1 [$_{VP}$ *Bill answered t_1*]]]]]]]^s
            = 1 iff
            card({x: x is a question in s and Bill answered x in s})
            is not large

⊕ **Exercise.** *Practicing the interpretation of structures with QR.* Provide a step-by-step compositional interpretation of (26).   □

⊕ **Exercise.** *Interpreting quantified objects.* The interesting aspect of (26) is that the object NP is not interpreted in its Surface Structure position. Try to compositionally interpret the Surface Structure of *Bill answered many* *questions*. Explain (in your own words) where you run into problems and why. The conclusion linguists have drawn from the problem you have discovered is that object quantifiers cannot be interpreted in their surface position, but rather have to be QRed in order to be interpretable.   □

A final remark on inflection-object quantifier type ambiguities: we have seen in the preceding subsection that modal verbs may give rise to scope ambiguity relative to subjects. In view of this, you may wonder about ambiguities created by the interaction of modals and quantified objects. Consider the following examples:

(26") a. *I should visit a family member tonight.*
b. *Jones could have committed all crimes.*

Try to detect and paraphrase the ambiguity.

2.4. Subject-object ambiguities

We discuss the following example (taken from Heim and Kratzer 1998) as a clear case of scope ambiguity:

(27) *Exactly two publishers offended every linguist.*

(27') a. 'There are exactly two publishers who offended every linguist.'
b. 'Every linguist was offended by some two publishers or other.'

(27") a. card({x: x is a publisher and x offended every linguist}) = 2
b. {x: x is a linguist} ⊆ {x: x was offended by exactly 2 publishers}

⊕ **Exercise.** *Distinct truth conditions.* Describe a situation in which (27'a) is true and (27'b) is false, and another situation in which (27'b) is true and (27'a) is false.   □

We have now practiced these readings sufficiently to see that reading (27'a) is an interpretation in which the subject takes scope over the object, and (27'b) is the reverse. We suggest the following structure for (27'a):

(28)   [$_{IP}$ [*exactly 2 publ.*] [1 [$_{I'}$ _ [$_{VP}$ [*every ling.*] [2 [$_{VP}$ t_1 *offended* t_2]]]]]]

Reading (27'b) could come about by either of the structures below given everything we have said so far.

(29) [$_{IP}$ [*every ling.*] [2 [$_{IP}$ [*exactly 2 publ.*] [1[$_{I'}$ _ [$_{VP}$ t_1 *offended* t_2]]]]]]
[$_{IP}$ _ [$_{I'}$ _ [$_{VP}$ [*every ling.*] [2 [$_{VP}$ [*exactly 2 publ.*] *offended* t_2]]]]]

⊕ **Exercise.** *More QR practice.* Provide a step-by-step compositional interpretation of (28). *Hint*: A novel aspect of (28) for you is probably that the rule Predicate Abstraction applies twice. In your calculation, you will have to interpret the smallest VP [$_{VP}$ t_1 *offended* t_2] in such a way that t_1 is associated with the subject quantifier and t_2 is associated with the object quantifier – e.g.: [[[$_{VP}$ t_1 *offended* t_2]]]$^s_{[x/1][y/2]}$ = 1 iff x offended y in s. □

⊕ **Exercise.** *More quantifier ambiguities.* Each of the examples below is ambiguous. Paraphrase the two readings and draw two Logical Forms corresponding to the two readings. Pick one example and sketch a situation in which one of the readings is true while the other reading is false. Compositionally interpret your Logical Form for the reading of (E5a) in which the object quantifier takes wide scope.

(E5) a. *A linguist invited every philosopher.*
b. *A linguist introduced Bill to every psychologist.*
c. *Ellen introduced a linguist to every psychologist.* □

2.5. Inverse linking

You may still feel skeptical about the suggestion that quantified NPs move about at a level of syntactic representation that is invisible. The term "inverse linking" refers to a type of data that is traditionally used to support this idea. Inverse linking data are sentences of the following kind (with paraphrases):

(30) *A representative from every city was invited.*
'For every city x: a representative from x was invited.'
(31) *Exactly one apple in every basket is rotten.*
'For every basket x: exactly one apple in x is rotten.'

You will easily see now that the plausible interpretation of these sentences is one in which the universal quantifier *every* takes wide scope (as our paraphrases start with 'for every x...'). It is clear why this is so, too: for any given apple, it is impossible for that apple to be in every basket simultaneously. Similarly, it is impossible for any particular representative to be from everywhere. So only the reading with the wide scope universal quantifier makes sense. This is interesting because, when we look at the syntax of such examples, the quantifier that must take wide scope is the quantifier that is lower in the Surface Structure:

(32)   [NP a [N' representative [PP from [NP every city]]]] was invited

The structure of inverse linking data looks like this: we have a quantified NP which contains, inside the N' sister of the first quantified determiner, another quantified NP. This second, inner, NP intuitively takes scope over the larger, outer NP. The problem posed by such data is how to derive the plausible reading.

It is here that the proponents of the QR theory succeed easily. With QR, we can assume that syntax may derive the following structure:

(32')

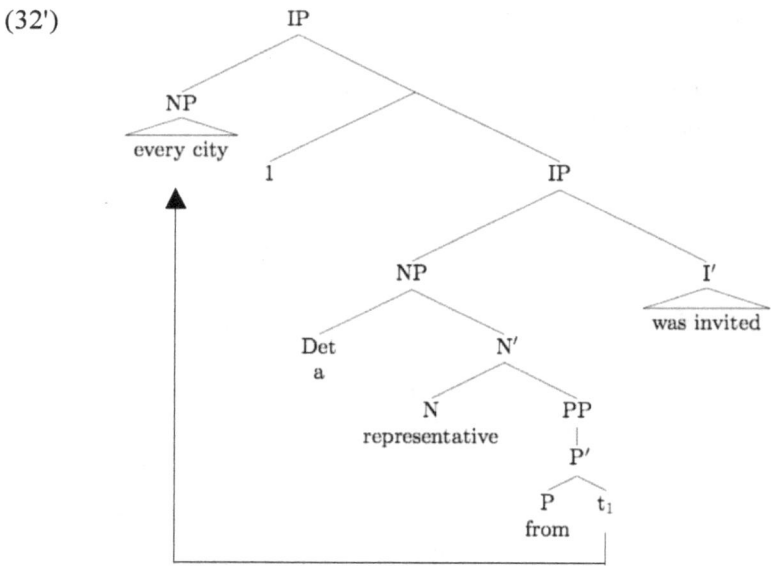

Suppose that the smaller IP provides us with the following set:

(33) {x: a representative from x was invited} =
{x: there is a y such that y is a representative and y is from x and y was invited}

(This is what our interpretation component predicts, as you can verify for yourself.) Then, the set in (33) can function as the second argument of *every* and the overall truth conditions are as in (34) – the desired result.

(34) {x: x is a city} ⊆ {x: there is a y such that y is a representative and y is from x and y was invited}
'For every city x: a representative from x was invited.'

The idea is, then, that QR allows us to extract the inner quantifier from the containing NP and adjoin it to IP, thus giving it widest scope and deriving the plausible reading.

3. Comparison with the German scope facts

The data on quantifier scope that we have considered so far were all from English. In this subsection, we compare them to parallel data from German. The discussion in this section, too, is organized according to syntactic configuration. Configuration is determined by the properties of German clause structure. We distinguish three syntactic circumstances: cases in which all relevant operators are in the middle field, cases in which a quantifier is in the prefield, and the inverse linking cases.

3.1. The middle field

The middle field, remember, is roughly the area in the German clause that follows the element in C and precedes sentence final verbs. We compare interpretive options in cases similar to the ones we have considered in English in section 2.

3.1.1. Negation

Remember that the following English example is ambiguous:

210 *Quantifiers and scope*

(35) *Bill didn't answer many questions.*
(35') a. 'There are many questions that Bill left unanswered.'
 b. 'It is not the case that Bill answered many questions – perhaps he just answered few.'

In German, word order disambiguates:

(36) a. ..., *weil   Bill   viele   Fragen   nicht*
  because Bill many.ACC questions.ACC not
  beantwortet hat.
  answered   has
 '..., because there are many questions that Bill didn't answer.'
 b. ..., *weil   Bill   nicht viele   Fragen*
  because Bill not   many.ACC questions.ACC
  beantwortet hat.
  answered   has
 '..., because it is not the case that Bill answered many questions.'

Note that the sentences chosen are direct translations (as close to the English structures as possible), except that an embedded clause structure was chosen. It looks as if German can choose to express unambiguously the intended meaning because the linear order of negation and quantifier is flexible. It can therefore reflect the intended scope. In English, on the other hand, this is often not possible. In the example at hand, we might consider (37).

(37) *Many questions, Bill didn't answer.*

(37) is a topicalization (compare Part I). This movement brings the quantified object to high structural position. In fact, (37') is precisely the structure we assume QR creates for the wide scope reading of *many questions*. (As we have noted, topicalization is rather restricted in terms of contextual appropriateness, though. We will come back to this briefly in Chapter II-5.)

(37') [$_{IP}$ [*many questions*] [1[$_{IP}$ *Bill* [2[$_{I'}$ *did* [*not* [$_{VP}$ t_2 *answer* t_1]]]]]]

More importantly for present concerns, the position of sentence negation in English seems fairly closely tied to the I domain. In German, we assume that negation is adjoined to VP. This gives rise to some flexibility. Structures for (36) are given below that give rise to the two interpretations paraphrased.

(36') [$_{VP}$ [$_{VP}$ *Bill* [2[$_{VP}$ *viele Fragen* [1[$_{VP}$ *nicht* [$_{VP}$ *t$_2$ t$_1$ beantwortet*]]]]]] *hat*]
(36") [$_{VP}$ [$_{VP}$ *Bill* [2[$_{VP}$ *nicht* [$_{VP}$ *viele Fragen* [1[$_{VP}$ *t$_2$ t$_1$ beantwortet*]]]]]] *hat*]

3.1.2. Two quantifiers

Next, we look at data with two quantified NPs. The English example is repeated in (38).

(38)   *Exactly two publishers offended every linguist.*

(38')   a.   There are exactly two publishers who offended every linguist.
      b.   Every linguist was offended by some two publishers or other.

It seems that once more, linear order in the middle field determines relative scope.

(39)   a.   ..., *weil   genau zwei   Verlage   jeden   Linguisten*
             because exactly two publ.   every.ACC   linguist.ACC
             beleidigt haben.
             offended have
    '..., because there are exactly 2 publ. who offended every linguist.'
      b.   ..., *weil   jeden   Linguisten   genau   zwei*
             because every.ACC linguist.ACC exactly two
             Verlage   beleidigt   haben.
             publishers   offended   have
    '..., because every linguist was offended by some 2 publ. or other.'

The next example, with different quantifiers, is parallel.

(40)   a.   ..., *weil   niemand fast   jede   Frage*
             because nobody almost   every.ACC   question.ACC
             beantwortet hat.
             answered has
    'because there is nobody who answered almost every question.'
      b.   ..., *weil   fast   jede   Frage   niemand*
             because almost every.ACC   question.ACC nobody
             beantwortet   hat.
             answered   has
    '..., because almost every question remained unanswered.'

We get a different result when we consider NPs with the determiner *ein* 'a'; those are called indefinites. In (41'), (41") below, both readings (41a) and (41b) are available. In particular, a wide scope of the universal/negative quantifier over the indefinite is possible (although the reading in which the indefinite takes wide scope seems to be more readily available).

(41)　　*A girl introduced every boy/ nobody.*
　　　　a.　'There is a girl who introduced every boy/nobody.'
　　　　b.　'Every boy/nobody was such that a girl introduced him.'

(41')　　..., *weil   ein   Mädchen   jeden   Jungen   vorgestellt hat.*
　　　　　　because a   girl   every.ACC boy.ACC   introduced has
　　　　'..., because a girl introduced every boy.'

(41")　　..., *weil   ein   Mädchen   niemanden   vorgestellt hat.*
　　　　　　because a   girl   nobody.ACC   introduced has
　　　　'..., because a girl introduced nobody.'

In sum, data with two quantified NPs in the middle field tend to be unambiguous, except perhaps cases in which the preceding quantifier is an indefinite.

The German scope facts suggest that QR is not as freely available in this language as in English. Now, QR means changing constituency and scope on the way to LF. As far as the German middle field is concerned, the relevant movement which would accomplish that is adjunction to VP. Remember though that German employs this same movement, adjunction to VP, at an earlier stage, namely on the way to the Surface Structure. It is called Scrambling. Scrambling is what creates the word order in (39b) and (40b), as illustrated below for (40b).

(40b')　　[$_{CP}$*weil* [$_{VP}$[$_{VP}$*fast jede Frage*] [1 [$_{VP}$ *niemand t$_1$ beantwortet*]] *hat*]]

This means that it is possible in German to overtly express the desired scope relations. Linguists have speculated that, since it is possible to do so, German has to be transparent in this sense. Something unclear about these data is the effect with indefinites. Indefinites must somehow be distinguished from (other) quantified NPs, and there is a lot of discussion in the literature arguing that, but it seems fair to say that linguistic theory does not yet offer a definitive answer as to how and why they are different.

3.2. The prefield

Remember that the prefield is the position in the German clause preceding C in V2 clauses, which contains just one constituent. In the following, we look at data that are quite parallel to the data in the preceding subsection, but a quantifier occurs in the prefield instead of the middle field.

3.2.1. Negation

Example (42) is another incarnation of the *questions* example, but now the quantifier is in the prefield.

(42)   *Viele   Fragen   hat Bill nicht beantwortet.*
           many.ACC questions.ACC has Bill not   answered
           'Bill didn't answer many questions.'

(42')   a.   'There are many questions that Bill left unanswered.'
           b.   'It is not the case that Bill answered many questions – perhaps he just answered few.'

(42")   *Alle Fragen hat Bill nicht beantwortet.*

(42) has both readings in (42'). Depending on intonation, one may be more prominent than the other. With a "normal" intonation, the reading corresponding to (42'a) is probably more salient. This is the reading that corresponds to the Surface Structure in terms of scope. Perhaps it is not surprising that this reading is easily available, given what we said in the last subsection. The other reading can be brought out in the following way (capitalization indicates stress):

(42')   *Bill hat ein paar Sachen gewusst, aber*
           Bill has a   few   things known   but
           VIEle   Fragen   hat er   NICHT   beantwortet.
           MAny.ACC questions.ACC has he   NOT   answered
           'It is not the case that Bill answered many questions.'

This is the reading in which Surface Structure does not match scope, that is, the quantifier that is high in the structure actually takes narrow scope rela-

214   *Quantifiers and scope*

tive to negation. The Surface Structure is given below to allow you to see this more easily.

(40b')   [$_{CP}$[*viele Fr.*] [2[$_C$ *hat*$_3$[$_{VP}$[$_{VP}$ *B.* [1[$_{VP}$ *nicht*[$_{VP}$ t_1 t_2 *beantwortet*]]]] t_3]

If you have doubts regarding the availability of this reading, note that this is the more prominent reading of (42"). So, if a quantifier is in the prefield, its scope doesn't have to match its surface syntactic position – it can be smaller. Next, we ask if this is a general phenomenon.

☕ **Exercise.** *Scope reconstruction.* You have come across a type of data before in which the scope position of an expression was below its surface position – remember subjects and negation in English. There, we resorted to reconstruction, i.e. we interpreted the subject in the position where it originated, not in the surface position. Try to extend this strategy to (40'b). That is, try to come up with a complete derivation including a Logical Form that will yield reading (42'b). *Hints*: For a complete solution, you need to remember the problem of quantifiers in object position and scrambling. Suppose for the purpose of this exercise that the auxiliary verb *hat* is semantically vacuous.   □

3.2.2. Two quantifiers

We will once more consider data parallel to the middle field data above except with one quantifier in the prefield:

(43)   a.   *Genau zwei Verlage haben jeden Linguisten*
exactly two publ. have every.ACC linguist.ACC
beleidigt.
offended
   b.   *Jeden Linguisten haben genau zwei Verlage*
every.ACC linguist.ACC have exactly two publ.
beleidigt.
offended
'exactly two publishers offended every linguist.' (ambiguous)

(44)   *Fast jede Frage hat niemand beantwortet.*
almost every.ACC question.ACC has nobody answered
'Nobody answered almost every question.'   (ambiguous)

(45)   *Ein Mädchen hat niemanden vorgestellt.*
       a   girl   has nobody.ACC introduced
       'A girl introduced nobody.'   (ambiguous)

We get ambiguity relatively easily here. The more accessible readings generally seem to be the one in which scope corresponds to surface word order. But the other reading (sometimes called "inverse scope" because scope does not correspond to surface word order) is possible and can be brought out in a good context (with possibly the help of intonation). These data are perhaps the best German parallel to the intuitions that English speakers tend to have about scopally ambiguous sentences.

Exercise. *Scope reconstruction once more.* We make a suggestion for the derivation of the (E6b) reading of the *publisher* example in (E7).

(E6)   *Genau zwei Verlage haben jeden   Linguisten beleidigt.*
       exactly two publ.   have every.ACC linguist.ACC offended
       a.   'There are exactly two publ. who offended every linguist.'
       b.   'Every linguist was offended by some two publ. or other.'

(E7)   Surface Structure:
       [$_{CP}$ [*genau 2 V*] 1 [$_C$ *haben$_3$* [$_{VP}$ [$_{VP}$ [*jeden L* 2 [$_{VP}$ t_1 t_2 *beleidigt*]] t_3]]]
       Logical Form:
       [$_{CP}$ _[$_C$ _[$_{VP}$ [$_{VP}$ [*jeden L*] 2 [$_{VP}$ [*genau 2 V*] t_2 *beleidigt*]] *haben$_3$*]]]

Argue that this is a possible derivation from a syntactic point of view. *Hint*: remember ways to mark that scrambling has taken place.   □

One way to describe the data is that the quantifier in the prefield can have surprisingly low scope. Maybe, it behaves as if it hadn't moved to the prefield, but is interpreted in its original position. This is similar to what we said about the subject and I in English: the subject needs to move to Spec-IP but it can be interpreted lower, in its original position in Spec-VP. And it is different from Scrambling/QR, which determines where a quantifier is interpreted.
Why should different kinds of movement come apart in this way? One might suppose that the movement of the subject in English is obligatory, no matter whether it makes semantic sense. Perhaps for this reason, it may be undone for the purpose of interpretation. Of course it would be useless to

ignore QR as its whole purpose is to provide the desired input for interpretation. If scrambling is similar to QR, then perhaps in cases like (46):

(46)   ..., weil   fast   jede   Frage   niemand
       because   almost   every.ACC   question.ACC   nobody
          beantwortet   hat.
          answered   has
       'because almost every question remained unanswered.'

it would be equally futile to ignore the movement: it was completely optional to scramble the object. We may have done it as a sort of early version of QR (early as in visible), which German allows. We cannot later undo its effects.

On this reasoning, movement to the prefield would have to be different from scrambling. Ideally, something would force us to move the constituent in question regardless of compositional interpretation. It is clear that there must be something in the prefield, but unfortunately for this line of thought, no particular thing is structurally obliged to move there (unlike subject movement in English). If there is a reason for a particular constituent to go there, it has to be external to syntax.

To sum up, there is variation between languages with respect to how pervasive scope ambiguity is. While English shows scope ambiguity under many syntactic circumstances, German appears to be more restricted in a way that relates to syntactic properties that distinguish it from English. Similar observations have been made about other languages.

Exercise. *Scope in Japanese.* Consider the Japanese data below. Can you extend the analysis sketched in the text to this language? What other data would you like to consider?

(E8)   a.   *On'nanoko*   *daremo-ga*   *dareka otokonoko-o*
            girl   every-NOM   some   boy-ACC
            tsukamae-ta.
            catch-PAST
            'Every girl caught some boy.'   (wide scope of *every girl*)
       b.   *Dareka*   *on'nanoko-ga*   *otokonoko daremo-o*
            some   girl- NOM   boy   every-ACC
            tsukamae-ta.
            catch-PAST
            'Some girl caught every boy.'   (wide scope of *some girl*) ☐

3.2.3. Inverse linking

In this subsection, we examine briefly and inconclusively inverse linking in German. We repeat some of the data from English first:

(47) a. *A representative from every city was invited.*
 b. *One apple in every basket is rotten.*

Below are the translations. Note that German offers the possibility of taking apart the complex NP and overtly moving out the inner quantifier. We are not certain with regard to intuitions here. The inversely linked reading may be possible in the (a) versions, but our judgment is that we would always prefer the (b) versions – which are once more the semantically transparent ones.

(48) a. *Ein Abgeordneter aus jeder Stadt war eingeladen.*
 a representative from every.DAT city.DAT was invited
 'A representative from every city was invited.'
 b. *Aus jeder Stadt war ein Abgeordneter eingeladen.*
 from every.DAT city.DAT was a representative invited
 'A representative from every city was invited.'

(49) a. *Ein Apfel in jedem Korb war angefault.*
 one apple in every.DAT basket.DAT was rotten
 'One apple in every basket was rotten.'
 b. *In jedem Korb war ein Apfel angefault.*
 in every.DAT basket.DAT was one apple rotten
 'One apple in every basket was rotten.'

The above examples have as the outer quantifier something that can be taken to be an indefinite. Let's try non-indefinite determiners for the outer NP. We might expect that the inverse linking reading is not possible below in German because inverse scope was possible above at best with indefinites. That does indeed seem to be the case: the example in (50) is odd and it should be ok on the inversely linked interpretation.

(50) ?? *Kein Produkt von jedem EU-Land verkauft sich gut.*
 no product of every.DAT EU-country.DAT sells REFL well
 'No product of every EU country sells well.'

(50')   For every EU country x: no product from x sells well.

We suspect that the corresponding English examples in (51) are also odd (and this is less expected), but we have not conducted a systematic investigation (nor are we aware that anyone else has). We use the ⁰ sign below for a sentence on which no judgment is marked.

(51) a.   ⁰ *No product of every EU country sells well.*
         For every EU country x: no product from x sells well.
     b.   ⁰ *Every apple in no basket is rotten.*
         For no basket x: every apple in x is rotten.

More empirical work is needed here. If we want to relate the inverse linking problem with the ideas presented above, there is some expectation that German scrambling could, and perhaps partly should, once more take the place of English QR.

The basics box summarizes the chapter very briefly:

☞ THE BASICS BOX: *Scope in English vs. German*
- ✓ quantified NPs denote a different kind of semantic object than referential NPs, namely sets of sets of individuals instead of individuals.
- ✓ quantified NPs give rise to scope ambiguities. Scope ambiguity is analyzed as syntactic ambiguity. Different structures can be the input to compositional interpretation. QR helps us generate the required structures, called Logical Forms.
- ✓ quantifier scope is more fixed by Surface Structure in German than in English, resulting in less ambiguity
- ✓ this seems intuitively related to the greater syntactic freedom that German has (position of negation, word order in the middle field)
- ✓ English makes up for a fairly fixed Surface Structure by a more liberal mapping to Logical Form.

---

4. Selected references

The semantics of quantifiers is the one introduced in Part I (Chapter I-8), a basic version of Generalized Quantifier Theory. We refer to the literature discussed there for the basic semantic analysis.

Recent decades have seen a lot of research on individual quantifiers, and revisions and refinements of Generalized Quantifier Theory. We cannot do justice to these developments and offer just a few references here. A recent overview of research on natural language quantifiers is Szabolcsi (2010). The Handbook of Semantics (2011, eds. Maienborn, von Heusinger, Portner) contains a whole section on noun-phrase semantics including a chapter specifically on quantifiers (see Keenan 2011). Penka (2011) concentrates on negative quantifiers and Hackl (2009) on *most*, to give just a few further references. Indefinites are often given a semantics different from quantifiers. See, e.g., Heim (1982, 2011), Kamp (1981), Reinhart (1997). Crossliniguistic discussion of quantifiers can be found e.g. in Matthewson (2001) and in Bach et al. (eds., 1995).

Similarly, there is a host of literature dealing with Logical Form, QR and reconstruction, as well as competing theories of the same scope phenomena. Haegeman (1994) introduces the syntactic theory on which the theory of Logical Form is built. Much of the analysis and most of the terminology presented in this chapter goes back to May (1985). Our version can basically be found in Heim and Kratzer (1998) along with many of the examples in the text. Aoun and Li (1989), Huang (1994), Johnson (2000), Fox (2003) offer a discussion of the properties of QR in English (and other languages), noting that English is comparatively flexible. Type shifting analyses compete with QR analyses. See, e.g., Partee (1987), Jacobson (1999) and de Hoop's (2012) overview for more on type shifting.

Regarding quantifier scope in German, important references include Pafel (1991, 2005) and Frey (1993). Jacobs (1982) discusses negation. Büring (1997) investigates scope involving the prefield position in great detail. Some relevant discussion can also be found in Diesing (1992), Beck (1996a, b) and Pesetsky (1989) (for an earliness principle perhaps similar to the one we allude to in the text). Problems related to Inverse Linking are discussed in Sauerland and Bott (2002), May and Bale (2005), Sauerland (2005).

The subscript introduced in the Predicate Abstraction rule and used for the interpretation of traces and pronouns is our introductory step towards a variable assignment function. Explanations of variables, variable assignment functions and so on can be found in standard introductions to logic (see e.g. Gamut 1991 and references therein). The discussion in Heim and Kratzer (1998) is in sync with how we have handled things here.

It is an open issue whether the traces left by head movement also produce interpretive effects. For many purposes, head movement can and ought to be undone for interpretive purposes. But cf. Lechner (2006) for evidence regarding the relevance of the traces of head movement, also Iatridou and Zeijlstra (2010).

Many of the intuitions in this chapter are fairly subtle, and the discussion in the literature has been controversial. We have presented the data as best we could and noted in places that intuitions are not completely clear. In recent years, linguists have employed more systematic empirical methods to establish what the facts actually are. With respect to quantifier scope, Anderson (2004) for English and Oliver Bott and colleagues (Bott and Radó 2009, Bott and Schlotterbeck 2012) for German represent this line of research. The Japanese data are from Han et al. (2008). Hackl et al. (2012) provide psycholinguistic evidence for the QR of object quantifiers. More generally, Bott et al. (2011) discusses the elicitation of semantic data. It has become clear in our discussion that there is still important work to be done in this area.

Chapter II-4
Negation and polarity

I'll answer him by law. I'll not budge an inch, boy;
(Christopher Sly in William Shakespeare's *The Taming of the Shrew*)

This chapter offers an introduction to negative and positive polarity items (NPIs and PPIs). Those are items that require a 'negative' or 'positive' environment, in a sense which we make precise below. The first section discusses the distribution of these elements. In the second section, we connect the topic of polarity items to the notion of scope, as developed in the previous chapter. Specifically, we consider the contrast between *some* and *any*. Section 3 provides references.

1. Negative and positive polarity items

1.1. Negative polarity items

Negative polarity items (NPIs) are expressions that require a special licensing context, in addition to meeting the distribution requirements of the category to which they belong. They can only occur in environments that are in some sense negative. Some examples of English NPIs are: *any*, *ever*, *a red cent*, *lift a finger*. The data in (1) illustrate that the NPI is acceptable in a negated sentence (e.g. *ever* in (1a)), but not acceptable in the corresponding plain affirmative sentence (e.g. (1a')). (1a") shows that adverbs like *often* can occupy the position that the adverb *ever* occurs in. So in addition to *ever* being an adverb, it comes with its own special distribution requirements. Negated sentences are a good environment for it. And similarly for (1b, c) with *any* and *lift a finger*. This observation explains the term NPI: these items appear to need a negative environment.

(1)   a.   *John hasn't ever been to Israel.*
         a'.   **John has ever been to Israel.*
         a".   *John has often been to Israel.*

b. *John didn't like anybody.*
b'. **John liked anybody.*
c. *John didn't lift a finger to help us.*
c'. **John lifted a finger to help us.*

NPIs exist in many languages (possibly in all). Some examples are given below.

(2) a. *Kai hat nicht versucht, [auch nur]*$_{NPI}$ *eine* [German]
Kai has not tried [even]$_{NPI}$ one.ACC
Aufgabe zu lösen.
problem.ACC to solve
'Kai hasn't tried to solve even one problem.'
a'. **Kai hat versucht, auch nur eine Aufgabe*
Kai has tried even$_{NPI}$ one.ACC problem.ACC
zu lösen.
to solve
'Kai has tried to solve even one problem.'
b. *Je n' ai pas compris* [French]
I NEG have NEG understood
[*un traitre mot*]$_{NPI}$
[a treacherous word]$_{NPI}$
'I didn't understand a single word.'
b'. **J' ai compris* [*un traitre mot*]$_{NPI}$.
I have understood [a treacherous word]$_{NPI}$
'I understood a single word.'
c. *Dhen idhe tipota o Janis.* [Greek]
Not saw anything the Janis
'Janis didn't see anything.'
c'. **Idhe tipota o Janis.*
saw anything the Janis
'Janis saw anything.'

There are other contexts besides negated sentences that allow NPIs. A lot of research has gone into describing precisely the environments that license NPIs. In this chapter we concentrate on sentences with quantified determiners, and we ask where NPIs can occur in such sentences. We first consider examples in which a quantified determiner is part of the subject and the NPI occurs within its second argument:

(3) a. *No students/less than seven people/few people*
  [ᵢ' *have* [ᵥₚ *ever been to Israel*]].
 b. * *Some people/all students/most professors/many people*
  [ᵢ' *have* [ᵥₚ *ever been to Israel*]].
(4) a. *Kein Student war* [ᵥₚ *jemals in Israel gewesen*]. [Germ.]
   no   student was   ever   in Israel been
   'No student had ever been to Israel.'
 b. * *Manche/viele/ alle Studenten*
   some/ many/ all students
   [ᵥₚ *waren jemals in Israel gewesen*].
     were ever in Israel been
   'Some / many / all students had ever been to Israel.'

In these examples, it depends on the quantifier whether the NPI is allowed within the predicate (that is, the I' or the VP), i.e. within the quantifier's second argument. For instance, NPIs are fine with *no*, but not with *some*. Next, we test whether an NPI is allowed in the first argument, the restrictor of a quantifier:

(5) a. *Every/no student who has ever been to Israel will be recruited.*
 b. * *Some student who has ever been to Israel will be recruited.*

The examples above teach us that it is possible to have NPIs also with quantificational structures, not just with negation. But their acceptability depends on two things: which quantifier is involved and where the NPI occurs, i.e. in the first or the second argument of the quantifier. For example, *no* licenses NPIs in both positions and *some* in neither. *Every* licenses the NPI in the first argument but not in the second. We expect an analysis of NPI licensing to account for these observations. The next subsection introduces such an analysis.

⊕ **Exercise.** *Finding more licensing contexts.* Try to find some further sentence contexts that allow NPIs. How does "negativity" fit as a description of your contexts? (You can continue this exercise after you have read the next subsection and see how the characterization of NPI contexts described there fits your data.) ☐

1.2. Downward entailing contexts

The preceding subsection has shown us that the NPI needs a licenser. *Ever*, for example, unlike *often*, is not happy in all the environments in which adverbs of this kind are happy. In addition to being in an appropriate position for an adverb, *ever* requires a special context. It is intuitively obvious that semantics is instrumental in defining the special context. That is, the difference between *no* and *some* in (3) above, for example, seems to lie in their meaning, not in the syntactic structure. Notice, however, that it is insufficient to say that the licensing environment is "negative". A clear illustration is *every*, which licenses NPIs in its first argument but not in its second argument. This should be seen vis-à-vis the fact that *no* licenses them in both, and *some* licenses them in neither argument. How is the first argument of *every* more "negative" than the second?

Interestingly, "negativity" of a linguistic environment in the relevant sense can be measured by the inferences that are permitted in that environment. An inference is "permitted", i.e. valid, remember, if every situation which makes the premise true also makes the conclusion true. A simple example of a valid inference is given in (6). Every situation that makes the first sentence in (6) true must also make the second sentence true. Hence, this is a valid inference.

(6) *John bought 'Ice Age II' and 'Finding Nemo'.*
 => *John bought 'Ice Age II'.*

We now consider the quantifiers that we have looked at above for the purposes of NPI licensing and ask what inferences they permit. We first look at the second argument of the quantified determiner. The quantifiers that allow NPIs in their second argument license a particular kind of inference, namely a superset to subset inference as illustrated by (7).

(7) a. *No student sang.*
  => *No student sang loudly.*
  b. *No more than 2/at most seven/few people sang.*
  => *No more than 2/at most seven/few people sang loudly.*
  BUT:
  c. *Some people/every student/most professors/many people sang.*
  ≠> *Some people/every student/most professors/many people sang loudly.*

Note that [[sang loudly]] ⊆ [[sang]]. In (7a, b), then, an inference from a superset to a subset is valid. (Examine your intuitions for other examples of superset-subset pairs (e.g. *sang or danced – sang*).) The same inferences are not permitted in the second argument of quantifiers that do not license NPIs in the predicate, cf. (7c). Linguists have taken this to suggest that NPIs are licensed only in sentence contexts that permit inferences from supersets to subsets.

This picture is confirmed when we look at the first argument of the same quantifiers. One way to go from sets to subsets is by using a modifier, e.g. a relative clause (again, try other superset-subset pairs, for example *student – tall student*):

(8)   a.   *Every/no student who sang was recruited.*
            => *Every/no student who sang loudly was recruited.*
           (first argument of the quantifier: *student who sang loudly*)
           BUT:
     b.   *Some student who sang was recruited.*
           ≠> *Some student who sang loudly was recruited.*

Every licenses inferences from supersets to subsets in its first argument, but not in its second. *No* licenses them in both, and *some* in neither. This matches the suggestion above that NPIs want to be in a sentence context in which inferences from supersets to subsets are permitted.

Our intuitions about valid inferences are predicted by our determiner meanings. This is shown below.

(9)   a.   For any s: $[[every]]^s = \{<P, Q>: P \subseteq Q\}$
     b.   For any s: $[[no]]^s = \{<P, Q>: P \cap Q = \emptyset\}$
     c.   For any s: $[[some]]^s = \{<P, Q>: P \cap Q \neq \emptyset\}$

(10)   *every*:   If $P' \subseteq P$ and $P \subseteq Q$, then $P' \subseteq Q$.
                       If $Q' \subseteq Q$ and $P \subseteq Q$, then nothing follows about P and Q'.
(11)   *no*:   If $P' \subseteq P$ and $P \cap Q = \emptyset$, then $P' \cap Q = \emptyset$.
                       If $Q' \subseteq Q$ and $P \cap Q = \emptyset$, then $P \cap Q' = \emptyset$.
(12)   *some*:   If $P' \subseteq P$ and $P \cap Q \neq \emptyset$, then nothing follows about P' and Q.
                       If $Q' \subseteq Q$ and $P \cap Q \neq \emptyset$, then nothing follows about Q' and P.

226   *Negation and polarity*

Environments that permit inferences from sets to subsets are called downward monotonic or downward entailing environments. They correspond to the environments where NPIs are licensed. Hence (13) characterizes NPI licensing.

(13)   **Condition on the Licensing of Negative Polarity Items** (NPIs)
An NPI wants to be in a downward monotonic environment
i.e. in the scope of an expression that creates a downward monotonic context.

Negation creates a downward monotonic environment and is therefore covered by the above NPI licensing condition:

(14)   *It is not the case that it rained.*
=> *It is not the case that it rained heavily.*

There is a lot more to be said about the distribution of NPIs. For example, the syntactic configuration also plays a role in NPI licensing. Also, not all NPIs are the same. We will not pursue the issue further. We stick here to the simplified view of the licensing condition for NPIs given in (13): that they want to be in a downward monotonic environment. This condition is incorporated into more sophisticated analyses of NPI-licensing, and it is therefore a good first step in understanding the grammar of NPIs.

It is interesting that inferential properties such as downward monotonicity are relevant for linguistic description. This means that we can never even state where e.g. *ever* in English sentences can occur without understanding the formal semantic properties of words like *no* and *every*. It also means that the grammar of English (and other languages) makes reference to inference patterns.

⌛ **Exercise.** *Testing more quantifiers for downward monotonicity.* Determine which of the following quantified determiners are downward monotonic by testing the superset-to-subset entailment patterns. Remember to consider both arguments. Do the lexical entries for the determiners predict the inferential behavior? Does the inferential behavior match the NPI licensing properties of the determiners?

(E1)   a.   *Less than four apples are rotten.*
       b.   *Exactly two apples are rotten.*

c.   *A few apples are rotten.* ☐

☕ **Exercise**. *Adverbial quantifiers as licensers.* Consider the examples in (E2). They should remind you of the data with *every*, *some* and *no*, except that we have an adverbial quantifier.

(E2) a.   *Sometimes when I see a dog I give it a treat.*
 a'. **Sometimes when I see any dog I give it a treat.*
 b.   *I always take an umbrella when there is a chance of rain.*
 b'. *I always take an umbrella when there is any chance of rain.*
 c.   *Bill never gardens when there is wind.*
 c'. *Bill never gardens when there is any wind.*
 e.   *Bill never does any gardening when there is wind.*
 f.   **I always take any umbrella when there is a chance of rain.*
 g.   **Sometimes when I see a dog I give it any treat.*

Suggest an analysis of these data. *Hints:* You need to come up with a semantics for the adverbs *sometimes*, *never* and *always*. Take them to quantify over situations, not individuals. Then you need to suggest interpretable Logical Forms for the examples. Do the data, under your analysis, fit the NPI generalization (13)? ☐

☕ **Exercise**. *Strawson entailments: extending downward entailment.* Determine the properties that may license the NPIs in (E3), by combining downward monotonicity with presuppositions. (Recall from Part I: presuppositions are appropriateness conditions on context and they can be triggered by different trigger words.). You may proceed as follows: (i) identify the presupposition and the trigger in each case; (ii) construct examples to see whether the contexts are downward monotonic.

(E3) a.   *Neither cat that has ever caught a mouse was taught by her mother.*
 b.   *Lisa was the youngest person in her class to win any prize.*
 c.   *Only Marge had any wine at the party.*

Hints and discussion: In example (E3a), the presupposition trigger is the quantified determiner *neither*. The presupposition is that there are exactly two elements in the set that is its first argument. Does *neither* create a downward monotonic context? Is the inference below (and others like it) valid?

(E4)   a.   *Neither cat ate potatoes.*
           b.   *Neither grey cat ate potatoes.*

The attempted inference in (E4) above does not hold intuitively. But what if we restrict our attention to those contexts in which (E4b) is defined?

(E5)   a.   *Neither cat ate potatoes.* AND
           a'.   *There are exactly two grey cats.*
           b.   *Neither grey cat ate potatoes.*

If our premises are (E5a) and (E5a'), then the so-called Strawson inference to (E5b) holds.   □

1.3. Positive polarity items

There is also what seems to be the reverse of an NPI: expressions that do not like negation in their vicinity. These are called PPIs. Examples are *some* and *already* in English and *sogar* in German.

(15)   a.   *Robin baked some cookies.*
           b. ^{??} *Robin didn't bake some cookies.*
(16)   a.   *John had already left.*
           b. ^{??} *Nobody had already left.*
(17)   a.   *Hans hat sogar gesungen.*   [German]
               Hans has even sung
               'Hans even sang.'
           b. ^{??} *Niemand hat sogar gesungen.*
                nobody has even sung
                'Nobody even sang.'

These expressions are not really the "reverse" of NPIs in any serious sense. They just don't want to be too close to a negation. If negation and PPI are separated by a clause boundary, for example, the PPI is acceptable. Downward monotonicity as such is not problematic either.

(18)   a. *I don't think that John has already left.*
       b. *Every student who had already left got an F.*

Again, more work would need to be done to properly characterize the environments in which PPIs are appropriate. We merely note:

(19)   **Condition on Licensing of Positive Polarity Items** (PPIs):
       A PPI does not want to be in the immediate scope of negation.

2. Scope in the distribution of *some* vs. *any*

Let us return to an example that we discussed when we first introduced scope ambiguity in the introduction to Part II, (20) together with its two interpretations (21a, b):

(20)   *I didn't invite one of her friends.*

(21)   a. *There is one friend of hers that I did not invite.*
       b. *It is not the case that I invited a friend of hers – i.e. I invited none.*

The ambiguity is in the relative scope of negation and the NP *one of her friends*. We derive two different LFs for the sentence, sketched below:

(22)   a. [[*one of her friends*] [1 [*NOT* [$_{VP}$ *I invite* t_1]]]]
       b. [__ [*NOT* [$_{VP}$ [*one of her friends*] [1[$_{VP}$ *I invite* t_1]]]]]

Step-by-step interpretation of these two structures according to the rules we discussed gives rise to the two readings observed.

We noted that German tends to disambiguate such structures through word order:

(23)   a. ..., weil   ich   einen   ihrer   Freunde   nicht
                because I   one.ACC   her.GEN   friends.GEN   not
                eingeladen   habe.
                invited   have
                '..., because there is a friend of her's that I didn't invite.'
       b. ..., weil   ich   keinen/   nicht einen   ihrer

because I none.ACC/ not one.ACC her.GEN
Freunde eingeladen habe.
friends.GEN invited have
'..., because I invited none of her friends.'

Actually, English also disambiguates, but it uses a different mechanism. Two unambiguous sentences that correspond to the two paraphrases are given below (we ignore number marking here for convenience).

(24) a. *I didn't invite some of her friends.*
      b. *I didn't invite any of her friends.*

Let us first consider the example with *some*. *Some* is a quantified determiner and has essentially the same semantics as *one* or *a*. A fairly intuitive suggestion for their interpretations might be (25):

(25) a. For any s: $[[some]]^s = \{<P, Q>: P \cap Q \neq \emptyset\}$
      b. For any s: $[[one]]^s = \{<P, Q>: card(P \cap Q) \geq 1\}$

The meanings in (25a) and (25b) above are identical: the intersection of the sets involved is different from the empty set if and only if its cardinality is at least 1.

The reading that is intuitively available for (24a) must then come from the structure in (26), parallel to (22a).

(26) [[*some of her friends*] [1 [*NOT* [$_{VP}$ *I invite* t_1]]]]
      'There are some friends of hers that I did not invite.'

The question is what excludes the other structure parallel to (22b), in other words, what disambiguates the example. That is the PPI status of *some*. The other LF is ungrammatical because it violates the constraint on PPIs. As a result, the sentence is unambiguous.

Next, we consider the version with *any*, (24b). We assume that *any* has the same meaning as *some*. We can infer this from the interpretation of (27), for example:

(27) a. *I did not promise to invite any of her friends.*
         = I did not make a promise with the following content:
         I will invite some of her friends.

b. *I did not try to invite any of her friends.*
= I made no attempt to do the following:
invite some of her friends.

Hence, *any* has the following meaning:

(28)   For any s: $[\![any]\!]^s = \{<P, Q>: P \cap Q \neq \emptyset\}$

This implies that the interpretation of the *any* version of our sentence arises through the LF below:

(29)   [__ [*NOT* [[*any of her friends*] [1 [$_{VP}$ *I invite* t_1]]]]]
'It is not the case that I invited a friend of hers – i.e. I invited none.'

And something must exclude the other LF. Here, we remember the NPI status of *any*. In the LF above, *any* is in the scope of negation and it is licensed. In the alternative LF, it would not be in the scope of negation, violating the licensing conditions on NPIs. It is thus the status of *some* and *any* as PPI and NPI respectively that disambiguates our example in the way described.

Here is what we are driving at with this example: Both sentences, the one with *some* and the one with *any*, are well-formed. They are distinguished in terms of interpretation. This means that the licensing condition on NPIs and PPIs applies at a level that determines interpretation – the level of Logical Form. Putting it differently: we cannot account for the distribution of NPIs and PPIs without the notion of scope, and that is an LF notion.

We are belaboring this point somewhat because traditional, simplified claims about the distribution of NPIs and PPIs tend to say things like the following:

(30)   Use *any* in negative sentences.
Do not use *some* in negative sentences.

Students will infer that when there is a negation in the sentence, you must use *any*. But this is not right: whether or not you use *any* depends on the meaning you want to convey! If what you want to say is *there is one friend of hers that I did not invite*, the lexical item to go for is *some*, despite the negation. Here are some real-life data collected informally from the web. They show that the phenomenon of *some* following negation is frequent and natural. Moreover, what we have said about scope captures the circumstances under which people give preference to *some* over *any* in negative contexts.

(31) a. *We didn't invite some friends and did invite others...*
  b. *I disagreed with and didn't buy some of the things they did in the movie...*
  c. *I didn't see some of the other great films...*
  d. *I didn't like some, but there were others I enjoyed...*
  e. *FNUC later agreed to cut the board, but hasn't followed some of the other recommendations...*
  f. *It is lucky that nobody followed some of the costly and misguided demands for policy...*
  g. *No one believed some of the facts he had dug up...*
  h. *No one liked some of his uniform designs...*

The first example is (i) a counterexample to the simple-minded statement about the distribution of *some* in (30); (ii) the context makes it clear that the interpretation is: 'there are some friends who we did not invite'. All examples are like that, i.e. in all examples, *some* takes scope over negation (*not, nobody, no one*). We observe the following empirical generalization:

(32) **Co-occurrence of *some* and negation**:
  some and negation can occur in the same simple clause only if *some* is not interpreted in the immediate scope of negation.

We learn from this discussion that no adequate description of the distribution of polarity items is possible without the notion of scope. Moreover, the set theoretic determiner meanings we introduced earlier have real descriptive power as well. They predict correctly inferential behavior that is instrumental to NPI licensing.

🕐 **Exercise** *Modals and negation.* Consider the English modals below and determine whether they can scope freely with respect to negation or whether they show restrictions, e.g. scoping only below or above negation. Can you apply what you learned about NPIs and PPIs to these facts?

(E6) a. *You need not smirk.*
  b. *John must not have another whiskey.*

c. *Nigel might not be the culprit.*
d. *You cannot pass.*

Hints: Paraphrase the meanings that these sentences have. Can you find two readings for each modal or just one? In the latter case: is your paraphrase one that shows wide scope of negation (e.g. 'It is not the case that...', 'It is not necessary...')? If so, you have identified an NPI modal. If, conversely, it is not possible for a given modal to find a paraphrase giving negation wide scope, you have identified a modal that resembles a PPI.

☐

☞ THE BASICS BOX: *Polarity items and interaction with negation*
- ✓ Negative polarity items require a downward-monotonic context, i.e. a context that licenses inferences from supersets to subsets. The licensors of NPIs include negation, but are not limited to it.
- ✓ Positive polarity items have the requirement that they should not be in the immediate scope of negation.
- ✓ *Some* is a PPI and *any* is an NPI. What traditional grammars teach about their distribution ("use *any* in negative sentences; use *some* in positive sentences") is false. *Some* can occur in negated sentence as long as it takes scope over negation. *Any* can occur in sentences that do not contain negation.

---

3. Selected references

The formal semantic analysis of NPIs as items that require a downward monotonic context is due to Ladusaw (1978), cf. also Ladusaw (1996). There is a large body of literature on the topic. Giannakidou (2011) offers a recent overview and many relevant references. An interesting question that we have not pursued here is why NPIs have this distributional requirement. Krifka (1995), among others, gives an answer to this question that links up with the topic of our next chapter: focus.

The suggestion that downward entailment should be extended to incorporate presupposition can be found in von Fintel (1999), Chierchia (2013).

These linguistic insights do not seem to have found their way into language teaching yet. Versions of what is attributed in this chapter to traditional grammars can be found for example in Red Line 2 (Ernst Klett Verlag Stuttgart 2007) and in Campden Town 1 (2013 Braunschweg:

Diesterweg) (English textbook targeting approx. 11-12 year old English learners in Germany) as well as in English Grammar in Use (Cambridge University Press, Cambridge, 1994) (an English Grammar targeted at upper level high school students) and various online grammars. A similar 30 to 40 year time lag in the introduction of scientific insights into school curricula would be deemed quite problematic in fields like biology or chemistry. Our goal in drawing attention to this point is to invite our readers to improve on this state of affairs. We hope to have convinced you that modern linguistic analysis characterizes the facts better than the traditional descriptions. If you are in a position to help develop teaching materials or descriptive grammars, hopefully we have motivated you to integrate insights like the ones discussed in this chapter. We would like to encourage you to take on this project.

The observation that certain modals must be in or outside the scope of negation has been made several times, but a recent research paper to investigate them as polarity items is Iatridou and Zeijlstra (2010).

Chapter II-5
Focus

> *'When I use a word,' Humpty Dumpty said in rather a scornful tone, 'it means just what I choose it to mean – neither more nor less.'*
> (Lewis Caroll, *Through the Looking-Glass*)

This chapter introduces the notion of focus. Section 1 gives an informal description of focus and its interpretive effects. In section 2, we offer a semantic analysis in terms of alternatives. A glimpse of crosslinguistic differences related to focus is given in section 3, followed by references in section 4.

1. What is focus?

The string *Molly met Bill* can be pronounced in different ways. Below, capitalisation indicates the syllable on which the main stress of the sentence (called the pitch accent) falls.

(1) a. *Molly met BILL.*
     b. *MOLly met Bill.*

Different ways of assigning stress to the sentence make no immediate difference to the truth conditions. No matter how you pronounce (1), the sentence is true if Molly met Bill and false otherwise. Still, one has the intuition that there is a meaning related difference between (1a) and (1b). The intuition probably has something to do with what is important, or what is new in (1). We work at pinning down what the difference is below. A few words on terminology: We say that in (1a) *Bill* is focused and in (1b) *Molly* is focused. The focus (or a focus) of a sentence is the word or constituent containing the main stress. Following convention, we use a subscript capital *F* in order to identify the focused constituent as shown in (2).

(2) a. *Molly met [BILL]$_F$.*

b. [MOLly]$_F$ met Bill.

Next, we examine some of the effects that focus can have.

1.1. Focus can make a difference in discourse appropriateness

1.1.1. Questions and answers

The string *Sally invited Bill* is appropriate as the response to two different questions depending on how it is pronounced. (4a) is appropriate as an answer to (3a) but not to (3b). Conversely, (4b) is an appropriate answer to the question in (3b), but it is not an appropriate answer to the question in (3a).

(3)   a.   *Who did Sally invite to the party?*
           b.   *Who invited Bill to the party?*
(4)   a.   *Sally invited BILL$_F$.*
           b.   *SALly$_F$ invited Bill.*

1.1.2. Contrast

Another discourse-related effect of focus is contrast. Imagine that person A states (5a), and person B intends to correct A. Uttering (6a) is appropriate as a contradiction. *Sally* is focused and contrasts with *Peter* in (5a). (6b) with focus on *syntax* instead is not an appropriate reply to (5a). Conversely, person B may contradict an utterance of (5b) by saying (6b), but not (6a). An intuitive notion of contrast is involved, where *Sally* contrasts with *Peter* and *syntax* contrasts with *semantics*. Section 2 makes this notion precise.

(5)   a.   *Peter taught Syntax last year.*
           b.   *Sally taught semantics last year.*
(6)   a.   *(No –) SALly$_F$ taught syntax last year.*
           b.   *(No –) Sally taught SYNtax$_F$ last year.*

More generally, we note that the focus of a sentence restricts what contexts the sentence can be used in. Different foci impose different conditions on the context.

1.2. Focus can make a truth conditional difference

1.2.1. Focus sensitive adverbs

A more obvious interpretive effect of focus can be detected when we consider certain adverbs like *only* and *even*. Such sentences have different truth conditions depending on what is focused. The meaning of (7a) is paraphrased in (7'a), the meaning of (7b) in (7'b).

(7) a. *Molly only introduced BILL$_F$ to Sue.*
     b. *Molly only introduced Bill to SUE$_F$.*
(7') a. *Molly didn't introduce anyone other than Bill to Sue.*
     b. *Molly didn't introduce Bill to anyone other than Sue.*

(8a) describes a situation in which (7a) would be true and (7b) false. In (8b) it's the reverse.

(8) a. *Molly hosts Bill, Sue, Tom and Paul. She introduces Bill to Sue, and to Tom. No other introductions are performed.*
     b. *Molly hosts Bill, Sue, Tom and Paul. She introduces Bill and Tom to Sue. No other introductions are performed.*

These data show that focus has a semantic effect. Some difference in the meaning of the VP *introduce BILL to Sue* compared to *introduce Bill to SUE* must exist that *only* can access, so that (7a, b) mean different things.

🕒 **Exercise.** *The focus-sensitive adverb* even. A parallel effect arises with the adverb *even*. Formulate your intuitions regarding the meanings of (E1a, b):

(E1) a. *Molly even introduced BILL$_F$ to Sue.*
     b. *Molly even introduced Bill to SUE$_F$.* □

1.2.2. Focus can disambiguate ellipsis

In preparation of things to come (see Chapter II-6 on ellipsis), we mention one other effect that focus has on interpretation. This effect concerns ellipsis. (9a) is an example of comparative ellipsis; a more spelled-out version would be either: *more often than he called Christian* or *more often than Christian called me*. (9a) as a string is ambiguous, but, depending on how it is pronounced, only one interpretation arises.

(9)   a.   *Thilo called me more often than Christian.*
         b.   *Thilo called ME$_F$ more often than Christian.*
             = Thilo called me more often than he called Christian.
         c.   *THIlo$_F$ called me more often than Christian.*
             = Thilo called me more often than Christian called me.

(10) involving so-called bare argument ellipsis shows a parallel effect.

(10)   a.   *I met Katie, and Robin, too.*
         b.   *I$_F$ met Katie, and Robin, too.*
             = I met Katie and Robin met Katie.
         c.   *I met KAtie$_F$, and Robin, too.*
             = I met Katie and I met Robin.

In sum, there are plenty of reasons to think that focus has some interpretive effect. The next section identifies an interpretive contribution of focus that allows us to capture the effects illustrated by the above data.

2. Focus introduces alternatives

2.1. Alternatives: The idea

The interpretive effect of focus is that it introduces alternatives. When you hear (11a), for example, you find yourself contemplating alternatives to Bill: Tom, Sam,... – whoever is around. More accurately, you find yourself contemplating alternatives to Bill in the role of someone being introduced to Sue. When you hear (11b), on the other hand, you contemplate alternatives to Sue: Mary, Peggy,... Again more precisely, you consider Bill being introduced to Mary, Bill being introduced to Peggy and so on.

(11)   a.   *Molly only introduced BILL$_F$ to Sue.*
         b.   *Molly only introduced Bill to SUE$_F$.*

The adverb *only* seems to operate on these alternatives as follows:

> ***only*** (informal version)
> The alternative actually mentioned is the unique true alternative.

Let us apply the alternatives idea to the examples in (13) repeated from above. Imagine again the question context in (12).

(12)   a.   *Who did Sally invite to the party?*
           b.   *Who invited Bill to the party?*
(13)   a.   *Sally invited BILL$_F$.*
           b.   *SALly$_F$ invited Bill.*

Focus on *Bill* in (13a) triggers the following set of alternative propositions:

(14)   {that Sally invited Bill, that Sally invited Tom, that Sally invited Sam}

More generally, the set of alternatives is (15) (recall that D is the domain of discourse, a set of individuals):

(15)   {that Sally invited x | x $\in$ D and x is a relevant person}

This is a set of alternative claims that could have been made, or in terms of our semantics, a set of propositions. Remember that a proposition is a sentence meaning – the intension of a sentence. This is a set of situations. The proposition that Sally invited Bill is the following set of situations:

(16)   {s: Sally invited Bill in s}

Back to (15); with this understanding of what a proposition is, the alternative "claims" amount to the following set:

(17)   {{s: Sally invited x in s} | x $\in$ D & x is a relevant person}

(15) and (17) are read as "the set of propositions which are 'that Sally invited x' for some x such that x $\in$ D and x is a relevant person." (Below, we sometimes use the representation in (15) as simplification of (17).) When we compare (13a) and (13b), we see that while the truth conditions are the same, the alternatives introduced differ:

(18) a. {that Sally invited x to the party | x ∈ D & x is a relevant person}
 b. {that x invited Bill to the party | x ∈ D & x is a relevant person}

We can use this difference to characterize question/answer congruence. We want to say that the focus in the answer must match the preceding question. What does "match" mean? Intuitively, what the question asks for (marked by the wh-phrase in (12)) is where the focus falls. Semanticists propose that a question sets up a choice situation: it contributes the set of possible answers to the question, and it invites the hearer to specify the true one(s) among the possible answers. Thus, the questions in (12) have the following meanings:

(19) a. {that Sally invited x | x ∈ D & x is a relevant person}
 b. {that x invited Bill | x ∈ D & x is a relevant person}

Now it is easy to see what the condition on question/answer congruence is:

> **Question/answer pairs** (informal version)
> The set of alternatives to the answer must be identical to the set provided by the question.

In this subsection, we have specified what we want as the semantic contribution of focus. We still need to say how this comes about. That is, we need a compositional semantics that derives focus alternatives and interprets operators that are sensitive to focus, like *only*.

2.2. Deriving focus alternatives

We limit the compositional calculation of focus alternatives to some basic cases in this chapter. Our framework will be able to deal with very simple examples only, like (20) below.

(20) a. *BILL left.*
 b. [$_{IP}$ [$_{NP}$ *BILL*]$_F$ [$_{I'}$ *left*]]

We need to be able to calculate the alternatives of the sentence based on the focused items contained in the sentence, the non-focused items and their combination. To our compositional semantics we add, for each way of specifying the "normal" meaning, a way of specifying the "focus" meaning. The two meanings are called the ordinary semantic value and the focus semantic value. The notation is as follows:

(21)   a. $[[\alpha]]_o^s$: the ordinary semantic value of α
      b. $[[\alpha]]_f$: the focus semantic value of α

The set of rules given below considers the ingredients of our basic type of example. (22a) states how to assign an ordinary and a focus semantic value to terminal nodes in the tree (the lexical items). (23) is the rule needed for composition in this example, the subject predicate rule Part 1, with instructions for the focus semantic value added.

(22)   a.   For any lexical terminal node α and any situation s:
          $[[\alpha]]_o^s$ is defined in the lexicon
          $[[\alpha]]_f = \{ [[\alpha]]_o \}$
      b.   For any constituent α_F and any situation s:
          $[[\alpha_F]]_o^s = [[\alpha]]_o^s$
          $[[\alpha_F]]_f = \{x: x$ is a relevant thing of the same kind as $\alpha\}$

(23)   Subject-Predicate rule Part 1 (with focus semantic values):
      For any IP with daughters β and γ and any s:
          $[[IP]]_o^s = 1$ iff $[[\beta]]_o^s \in [[\gamma]]_o^s$
          $[[IP]]_f = \{ p: p = \{s: \beta'_s \in \gamma'_s\} \mid \beta' \in [[\beta]]_f$ and $\gamma' \in [[\gamma]]_f \}$
          (where, if $\beta' = \{s: [[\beta]]_o^s \}$, then $\beta'_s = [[\beta]]_o^s$)

Suppose that the relevant individuals are Bill, Lydia and Pat. The rules allow us to calculate:

(24)   a. $[[BILL_F\ left]]_o^s = 1$ iff Bill left in s
      b. $[[BILL_F\ left]]_f$
          $= \{ p: p = \{s: \beta'_s \in \gamma'_s\} \mid \beta' \in [[BILL_F]]_f$ and $\gamma' \in [[left]]_f \}$
          $= \{ p: p = \{s: \beta'_s \in \gamma'_s\} \mid \beta' \in \{x: x \in D$ & x a relevant person$\}$
                                          and $\gamma' \in \{[[left]]_o\}\}$
          $= \{p: p = \{s: x \in [[left]]_o^s\} \mid x \in D$ & x is a relevant person$\}$
          $= \{p: p = \{s: x$ left in s$\} \mid x \in D$ & x is a relevant person$\}$

= {{s: x left in s} | x ∈ D & x is a relevant person}
= {that x left in s | x ∈ D & x is a relevant person}
= {that Bill left in s, that Lydia left in s, that Pat left in s}

To convince yourself that composition of focus semantic values is necessary, you may consider (25) with stress on the verb instead of the subject:

(25)   a.   *Bill LEFT.*
       b.   [$_{IP}$ [$_{NP}$ *Bill*] [$_{I'}$ *LEFT*]$_F$]

We need to be able to predict that while (20) and (25) have the same truth conditions (i.e. the same ordinary semantic value), they have different focus semantic values. That is, they introduce different alternatives. The rules in (22) and (23) are able to predict this. Suppose that the relevant alternatives to leaving are staying and screaming. Then we predict that:

(26)   [[*Bill LEFT*$_F$]]$_f$
       = {p: p = {s: Bill Q'ed in s} | Q a relevant property}
       = {p: p = that Bill Q'ed | Q a relevant property}
       = {that Bill left, that Bill stayed, that Bill screamed}

🕐 **Exercise.** *Practicing composition of focus semantic values.*
   a.   Show this step by step.
   b.   What did we assume in (24) about the rule for non-branching trees with focus semantic values? State the extended version of the rule.
                                                                                    □

☕ **Exercise.** *Extending the framework.* Parallel to the version of the subject predicate rule with focus semantic values, we need versions of other rules of composition. Get us started on this enterprise by formulating the relevant version of the rule for sentential negation.   □

Here is, in short, how we have updated our semantic system: there are two semantic values associated with an expression: an ordinary semantic value and a focus semantic value, where the latter contains alternatives. Both are determined compositionally.

2.3. Applying focus alternatives

Next, we come back to the observations about focus effects we made above. We apply an analysis in terms of focus alternatives to them.

2.3.1. Only *revisited*

The most striking interpretive effect focus can have is to affect the truth conditions of a sentence. Remember the example in (27).

(27)   *Molly only introduced BILL$_F$ to Sue.*

We can now make the semantics of *only* explicit. Assume that the VP in the example is interpreted as in (28).

(28)   a. $[\![[_{VP}$ *Molly introduced BILL$_F$ to Sue*$]]\!]_o =$
             {s: Molly introduced Bill to Sue in s}
       b. $[\![[_{VP}$ *Molly introduced BILL$_F$ to Sue*$]]\!]_F =$
             {{s: Molly introduced Bill to Sue in s},
              {s: Molly introduced John to Sue in s},...}
             = {p: p ={s: Molly introduced y to Sue in s} | y $\in$ D}
             the set of all propositions which are 'that Molly introduced y to Sue' for some relevant individual y

Adverbs like *only* are focus sensitive, meaning that they operate on the focus semantic value as well as the ordinary semantic value of their sister. The composition rule given below that interprets VP adjoined *only* captures that.

---
only
If $\alpha = [$ only β_{VP} $]$, then for any s: $[\![\alpha]\!]_o^s = 1$ iff
for all p such that p $\in [\![\beta]\!]_F$: if s $\in$ p then p = $[\![\beta]\!]_o$

The truth conditions predicted for our example are:

(29) $[\![$*Molly only introduced BILL$_F$ to Sue*$]\!]_o^s = 1$ iff
       for all p such that p $\in [\![$ *Molly introduced BILL$_F$ to Sue*$]\!]_F$: if s $\in$ p

then p = [[*Molly introduced BILL*$_F$ *to Sue*]]$_o$ iff
for all p s. that p∈{q:q={s:Molly introduced y to Sue in s}|y∈D}:
if s ∈p then p = {s: Molly introduced Bill to Sue in s} iff
for all propositions p that are 'that Molly introduced y to Sue' for some y: if p is true, then p is: 'that Molly introduced Bill to Sue'.

You see in the above semantics that *only* is a quantificational expression, and focus alternatives provide the restriction of the quantifier.

🕒 **Exercise**. *More examples*. Consider the sentences below.

(E2) a. *Sonja only [WATCHed]*$_F$ *'Pride & Prejudice'*.
  a'. *Sonja only watched ['Pride & Prejudice']*$_F$.
  b. *Sonja always showed TIM*$_F$ *treeferns*.
  b'. *Sonja always showed Tim TREEferns*$_F$.

Give a paraphrase for each example. Specify the set of alternatives that each example works with. For (E2a, a'), apply the *only*-rule and show that it derives interpretations amounting to your paraphrases. What could be the analysis of (E2b, b')? (*Hint:* You need to come up with an *always*-rule.) ☐

2.3.2. Contrast

Let us now return to the non-truth-conditional effects that focus can have and let us be more precise about what happens, using the focus semantic values we now have at our disposal.

We begin with the notion of contrast. Remember the examples in (30)–(31):

(30) a. *Peter taught syntax last year.*
  b. *Sally taught semantics last year.*

(31) a. *(No –) SALly*$_F$ *taught syntax last year.*
  b. *(No –) Sally taught SYNtax*$_F$ *last year.*

We add the example in (32) (from Rooth (1992)), which shows that a contrast relationship can hold below the sentence level:

(32) An aMERican farmer was talking to a caNAdian farmer...

Intuitively, the phrase you are using contrastively has to follow upon a phrase that is a focus alternative and not the same. This is expressed below in terms of ordinary and focus semantic values.

> **Contrasting phrases**
> Construe a phrase α as contrasting with a phrase β if $[[\beta]]_o \in [[\alpha]]_f$ and $[[\beta]]_o \neq [[\alpha]]_o$.

(33) a. $[[SALly_F \text{ taught syntax}]]_f =$
{that Sally taught syntax, that Peter taught syntax,...}
b. $[[(30a)]]_o \in [[(31a)]]_f$
- congruent pair
c. $[[Sally \text{ taught } SYNtax_F]] =$
{that Sally taught syntax, that Sally taught semantics,...}
d. $[[(30b)]]_o \in [[(31b)]]_f$
- congruent pair
e. $[[(30b)]]_o \notin [[(31a)]]_f$, $[[(30a)]]_o \notin [[(31b)]]_f$
- incongruent pairs

2.3.3. Question/answer congruence

We have already described the question/answer relationship illustrated in (34) and (35) informally as in (36) below.

(34) a. *Who did Sally invite?*
b. *Who invited Bill?*

(35) a. *Sally invited BILL$_F$.*
b. *SALly$_F$ invited Bill.*

(36) Question/answer pairs:
The set of alternatives to the answer must be identical to the set provided by the question.

246 *Focus*

Recall that the meaning of a question is the set of possible answers to the question. This makes the semantics of focus and questions very close to each other. The more formal version of (36) is given below.

> **Question-answer congruence**
> In a question-answer pair <Q, A>, $[[Q]]_o^s = [[A]]_f$.

2.3.4. Implicatures

A final discourse effect of focus that illustrates rather nicely the role of alternatives is implicatures. The example below is once more from Rooth (1992) and we take Mats Rooth to be speaker.

(37) a. Contextual background: *How did the exam go?*
     b. *Well, I PASSed$_F$.*
     c. *Well, I$_F$ passed.*

(37b) suggests (38a) while (37c) suggests (38b).

(38) a. *Mats did not do very well.*
     b. *The others did not pass.*

Both answers thus give rise to implicatures. Note that the meaning components in (38) can be canceled (that is, the speaker could continue (37c) with: "But I didn't mean to imply that the others did not pass."). So they are not part of the truth conditions. Instead, they are implicated. Importantly, which implicatures arise is different in (37b) vs. (37c), and it depends on focus.

Plausible focus alternatives of (37b) are (39a), while alternatives of (37c) might be the ones in (39b).

(39) a. {that Mats passed in s, that Mats did well in s, that Mats excelled in s}
     b. {that Mats passed in s, that Steve passed in s, that Paul passed in s, that Mats & Steve passed in s, that Mats & Paul passed in s, that Steve & Paul passed in s, that Mats & Steve & Paul passed in s}

One seems to exclude those alternatives that would make stronger claims than the claim actually made. This is the hallmark of a so-called scalar implicature – cf. (40).

(40)   *I make 1500.- a month.*
       Implicature: *I do not make more than 1500.- a month.*

Focus seems to determine the content of the implicature:

> **Constraint on scales**
> In construing a scale of alternative assertions determining scalar implicatures of a sentence α, choose an underlying set C such that $C \subseteq [[\alpha]]_f$.

To sum up this section: We call a linguistic expression a focus if its role is to introduce alternatives. Pitch accent in English indicates what the focus of a sentence is. The alternatives triggered by focus can be used in various ways. They can influence truth conditions by forming the restriction of a quantificational adverb (cf. *only*). The alternatives furthermore affect discourse appropriateness (cf. question/answer congruence and contrast). And they can trigger implicatures. When we talk about ellipsis in Chapter II-6, we will return to another role that focus alternatives play. This will explain the disambiguation effect we have seen in this chapter.

More generally, understanding focus effects has a very significant impact on our semantic theory. A complete analysis has to "double" all rules of compositional interpretation, in the sense that each linguistic expression is assigned an ordinary and a focus semantic value.

3. Some remarks on focus across languages

Focus introduces alternatives – this understanding of focus has recently been taken as a definition of focus by semanticists and on this understanding, probably all of the world's languages express focus. That is, all languages have a means of introducing alternatives into the semantics. What that is, however, varies widely. While in English, stress is instrumental, other languages may instead mark focus morphologically. To give one example: In Gùrùntùm, the marker *a* precedes the focus constituent (Hartmann and Zimmermann 2009):

(41) a. Á   fúrmáyò   bà   wúm   kwálíngálá.
       FOC fulani   PROG   chew   colanut
       '[The Fulani]_F is chewing colanut.'
    b. Tí   bà   wúm-á   kwálíngálá.
       3SG PROG chew-FOC   colanut
       'He is chewing [colanut]_F.'

Yet other languages (e.g. Hungarian) have a syntactic strategy of marking focus, namely in terms of reordering. Mixed strategies also occur (and Hungarian is once more an example). The different ways of marking focus do not all give rise to exactly the same interpretive effects, but in order for us to call them focus marking, they all have to trigger the introduction of alternatives.

English and German both mark focus intonationally, using pitch accent. They differ somewhat with respect to the empirical behavior of focus. Below, we observe some differences regarding where a focused element can be in the sentence structure.

☕ **Exercise**. *More means of expressing focus: focus constructions*. Consider the examples below:

(E3) a. *It was Sally who taught syntax.*
     b. *It was syntax that Sally taught.*

These constructions are called clefts. Intuitively, clefts are similar to focus in that the clefted constituent (*Sally* in (E3a) and *syntax* in (E3b)) seems to play a focus-like role. Examine this intuition. Do you find data that (i) support the similarity and (ii) differentiate between intonational focus and clefts in English? Take the interpretive effects of focus described in this chapter as your starting point. What is the semantic analysis of clefts, given your data? Be as precise as possible. ☐

3.1. Topicalization vs. prefield

The constituent in the German prefield can be a focus, as the question-answer sequence in (43) shows. A topicalized nominal constituent in English cannot easily be a focus, cf. the oddness of (42).

(42) a. *Who did you invite?*
b. $^{??}$ *[My cousin]$_F$, I invited.*

(43) a. *Wen   hast   Du   eingeladen?*
who.ACC   have   you   invited
'Who did you invite?'
b. *Meinen Cousin   hab   ich eingeladen.*
my.ACC cousin.ACC have I   invited
'I invited [my cousin]$_F$.'

This is part of the discourse related constraints on English topicalization that we alluded to in Chapter II-2. We now understand such effects a little better: information structural elements like focus influence discourse appropriateness, and English topicalization seems to be sensitive to that.

3.2. Focus in the middle field

There is a tendency for a focus in the German middle field to occur towards the right, as the question/answer pairs given below indicate.

(44) *Wem   hast   du   das   Buch   gezeigt?*
whom   have   you the.ACC book.ACC shown
'Who did you show the book to?'
a. *Ich hab   das   Buch   dem   KIND   gezeigt.*
I   have the.ACC book.ACC the.DAT child.DAT shown
'I showed the book to the CHILD.'
b. $^{(?)}$ *Ich   hab   dem   KIND   das   Buch   gezeigt.*
I   have the.DAT child.DAT the.ACC book.ACC shown
'I showed the book to the CHILD.'

(45) *Was hast du   dem   Kind   gezeigt?*
what have you the.DAT child.DAT shown
'What did you show to the child?'
a. *Ich hab   dem   Kind   das   BUCH   gezeigt.*
I   have the.DAT child.DAT the.ACC book.ACC shown
'I showed the BOOK to the child.'
b. $^{??}$ *Ich   hab   das   BUCH   dem   Kind   gezeigt.*
I   have the.ACC book.ACC the.DAT child.DAT shown

'I showed the BOOK to the child.'

Contrast confirms this:

(46)   Du   hast   dem   Kind   die   DVD   gezeigt.
       you have   the.DAT   child.DAT   the.ACC   DVD.ACC   shown
       'You showed the DVD to the child.'
   a. Ich hab   dem   Kind   das   BUCH   gezeigt.
       I   have   the.DAT   child.DAT   the.ACC   book.ACC   shown
       'I showed the BOOK to the child.'
   b. ??Ich   hab   das   BUCH   dem   Kind   gezeigt.
       I   have   the.ACC   book.ACC   the.DAT   child.DAT   shown
       'I showed the BOOK to the child.'

In English, there is no word order difference, merely a difference in where the main stress is.

(47)   a.   *Who did you show the book to?*
       b.   *I showed the book to the CHILD.*
(48)   a.   *What did you show to the child?*
       b.   *I showed the BOOK to the child.*

In German, word order helps to indicate focus. Descriptively speaking, the focus tends to occur to the right. In terms of syntactic analysis it seems that when the focused constituent is not immediately preceding the verb, other material can be scrambled out of the way. Scrambling focused constituents leads to degraded structures.

English, not having the option of scrambling and free word order, uses intonation alone to mark focus. Thus, intonation bears a heavier burden in English (it seems that that makes it more marked, something that is not easy to acquire for e.g. German speakers).

We will not try to offer an explanation for why the facts are as they are. Whatever the explanation turns out to be for the above data: it is pretty clear that it must make recourse to the concept of focus, since that must feature even in a plain description of the facts. You can take the data discussed in this section as an illustration of how the semantic analysis of focus helps us to describe crosslinguistic differences.

> **THE BASICS BOX:** *Focus*
> - ✓ Focus introduces alternatives.
> - ✓ In English, focus is marked by pitch accent. Other languages have other focus marking strategies.
> - ✓ Alternatives matter for discourse appropriateness and for restricting quantifiers. Hence focus restricts appropriate contexts of use for a sentence, and affects the interpretation of adverbs.
> - ✓ Focus interacts with syntax: English topicalized constituents and German scrambled constituents do not want to be foci.

4. Further readings

Our discussion in this chapter is based on Rooth (1985, 1992). The observations, analysis and many of the examples can be found there.

Alternative semantics exists in different guises. Besides Rooth, Krifka (1991) and von Stechow (1990) have also developed semantic analyses of focus. For question semantics, see Hamblin (1973) and Karttunen (1977), or Krifka (2011) for recent discussion. For those interested in a complete system of interpretation, Beck (to appear) offers a recent version of a compositional system for the calculation of Roothian alternatives (the paper also contains an explanation of why the compositional system in this chapter is (necessarily) incomplete).

The literature on focus marking, typology and the semantic effects of focus is vast. Look at Hinterwimmer (2011), Zimmermann and Onea (2011) and Krifka (2008) for introductions to central issues. Recent handbooks (cf. Zimmermann and Féry 2009 and Féry and Ishihara forthcoming) illuminate the different aspects of research on focus.

There is a considerable body of literature and much controversial discussion about word order in the German middle field. A foundational reference is Lenerz (1977). Fanselow (2008) offers a perspective on the middle field data observed above, as well as a lot of further relevant references.

Fanselow & Lenertová (2011) show that German focused constituents can occur in the prefield position. They offer further data and discussion regarding left peripheral positions and information structure in German and Czech (as well as further references).

The full range of cases of topic- (and partly focus-)based fronting in English are subtler than they could be presented here at the textbook level.

There are rare contexts in which focus fronting is claimed to be allowed, and e.g. topic-based fronting comes with its restrictions, too. Relevant recent references on the interaction between pertinent discourse factors, semantics, prosody and word order in English are Büring (2012), Birner and Ward (2009), Wagner (2012), Ward and Birner (2011). As for the question why the English topicalized position may dislike focus, see Speyer (2010) for important observations that are historically grounded.

A historical connection has also long been observed more generally between the rise of specialized focus constructions in English (e.g. clefts) and the loss of word-order flexibility and in particular the vanishing possibility to have focus in the prefield. This possible tendency has been observed by one of the leading figures in linguistics Otto Jespersen (Jespersen 1937) and it has recently been investigated e.g. by Los and Komen (2012).

Chapter II-6
Ellipsis

Mabel Minerva, a Central Park rental horse, begins galloping at full speed with the terrified Fred atop. Fred: "No, no! Don't _!"
(From Johnson 2001)

This chapter presents an analysis of ellipsis in the framework we have developed in the preceding chapters. Section 1 is an introduction to the topic. In sections 2 and 3 we discuss two well-known constraints on ellipsis, the LF identity condition and the contrast condition, respectively. We introduce Antecedent Contained Deletion ACD as a special case in section 4, concluding with section 5, which offers pointers to the literature.

1. What is ellipsis?

Remember from Part I (Chapter I-2) the phenomenon of VP ellipsis illustrated by (1) and (2). A VP remains unpronounced in a sentence, but it is understood to be there. Its meaning is the meaning of another VP in the context. An intuitively similar effect can be achieved with *do so*, a VP pro-form, in (3).

(1)   a.   *Did you invite Karen?*
            b.   *Yes I did.*
                 ... I did ~~invite Karen~~

(2)   a.   *Lizzy will go to Lambton before Jane will.*
                 ... before Jane will ~~go to Lambton.~~
            b.   *Lizzy will go to Lambton and Jane will, too.*
                 ... and Jane will ~~go to Lambton~~ too.

(3)   a.   *Lizzy will go to Lambton before Jane will do so.*
            b.   *Lizzy will go to Lambton and Jane will do so, too.*

VP ellipsis is interesting for us because it provides further illustration of the work that two concepts central to this textbook do – the concepts of **scope** and of **focus**. Both are involved in any proper understanding of VP ellipsis.

Before we turn to their relevance, we first make the intended analysis a bit more precise. Since we understand the VP in the semantics, we assume that it is in fact present at the level which we interpret – Logical Form (LF). That is, the sentence in (1) containing the ellipsis – the ellipsis clause – has the LF in (1').

(1')   [IP *I* [I' *did* [VP *invite Karen*]]]

This is permitted because there is just such a VP in the preceding sentence in (1). An analysis of the parallel example (2b) is given in (2b') with LFs for the sentence containing the antecedent VP – the antecedent clause – as well as the ellipsis clause.

(2b')   [IP *Lizzy* [I' *will* [VP *go to Lambton*]]] and
         [IP *Jane* [I' *will* [VP *go to Lambton*]]]

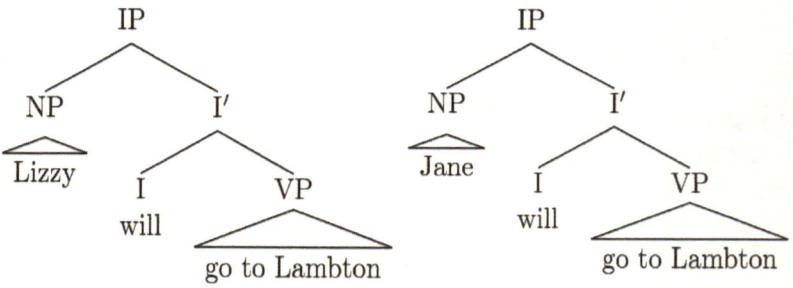

We take the following to describe VP ellipsis:

VP ellipsis
A VP may remain phonologically empty only if it is identical at LF to another VP in the context.

Here is one more example of VP ellipsis:

(4)   a. *Laura showed Ana a drawing but Lena didn't.*
        b. [IP *Laura* [I' PAST [VP *show Ana a drawing*]]] but
           [IP *Lena* [I' *didn't* [VP *show Ana a drawing*]]]

2. Structural identity at LF

2.1. Why LF?

The point about ellipsis is that the deleted/silent material that is understood to be there is understood to be the same as overt material in the linguistic context. (For example, in (4) the second sentence must mean "but Lena didn't show Ana a drawing"; it cannot mean anything else, like "but Lena didn't show around anything".) Much work in linguistics is devoted to the question of what "the same" in the statement above means exactly. One important fact concerns data like the following (example taken from Heim and Kratzer):

(5) *Laura showed a drawing to every teacher, but Lena didn't.*

Let's first consider the antecedent sentence in isolation. It is ambiguous between (5'a) and (5'b).

(5') a. *There is a drawing that Laura showed to every teacher.*
b. *To every teacher, Laura showed some drawing or other.*

That is, there are two different relative scopes possible. According to our analysis of scope ambiguity, there are two different LFs available for the sentence, distinguished by which quantifier takes wide scope.

(6) a. [$_{VP}$ [*a drawing*] [1 [[*every teacher*] [2 [*Laura show t_1 to t_2*]]]]]
b. [$_{VP}$ [*every teacher*] [2 [[*a drawing*] [1 [*Laura show t_1 to t_2*]]]]]

a.

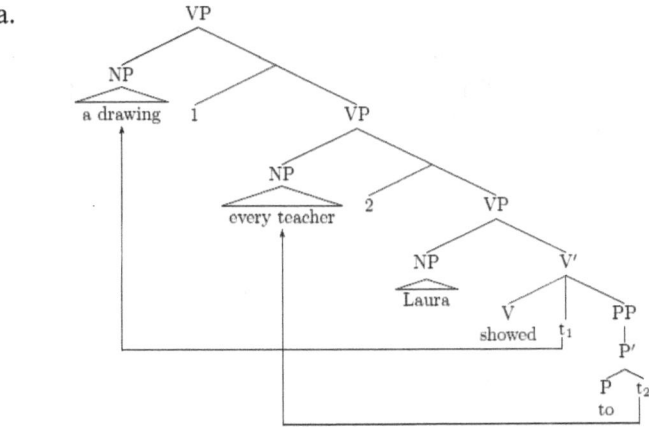

b.

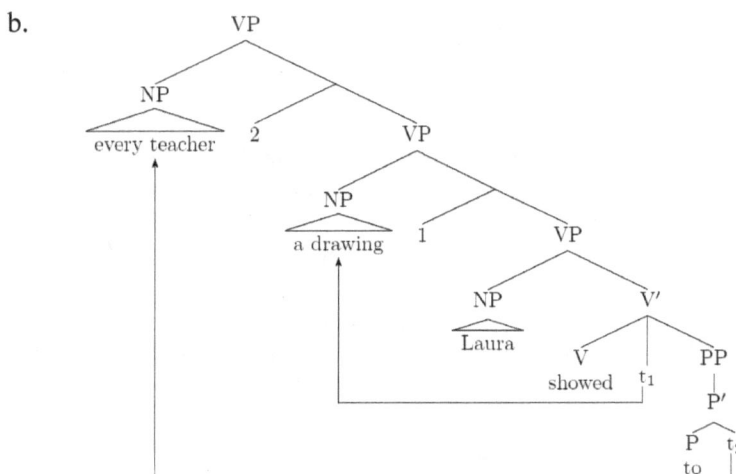

Let's now turn to the second conjunct, the ellipsis clause. This, also, can be understood in the two ways described for the first conjunct, the antecedent. However, when the antecedent has the a-reading (with wide scope of *a drawing*) so does the ellipsis clause, and when the antecedent has the b-reading (with wide scope of *every teacher*), the ellipsis clause has the parallel reading. It is not possible to read the first conjunct with one scope order and the second one with the other (this is referred to as the parallelism constraint). From this we conclude that "the same" must mean: is identical at LF. Identity, in short, means interpretive identity. A related phenomenon is:

(7)   *Jim invited her and Bill did, too.*

The referent of the pronoun must be the same in the antecedent clause and in the ellipsis clause. A detailed analysis of the interpretation of pronouns makes this follow from LF identity, too. For now, we just note that the two VPs express the same property.

🕒 **Exercise.** Use the interpretation of pronouns from Chapter II-3, section 2.2., to analyze how the observation regarding (7) can be accounted for. ☐

🕒 **Exercise.** Show how the parallelism constraint is at work in (E1):

(E1)   *Karen identified one patient with every symptom, and Ellen did, too.* ☐

2.2. A note on other kinds of ellipsis and crosslinguistic variation

There are many different kinds of ellipsis processes. VP ellipsis refers specifically to data where a VP category is silent. At the same time, Infl (the Inflection node) is present. This is a pretty common and wide spread phenomenon in English. German, on the other hand, does not have this particular kind of ellipsis.

(8) a. * *Lizzy kann Fahrrad fahren und Jane kann auch*
  Lizzy can bike ride and Jane can too
  'Lizzy can ride a bike, and Jane can, too.'
 b. * *Lizzy konnte Fahrrad fahren bevor Jane konnte.*
  Lizzy could bike ride before Jane could
  'Lizzy could ride a bike before Jane could.'

VP proforms, on the other hand, are also possible in German.

(9) *Lizzy konnte Fahrrad fahren, bevor Jane **das** konnte.*
  Lizzy could bike ride before Jane that could
  'Lizzy could ride a bike before Jane could do so.'

Suppose that the Infl node in English functions as a sort of syntactic flag – the last node visible on the surface before deletion of its complement VP takes place – and suppose that the availability of VP ellipsis hinges on it. Then the lack of VP ellipsis in German falls neatly into place: the lack of VP ellipsis is yet another indication of the lack of an Infl node in this language.

Other forms of ellipsis that English and German share include the following:

(10) a. *Laura drank the milk, or perhaps the juice.*
     (bare argument ellipsis)
  ... perhaps ~~Laura drank~~ the juice
 b. *I gave Jane a book, and him too.* (bare argument ellipsis)
  ... and ~~I gave~~ him ~~a book~~ too
 c. *They invited someone, but I don't know who.* (sluicing)
  ... but I don't know who ~~they invited~~
 d. *I bought a book and Jane a magazine.* (gapping)
  ... and Jane ~~bought~~ a magazine

258 *Ellipsis*

Let us look at bare argument ellipsis a little more closely. An analysis of (10a), analogous to our analysis of VP ellipsis, requires us to find an antecedent for the ellipsis that is structurally identical at LF. This type of ellipsis deletes more than just a VP. There is no Infl node present in (10a). Moreover, we know that ellipsis processes tend to target constituents (they are structure sensitive, as discussed in Part I). So which constituent could be targeted by ellipsis in (10a)? The first constituent that contains the subject and Infl is the IP, so we assume that bare argument ellipsis is a case of IP deletion. What remains undeleted – the remnant – must have moved out of the IP. We have two precedents for this kind of movement: one is QR, the other is topicalization – cf. (11). Both adjoin a constituent to IP.

Following this reasoning, the structures for antecedent and ellipsis clause in (10a) are given in (12). Since we assume the same identity condition as for VP ellipsis, *the juice* in the ellipsis clause is topicalized, and we have to suppose that at LF the antecedent clause provides a structure with parallel QR of *the milk*, as indicated in (12).

(11)   *I think that the green stuff, you shouldn't eat.*

(12) $[_{IP}$ *the milk* $[1\ [_{IP}$ *Laura* $[PAST\ [drink\ t_1]]]]$
  or perhaps $[_{IP}$ *the juice* $[1\ [_{IP}$ ~~*Laura* [*PAST* [*drink* t_1]]~~$]]$

We generalize the identity condition to categories other than VP:

LF identity condition on ellipsis
A constituent may remain phonologically empty only if it is identical to another constituent at LF.

🕒 **Exercise.** Determine the type of ellipsis in the following sentences and then perform the tasks described below.

(E2)   a. *Tony will pass this exam, and probably Kim will, too.*
   b. *I have bought 'The Hunger Games' and Thilo 'Cranford'.*
   c. *Karen will get the job or perhaps Ellen.*
   d. *Thilo has bought the best book about some New Zealand author, and I know which one.*

First, provide the syntactic analyses of the VP ellipsis and the bare argument ellipsis examples. Second, state informally how the gapping example differs from the example in the main text; what problem does it present for syntactic analysis?

3. Focus in ellipsis

3.1. The contrast condition

With the background on structural conditions on ellipsis from the preceding section, we now consider the VP ellipsis examples below:

(13) a. *Lizzy will go to Lambton tomorrow and Jane will on Tuesday.*
   b. *??Lizzy will go to Lambton tomorrow and Jane will tomorrow.*

(14) a. *Pat invited Karen on Wednesday because Sandy did on Tuesday.*
   b. *??Pat invited Karen on Tuesday because Sandy did on Tuesday.*

The a- and b-sentences differ with respect to the things left behind by the ellipsis, the remnants. It seems that there is a condition that what is left behind is focused. Intuitively, it is focused because there is a contrast with a parallel item in the antecedent clause. Below is a constraint that captures this intuition in terms of alternative semantics. It relies on what we have learnt about focus in Chapter II-5. Note how it makes use of both ordinary and focus semantic values, and the same notion of contrast that we have discussed in Chapter II-5.

Contrast Condition on ellipsis
When a category Y contains an ellipsis that finds its antecedent in a category X, Y must stand in a contrast relation to X – i.e.
$[[X]]_o \in [[Y]]_f$ and $[[X]]_o \neq [[Y]]_o$

Applied to examples (13) it is clear that the condition is met in (13a) but not (13b):

(15) a. $[[\text{go to L tomorrow}]]_o \in [[\text{go to L [on Tuesday]}_F]]_f$ and
      $[[\text{go to L tomorrow}]]_o \neq [[\text{go to L [on Tuesday]}_F]]_o$
   b. $[[\text{go to L tomorrow}]]_o \in [[\text{go to L tomorrow}_F]]_f$ but NOT:
      $[[\text{go to L tomorrow}]]_o \neq [[\text{go to L tomorrow}_F]]_o$

260 *Ellipsis*

It seems that the contrast requirement must hold for the smallest constituent above the ellipsis, because otherwise it ought to be sufficient that *Jane* contrasts with *Lizzy*.

The contrast condition not only helps us with the VP ellipsis data above; its application extends to other kinds of ellipsis besides VP ellipsis. In fact, we have already come across the phenomenon in the shape of (16) when we talked about focus.

(16) a. *I met Katie, and Robin, too.*
      b. *I_F met Katie, and Robin, too.*
      c. *I met KAtie$_F$, and Robin, too.*

We now recognize the example as bare argument ellipsis. Here is the structural analysis of the two readings.

(17) a. [$_{IP}$ I_F [1 [t_1 met Katie]]]   and
          [$_{IP}$ Robin$_F$ [1 [$_{IP}$ t_1 met Katie]]] too.
      b. [$_{IP}$ KAtie$_F$ [1 [*I* met t_1]]]   and
          [$_{IP}$ Robin$_F$ [1 [$_{IP}$ *I* met t_1]]] too.

The disambiguiating effect of focus in (16) can be explained by the contrast condition. It looks like there must be a mutual contrast relationship between antecedent and ellipsis clause. "I_F met Katie" contrasts with "Robin$_F$ met Katie". "I met Katie$_F$" contrasts with "I met Robin$_F$". But "I_F met Katie" and "I met Robin$_F$" do not stand in a mutual relation of contrast. Hence focus disambiguates, because the foci in the antecedent and the ellipsis clause must be parallel.

(18) a. $[[Robin_F \text{ met Katie}]]_o \in [[I_F \text{ met Katie}]]_f$ and
          $[[Robin_F \text{ met Katie}]]_o \neq [[I_F \text{ met Katie}]]_o$
      b. $[[I \text{ met Robin}_F]]_o \in [[I \text{ met KAtie}_F]]_f$ and
          $[[I \text{ met Robin}_F]]_o \neq [[I \text{ met KAtie}_F]]_o$
      c. $[[Robin_F \text{ met Katie}]]_o \notin [[I \text{ met KAtie}_F]]_f$
      d. $[[I \text{ met Robin}_F]]_o \notin [[I_F \text{ met Katie}]]_f$

3.2. Pseudogapping

We discuss a final kind of ellipsis in this section that also brings together structural and focus conditions in an interesting way. The remnants in the VP ellipsis examples we saw in (13) and (14) were perhaps not too surprising. An adverb like *tomorrow* can easily be somewhere above VP (for instance adjoined to VP, as we have assumed in Chapter II-2 for such adverbs) and thus not be affected by the ellipsis. More surprising, perhaps, is the acceptability of (19). Some kind of ellipsis affected the verb but not its object.

(19)   *While I don't like kumara, I do _ chocolate.*

This phenomenon is called pseudogapping (it looks like gapping because just the verb vanishes, but the finite verbal category in Infl is not deleted). Notice that it is subject to the same contrast condition as the examples with the adverb, (13) and (14).

(20)   a.   *Lizzy likes kumara and Jane does chocolate.*
       b. $^{??}$*Lizzy likes chocolate and Jane does chocolate.*

Here is another way to test the contrast requirement: The pronoun in the ellipsis clause in (21b) cannot be understood as referring to Tom.

(21)   a.   *Jill will like Tom and Fanny will Edmund.*
       b.   *Jill will like Tom and Fanny will him (*too).*

This shows that we are right in analysing the contrast condition as a constraint that operates on a semantic level.

It has been suggested that pseudogapping is VP ellipsis. How could that be? It could only work if there was a process in English that creates a VP from which the object NP is removed. This VP can then elide. Notice that the movement of the object NP stays below the Infl node because that node is still present in pseudogapping. In fact, we know that there is such a movement: we have called it scrambling. So, one hypothesis would be that English, under very limited circumstances, has a scrambling-like process. (Why this is acceptable in English only when the VP elides is not obvious.) (20a) is analyzed below, with scrambling occuring in the ellipsis clause and parallel QR occuring in the antecedent clause. Similar to bare argument ellipsis, pseudogapping allows us to see the close connection between overt

(Surface Structure) and covert (LF) movement, in this case adjunction to VP in the shape of scrambling and QR.

(22)   [$_{IP}$ *Lizzy* 2 [$_{I'}$ *-s* [$_{VP}$ *kumara* [1 [$_{VP}$ t_2 *like* t_1]]]]]
        and   [$_{IP}$ *Jane* 2 [$_{I'}$ *does* [$_{VP}$ *chocolate* [1 [$_{VP}$ t_2 ~~*like* t_4~~]]]]]

🕒 **Exercise.** *Irish - movement and ellipsis.* Grammars of Irish sometimes state that Irish has no words for 'yes' or 'no'. This claim should be considered in connection with ellipsis. Consider the following sentences and first describe the type of omission. Then provide an analysis.

(E4)   a.   Q: *Ar*   *chuir*   *tú*   *isteach air?*   A: *Chuir.*
                INTERR.COMP put.PAST you   in   on-it   put.PAST
                Q: 'Did you apply for it?'   A: 'Yes.'

          b.   *Dúirt mé go*   *gceannóinn*   *é agus cheannaigh.*
              said   I   COMP buy. COND.S1 it and   bought
              'I said that I would buy it and I did.'

Hints: Some facts about the structure of Irish: it includes an IP level in the clause structure, it allows null subjects, and it has V-to-I movement. How does the latter fact compare to English, where only auxiliaries appear under the I node? Put this together with the kind of ellipsis that can be observed underneath the I node to come up with syntactic trees.

Further suggestions: There are other languages that display an interesting interaction between ellipsis and movement. For instance, if you have access to speakers or a grammar of a Bantu language, a variety of Portuguese, or some South-Slavic languages, you can look into phenomena of the kind observed above in those languages.   □

4. Antecedent Contained Deletion (ACD)

4.1. The phenomenon

This section discusses a special kind of VP ellipsis called Antecedent Contained Deletion (ACD), which provides interesting further support of important aspects of the syntactic and semantic theory we have introduced. Here are some examples of the phenomenon:

(23)   a.   *I read every book you did.*
                 'I read every book you read.'

b. *I visited every city that you did.*
'I visited every city that you visited.'

ACD is an instance of VP ellipsis. Below are ordinary VP ellipsis examples similar to the ACD examples in (23):

(24) a. *I read this book before you did.*
... before you did [$_{VP}$ ~~read this book~~]
b. *I visited every city because you did.*
... because you did [$_{VP}$ ~~visit every city~~]

In each case, a constituent that corresponds syntactically to a VP is phonologically empty, but understood to be there. Here is our analysis of VP-ellipsis once more.

> **VP ellipsis**
> A VP may remain phonologically empty only if it is identical at LF to another VP in the context.

The additional feature that our ACD examples exhibit is this: The VP ellipsis is inside a relative clause modifying the object NP of the only VP in the sentence. For the interpretation of (23a), we need a VP [*read t_3*]. The reconstructed NP with the relative clause that has undergone VP ellipsis looks like this:

(25) [$_{NP}$ *every* [$_{N'}$ *book* [$_{CP}$ *wh$_3$ that* [$_{IP}$ *you did* [$_{VP}$ *read t_3*]]]]

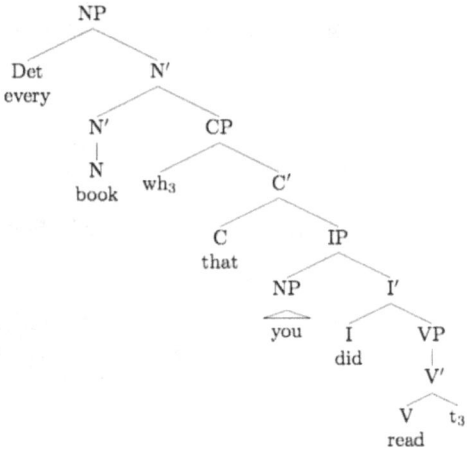

264   *Ellipsis*

This will have the desired meaning:

(26)   {P: {x: x is a book and you read x} ⊆ P}

That is, the sister of *every* contributes the following set:

(27)   {x: x is a book and you read x}

Once we have this, the truth conditions for the whole sentence will be the appropriate ones.

(28)   {x: x is a book and you read x}⊆{x: x is a book and I read x}
'Every book that you read, I read as well.'

In other words, the example with the ellipsis (23a) has the same meaning as (29), which contains no ellipsis.

(29)   a. *I read every book that you read.*
        b. *I* [$_{VP}$ *read*
           [$_{NP}$ *every* [$_{N'}$ *book* [$_{CP}$ *wh$_3$ that* [$_{IP}$ *you* [$_{VP}$ *read t$_3$*]]]]]]

The problem is to find the required VP [*read t$_3$*] in the linguistic context. Example (23a) contains just one VP that could potentially function as an antecedent – the VP "read every book you did." If we were to suppose that this VP is what is silent at the ellipsis site, we would get "I read every book you did read every book you did". This contains another ellipsis, the filling of which would lead to further, infinite regress. The problem that the ACD examples pose is that the ellipsis is contained within its own antecedent. There is no independent VP.

4.2. The analysis and some consequences

The standard solution to the problem of ACD is to QR the whole quantified NP:

(30)   [$_{IP}$ [$_{NP}$ *every* [$_{N'}$ *book*   [CP *wh$_3$ that*   [$_{IP}$ *you did* [VP ~~read t$_3$~~]]]]]
                                    [3   [$_{IP}$ *I PAST* [$_{VP}$ *read t$_3$*]]]]

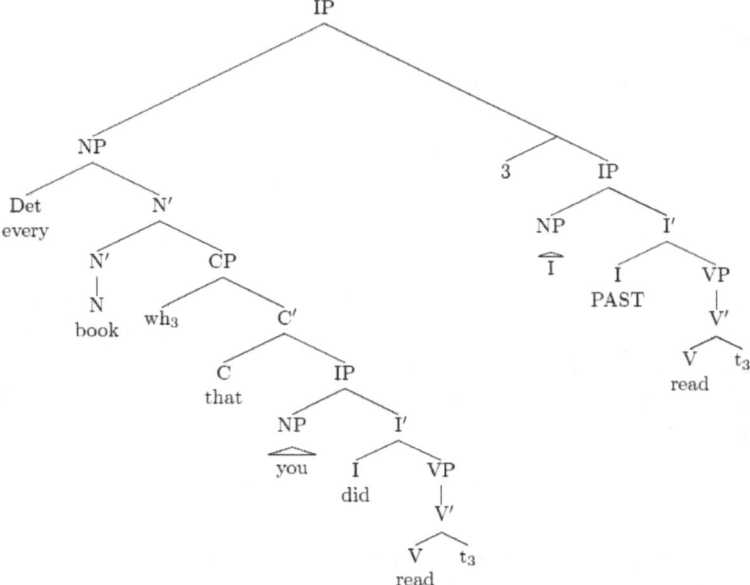

QR creates the required VP. It removes the ellipsis from the antecedent and solves the problem of infinite regress. This is a strong argument in favor of this invisible movement: the antecedent requirement in VP ellipsis cases is a well-motivated licensing condition. QR helps us reconcile this requirement with the ACD facts.

There is one further observation we mention here that speaks in favour of QR. Remember that we linked QR to scrambling. Now, scrambling cannot apply everywhere. Clause boundaries are a limit for scrambling in German:

(31) a. * *Ich habe den   Hund   gesagt,   dass der*
      I   have the.ACC dog.ACC said   that the
      Junge   gefüttert   hat.
      boy   fed   has
      'I said that the boy fed the dog.'
  b. * *Ich habe der   Junge   gesagt,   dass   den*
      I   have the   boy   said   that   the.ACC
      Hund   gefüttert hat.
      dog.ACC   fed   has
      'I said that the boy fed the dog.'

Compare (32), by contrast, where scrambling within a simple clause is well-formed:

(32) Ich   habe gesagt, dass den   Hund   der
     I   have said   that the.ACC   dog.ACC   the
     Junge gefüttert   hat.
     boy   fed   has
     'I said that the boy fed the dog.'

Clause boundedness is a property of QR as well. The example in (33) only permits a reading in which the quantifier *nobody* is interpreted in the embedded clause. In the framework presented here, this means that it cannot be QRed beyond the embedded clause into the matrix – quite parallel to scrambling in (31).

(33) *I said that nobody had passed.*

(33') a. I made the following claim: nobody passed.
         content of my claim: {x: x is a person} & {x: x passed}=∅
      b.*There is no x such that I said that x had passed.
         {x: x is a person} & {x: I said that x had passed}=∅

We understand this in terms of a restriction on movement: the movement that shows up as scrambling overtly and QR covertly can only apply inside a simple clause.

ACD makes this constraint visible in terms of grammaticality. This is useful because acceptability can be easier to judge than interpretation.

(34) **I said that everyone you did passed.*
      ≠ For every x such that you said that x passed: I said that x passed.

The LF underlying this reading would be the one in (35). This LF is ruled out by the constraint on QR. Thus, the facts about scrambling, scope, and ACD as an instance of ellipsis come together very nicely.

(35) [[*everyone*   *that you did* ~~VP~~]
                        [1 [$_{IP}$ *I* [$_{I'}$ *PAST* [$_{VP}$ *say that t_1 passed*]]]] =
      [[*everyone*   *that you did* [$_{VP}$ *say that t_1 passed*]]
                        [1 [$_{IP}$ *I* [$_{I'}$ *PAST* [$_{VP}$ *say that t_1 passed*]]]]]

☺ **Exercise.** *ACD ambiguity.* The example below is ambiguous:

(E5)   *John wants to study every subject Karen does.*

Paraphrase the two readings. Draw the two Logical Forms that give rise to the two readings. Consider the QR movements you applied to create these Logical Forms. What do you predict for (i) scope and (ii) scrambling given those movements? In so far as you are able to, check your predictions (i.e. construct some relevant data and check their acceptability and interpretation with native speakers). ☐

Let us sum up some important points made in this chapter. We have applied the syntactic and semantic theory developed so far to various ellipsis phenomena. The data according to this analysis provide further support for some important aspects of the theory. First of all, they support our assumption of a level of Logical Form. Structural identity conditions were shown to hold at that level. More specifically, the movement process QR has received further support. ACD data follow straightforwardly from the existence of VP ellipsis plus QR. The close relationship we have seen between overt (Surface Structure) and covert (LF) movements is emphasized by bare argument ellipsis and pseudogapping. Besides structure, constraints on meaning play a role in ellipsis. The contrast condition is an application of our focus semantics that explains acceptability and interpretation of some ellipsis data, including the disambiguating effect focus can have. Since a whole set of further data falls neatly into place, we take this as support of the theory developed in the preceding chapters.

☞ THE BASICS BOX: *Ellipsis*
- ✓ Ellipsis processes in natural language allow linguistic material to be unpronounced if it is the same as material that is overtly given.
- ✓ Ellipsis is subject to a structural identity condition, which applies at the level of Logical Form. It is also subject to the contrast condition, which requires the focus semantic notion of contrast to hold between ellipsis and antecedent clause.
- ✓ The analysis accounts for a range of data, from different kinds of ellipsis like bare argument ellipsis and pseudogapping, to scope phenomena in ellipsis, as well as antecedent contained deletion and disambiguating effects of focus.

5. Selected references

Ellipsis is another large topic in linguistics, and we have only begun to scratch the surface here. For a recent syntactic overview, see Merchant (to appear), which also contains pointers to work on processing (e.g. Frazier and Clifton 2005). The structural discussion of ellipsis in this chapter is basically taken from Heim and Kratzer (1998), along with their definitions and several examples. Some key studies in the line of research focusing on the level of LF in ellipsis are Sag (1980), May (1985), Fox (1995, 2003). For a taste of up-to-date explorations in the field, see the papers collected in Johnson (2010). For example, Kennedy (2010) in the volume focuses on the phenomenon of ACD discussed above. Reich's (2011) overview provides a useful and rich vista of the issues relevant in semantics today.

Hankamer and Sag (1976) is an accessible and influential classic paper that deals with different classes of ellipsis, but also proforms. See e.g., Ross (1969), López and Winkler (2000) on the properties of the *es* substitute in German, which does not have a systematic form of VP ellipsis. The syntactic properties of VP ellipsis are discussed in Johnson (2001); see also Lobeck (1995) and Gergel (2009), among many others. Johnson (1996/2003) offers a detailed discussion of gapping.

The contrast condition in the main text is adapted from Rooth (1992). See also Fox (1999) and Tomioka (1997) for related discussion. It has also been proposed on the basis of syntactic and prosodic evidence that only a subclass of ellipses may be contrastive; cf. Winkler (2005) for an overview.

For a discussion of scrambling, QR and pseudogapping, see Johnson (2001). Ellipsis phenomena that have been analyzed as VP ellipsis plus movement of the verb itself are attested in some languages that have both VP ellipsis and V-to-I movement; see, e.g., McCloskey (1991) on Irish and Ngonyani (1996) on the Bantu languages Ndendeule and Swahili.

Chapter II-7
Tense and aspect

> *For a moment, nothing happened.*
> *Then, after a second or so, nothing continued to happen.*
> (Douglas Adams, *The Hitchhiker's Guide to the Galaxy*)

This chapter introduces the concepts of tense and aspect and fits them into our syntactic and semantic analysis. Section 1 introduces the basic ideas and section 2 extends the theory from the preceding chapters to include them. In section 3 we discuss the English Perfect. Section 4 is devoted to a contrastive look at tense and aspect. The chapter concludes with references.

1. What are tense and aspect?

1.1. Tense

Tense is the grammatical reflex of the concept of **time** that humans refer to when talking about situations – writing a paper, listening to music, driving to the beach, or falling off one's bike. Situations have a temporal location. We have ignored this so far for simplicity, but a theory of natural language semantics has to include it – cf. the simple fact that (1a) may be true while (1b) is false and vice versa. It's high time (!) to add reference to time to our semantics component.

(1)   a.   *It is raining.*
           b.   *It was raining.*

We think about time here as an infinite scale (similar to the real numbers): a straight arrow towards the future, so that a point to the left will always be followed by a point to the right. We add times to our ontology of semantic objects. To be precise, we add time intervals, i.e. sets of connected points on the timeline. Some examples of such intervals are given schematically below:

(2)   Examples of relations for temporal intervals on the timeline
        --->
        t_1 (   )
        t_2 (   )
        t_3 (   )
        t_4 ( )

        (t_1 and t_2 overlap; t_3 abuts t_2; t_3 includes t_4; t_1 precedes t_3 and t_4)

In the interpretation of natural language sentences, certain times serve as 'anchors'. The first such time is the **utterance time (UT)**. UT is the time at which a sentence is uttered (spoken, written, or signed in a sign language). Tense systems of languages, as we understand them, put the situations described in a sentence into perspective relative to this time. A situation of being on a vacation in August can be talked about, for example, in the past or the present. This depends on when the sentence in which this situation is linguistically packaged is uttered. Past or present tense will be chosen depending on whether the situation described is before the utterance time, or simultaneous to it, as illustrated in (3).

(3)   a. *Marge was on vacation (in/as of August 2013).*   (Past)
        b. *Marge is on vacation (in/as of August 2013).*   (Present)

In (3a), the time of Marge's vacation precedes UT. This is expressed by the past tense. In (3b), on the other hand, the time of Marge's vacation includes UT. Besides the utterance time, another important time is the so-called **event time**, i.e. the time for which an eventuality or situation extends. That is Marge's actual time of being on vacation in the example, and we abbreviate it as ET in what follows. We write ET(s) for the time during which a situation/eventuality s occurs. A note on our terminology: we have talked about situations so far. What we have called situations is often called eventualites in the literature on tense and aspect. The term eventuality is used to cover genuine events (e.g. *Mary is singing*) as well as states (e.g. *Mary is French*). We make no systematic distinctions in this chapter.

In short: tenses serve to relate times at which situations are located with the utterance time UT.

1.2. Aspect

Aspect is defined as the **viewpoint** taken on an event or situation. Consider (4a,b):

(4)   a.   *Bart was watching his favorite show.*
        b.   *Bart watched his favourite show.*

(5)   *Lisa has known the answer all along.*

Suppose we are talking about yesterday evening and suppose the show was on from 7 pm to 8 pm. The event of Bart watching his favorite show occurs then, but it is presented from two different perspectives in (4). Sentence (4a) has a progressive or imperfective aspect (for the moment, we use the two interchangeably), one that presents the situation of the VP as ongoing or incomplete in some sense. For (4a), a natural continuation is, e.g., *when Marge came into the room*. Importantly with the progressive, the time interval associated with Marge's entering the room is included in the larger situation interval in which Bart is watching his favorite show (so the entering falls within 7pm to 8pm last night). So the **imperfective** aspect says that ET **includes** some other time. Sentence (4b) is in the perfective aspect. It presents the situation described as complete. A natural context would be, for instance, for the sentence to be preceded by the temporal phrase *last night*. The time interval of Bart watching the show now is included in the other time interval. So the **perfective** aspect says that ET **is included in** some other time interval.

English has past tense morphology and explicit means to mark the progressive (*be* with verb +-*ing*, as in (4a)), but – unlike other languages, such as Hindi or French – it does not have an overt piece of morphology that is specifically perfective. So we assume that this aspect is marked covertly. (We return to the issue in section 2.)

With the present perfect, in (5), things are a bit more complex. We develop the main ideas in section 3 below; but as a first approximation, the contribution of the perfect seems to be that there is an interval extending back into the past, which reaches up to (i.e. 'abuts') the relevant time (here: the utterance time).

In short: aspect tells us whether the event time ET includes or is included in some other time interval.

2. Compositional semantics for tense and aspect

2.1. Tenses are time pronouns

We introduce here an analysis of tense according to which tenses are time pronouns. The following example due to Barbara Partee motivates such an analysis. Let's imagine that Marge leaves home and then she realizes:

(6)   *I didn't turn off the stove!*

The intuition that this example elicits is that there is a specific time that this sentence is about, namely the time of Marge leaving the house, at which the stove should have been turned off - say the interval (9:42-9:51). The sentence says that Marge didn't turn the stove off at this time. Partee's suggestion is to treat tenses as pronouns. The meaning of (6) can be described as in (7):

(7)   Marge didn't turn off the stove at t_c
        (where t_c is the salient time interval, e.g. (9:42-9:51)).

The idea is that a tense such as the past above denotes a time interval. But it is not fixed once and for all which interval is referred to. The interval that is referred to in (6) depends on the context. (We use subscript c on t_c to indicate that the relevant time span depends on context). Hence the suggestion is that tenses are variables, like natural language pronouns *she, he, they* etc. (remember Chapter II-3). Tense pronouns refer to times instead of individuals.

Moreover, it is relevant that the tense in (6) is past as opposed to present. An appropriate time interval is one that precedes the utterance time (UT). We recognize this as a presupposition. Recall that sentences containing presupposition triggers can only be used under appropriate contextual conditions. For example, the form of the pronoun *he* indicates that that expression can only be used when there is a relevant referent that is singular, male and third person, i.e. distinct from both the speaker and the addressee (cf. again Chapter II-3). We can extend this presuppositional analysis from pronouns that range over individuals and transfer it to tense pronouns. Consider (8).

(8)   a. *Maggie was awake.*   b. *Maggie is awake.*

Compositional semantics for tense and aspect 273

Similar to the way pronouns impose restrictions on individuals to which they can refer, tenses place restrictions on time intervals. The first sentence can only be used if the relevant time t_c is before the utterance time, UT. Conversely, the second sentence, containing a present tense, can only be used if the relevant time interval t_c includes UT. More formally, we interpret the major tenses as follows:

Past (PAST):
For any t: $[[\text{Past}_i]]_{[tc/i]}^{t}$ is defined only if t_c **precedes** the utterance time t.
Then $[[\text{Past}_i]]_{[tc/i]}^{t} = t_c$.

Present (PRES)
For any t: $[[\text{Present}_i]]_{[tc/i]}^{t}$ is defined only if t_c **includes** the utterance time t. Then $[[\text{Present}_i]]_{[tc/i]}^{t} = t_c$.

(An aside: focus semantic values will not play a role in this chapter. For simplicity, we write $[[\alpha]]$ for $[[\alpha]]_o$ in this chapter.)

Our next task is to develop the compositional system further in order to integrate these meanings of tenses into the surrounding structure and compositionally calculate sentence meanings. We begin by finding the appropriate Logical Form, a task undertaken in 2.2 below.

⊕ **Exercise.** *The future.* There are two ways to treat the future – one purely temporal, the other modal. First, establish a rule that is parallel to the rules we have had for present and past. Second, write a list of uses of the future for which such a rule will not make the right predictions. □

2.2. The LF-structure for tense and aspect

Let us take stock. The preceding subsection has introduced time pronouns. Their syntactic location in English is in the Infl position:

(9)   [$_{IP}$ subject [$_{I'}$ Past/Present [$_{VP}$ t$_{subject}$ V']]]

That is, we assume that the syntactic category of Past and Present is I. They are morphologically (as a rule) expressed as *-ed* and ∅ or *-s* and their meaning is a time interval. According to everything we have said so far, the syntactic representation of an English main clause is as in (9) (incorporating the VP internal subject hypothesis). For instance:

(10)   a. *Homer danced.*
       b. [₁ₚ [₁' *-ed* [ᵥₚ *Homer dance*]]]

It is quite obvious that we have a composition problem in (9)/(10). That is, the ingredients as they stand do not combine. This is because we have, as of now, no composition rules that apply to times.

Let us make the semantic problem more explicit. The VP (with the subject contained in it) has an intension and an extension. These are a set of situations (a proposition) and a truth value, respectively. For instance:

(11)   [[[ᵥₚ *Homer dance*]]] = {s: Homer dances in s}
       [[[ᵥₚ *Homer dance*]]]ˢ = 1 iff Homer dances in s

Neither of these combines with a time interval (the meaning of the sister constituent under Infl). So we are still missing something. Let us check our options and then try to go on deductively and connect the pieces of meaning available.

What we would expect to see, given the rules of composition we are familiar with, is one of two things: (i) either the sister of the Infl node being a set of times, or (ii) the sister of the VP constituent being a situation. Either option would allow composition in terms of set membership. Option (ii) can be ruled out immediately – we have had the opportunity to conclude that times are needed, so the meaning of the tenses will remain simply a time. But what about option (i)? By investigating the meaning of *Homer danced* more precisely and comparing it to the following sentence in (12), we can explore this question and find out about the part we are missing

(12)   *Homer was dancing.*

The two sentences share the tense (Past) and the VP core (*Homer dance*), but do not mean the same thing. What distinguishes them in the morphosyntax of English should be straightforward now: aspect. (12) contains the progressive form, an imperfective aspect: one under which the event is viewed as developing or ongoing rather than as a whole and completed. (We abbreviate the imperfective aspect with Imp.) Conversely, the sentence *Homer danced* describes a completed situation. This is the perfective aspect (Pfv for short). We need to include aspect information in our Logical Forms. In turn, we can capitalize on this information in terms of composition. Linguists assume that there is an aspectual head in the structure to be interpreted between the I node and the VP, which projects an aspectual phrase, as shown in (13). The Logical Form of (12) is given in (14).

(13)   [IP subject [I' Past/Present [AspP [Asp' Pfv/Imp [VP t_subject V']]]

(14)   a.   *Homer was dancing.*
       b.   [IP _ [I' Past [AspP [Asp' Imp [VP *Homer dance*]]]

It is the job of aspect to mediate between situations/eventualities and times. The next subsection explains how it does that.

2.3. Composition rules for tense and aspect

We have found out so far that the pieces minimally needed to put together our temporal semantics are a tense node, an aspectual node, and the VP itself. How do they combine?

In the previous subsection we have pointed out that the tense node (denoting a time) cannot combine directly with the VP. Instead, it would like to combine with a set of times. This is much like an individual has been combined with a set of individuals all along – truth conditions are checked as set membership. The rule below thus mirrors exactly our rules for combining individuals with predicates of individuals. In analogy, we call the rule the tense-predicate rule (where the right-branching sister is a set of times rather than individuals):

Tense-Predicate (TENSEPRED)
If X= [Z_i Y], where Y is an aspect phrase, AspP, then for any t:
$[\![X]\!]_{[tc/i]}^t = 1$ iff $[\![Z]\!]_{[tc/i]}^t \in [\![Y]\!]_{[tc/i]}^t$.

Next, how do we derive a set of time intervals as the meaning of the aspect phrase, AspP? The interpretive function of aspect is to turn the set of situations handed over by the VP into a set of times, which can then further combine with the higher tense head on the basis of the tense-predicate rule.

The specific impact of the aspectual head depends on which aspect is involved. Following up on the ideas from section 1, the imperfective aspect says that some time t is included in the event time; the perfective aspect says that some time t includes the event time. The two lexical entries below state just that. The subsequent composition rule for aspect distills the event time from the set of situations described by the VP and combines it with the aspect node:

Imperfective (IMP)
$[[\text{Imp}]] = \{<t',t>: t \subset t'\}$

Perfective (PFV)
$[[\text{Pfv}]] = \{<t',t>: t' \subset t\}$

Aspect (ASP):
If $X = [\text{Asp } Y]$, then:
$[[X]] = \{t: \text{there is a situation } s \in [[Y]] \text{ such that } <ET(s),t> \in [[\text{Asp}]]\}$

Recall that while the perfective aspect is needed at the level of LF in English, it is not tied to a specific overt morpheme. Perhaps (on a first approximation), the absence of the imperfective morphology is sufficient to indicate the perfective. It is also important to note that the English type of perfect is not a good candidate for perfective aspect. We will discuss in more detail in section 4 below that the perfect can go together with both perfective and imperfective aspect. So, in brief, we assume that the perfective Asp head is there at the level of interpretation.

We now have the rules for tense and aspect in place and can check that composition works out in the intended way. We calculate below the truth-conditions for the sentence *Homer was dancing*. The interpretable nodes are lined up as in (15) and we check in (16) that the presupposition related to the temporal node is satisfied. The calculation follows in (17).

(15) $[_{IP} \text{Past}_i [_{AspP} \text{Imp} [_{VP} \textit{Homer dance}]]]$

(16) $[[\text{Past}_i]]_{[tc/i]}^t$ is only defined if t_c precedes the utterance time t. Assume that that's the case. Then $[[\text{Past}_i]]_{[tc/i]}^t = t_c$.

(17) $[[\text{Past}_i \text{ Imp } \textit{Homer dance}]]_{[tc/i]}^t = 1$ iff   (TENSEPRED and PAST)

$t_c \in$ [[Imp *Homer dance*]] iff (ASP; IMP; SIMPL)
$t_c \in \{t:$ there is a situation $s \in$ [[*Homer dance*]] such that $t \subset ET(s)\}$
iff (INTENSION OF VP)
$t_c \in \{t:$ there is a situation $s \in \{s': $ [[*Homer dance*]]$^{s'} = 1\}$ such that $t \subset ET(s) \}$
   (SUBJPRED, NONBR within VP and 2 x within NP, 2 x LEX)
iff
$t_c \in \{t:$ there is a situation $s \in \{s':$ Homer $\in \{x: x$ dances in $s'\}\}$ such that $t \subset ET(s) \}$ (SIMPL)
iff
$t_c \in \{t:$ there is a situtation $s \in \{s':$ Homer dances in $s'\}$ such that $t \subset ET(s) \}$ (SIMPL)
iff
$t_c \in \{t:$ there is a situation s such that H. dances in s and $t \subset ET(s) \}$
   (PARAPHRASING)
iff
$t_c \in \{t:$ there is a situation of H. dancing the event time of which properly includes $t \}$ (SIMPL)
iff
there is a situation of Homer dancing the event time of which properly includes the time t_c.

To summarize, we obtain that the contextually relevant time t_c which precedes utterance time, must be properly included in the event time of an event/situation in which Homer dances.

⊕ **Exercise.** Calculate truth conditions for the following sentence (with the past tense and the perfective aspect):

(E1)   *Bart sneezed.*   ◻

≚ **Exercise.** We ought to check that the significant changes that we have made in the sentence architecture in this chapter do not mess up the compositional system that we had before. A good start would be to compositionally calculate the truth conditions of the examples below in the new system with tense and aspect. Proceed as follows: first, adopt all composition rules and lexical entries as they were presented in this book. Can you interpret the examples? What assumptions do you have to make in order to be able to do so? Second, examine those assumptions. Are they plausible? What revisions to the semantics could you make to come up with an alternative compositional analysis of the data in (E2)?

(E2) a. *Every boy sneezed.*
      b. *Many bottles didn't arrive.*
      c. *John didn't answer many questions.* □

2.4. Temporal intensions and extensions

Adding times to our semantics is a significant step. We have refined our view of intensions vs. extensions with respect to time: one 'intensional' feature of a situation is its temporal location, and tense systems (together with aspect) talk about that. Incorporating tense has lead us to calculate 'situational' extensions and intensions below the aspect node and temporal intensions and extensions above it. So [[IP]] is now a set of times; and evaluating it with respect to a particular time (the utterance time UT in our examples) $[[IP]]^t$ gives us a truth value (= an extension). A range of further questions could be pursued now – we only mention three areas:

– What about other temporal operators like *former*? Try to analyze (18) in more detail (cf. also Chapter I-7).

(18)   *John likes/liked a former teacher.*

– What about non-temporal intensionality? Expressions like *possible* and modals talk about (logical) possibility rather than temporal location. We now need to understand this as a separate thing. Think about the meaning of the examples below (Rosa pimpinellifolia and 'Stanwell Perpetual' are roses).

(19) a. *Rosa pimpinellifolia is a possible ancestor of 'Stanwell Perpetual'.*
      b. *Rosa pimpinellifolia may be an ancestor of 'Stanwell Perpetual'.*
      c. *Rosa pimpinellifolia must be an ancestor of 'Stanwell Perpetual'.*

– What about tenses in embedded sentences, and different times at which predicates in a sentence are true?

(20) a. *John said that Bill was ill.*
 b. *I saw a boy who was crying.*
 c. (I knew a lot of rugby players and boxers in the 80s, but now) *the rugby players play golf and the boxers are passionate cooks.*

We will not pursue these questions here. Take a moment to think about the examples, and check the references in section 5 for more discussion.

3. The perfect

In this section we explore the perfect in English, consisting of the auxiliary *have* and the past participle. A widely adopted view is that the perfect is something different from the perfective aspect we have considered so far. The perfect is not necessarily perfective, i.e. not necessarily bounded or completed. This can be seen in a phenomenon called the continuative reading. We can find it with statives and progressives, compare:

(21) *I've known Marge for ten years now.*

(22) *Lisa has been writing a paper (ever since this morning).*

The eventuality of Lisa writing a paper may still be ongoing, so its event time is not included in the salient time interval that (22) talks about. (22) is not perfective (and similarly for (21)). Continuative readings are not the only readings of the English perfect, but they are important for understanding its semantics. Therefore, we use the insight they provide in support of the so-called extended-now theory of the perfect.

If the perfect is not to be equated with the perfective, does the existence of the continuative readings then mean that we should go in the opposite direction in our search for the meaning of the English perfect? This would amount to the suggestion that it is in fact a realization of some sort of *imperfective* aspect. We cannot do that either. Here is why. In many cases when we use the perfect, we view the event as a completed, i.e. plainly as perfective:

(23)   Lisa has read 'Pride and Prejudice'.

Lisa's reading of *Pride and Prejudice* is done and over with. The viewpoint is not that of an event viewed as 'live' as was the case with the progressive/imperfective. An intuition that we will rely on, however, is that (23) is relevant for the present in some way. One such way is that the result of having read the book is relevant at utterance time if (23) is used.

If the perfect is neither perfective nor imperfective, then it must be something different altogether than these two classical types of aspect. An easy way out might be to ask whether the perfect is not a tense. (It is indeed often treated on a par with other tenses in some of the traditional literature.) But this should also be rejected. There is still clearly a distinguishable tense **on top** of the perfect (e.g. *has danced* vs. *had danced*). Hence the English perfect is not the same as a tense. What results from these observations is, however, a clear positioning at LF. The perfect combines with an aspectual phrase (perfective or imperfective) and the phrase it projects serves as the complement of the tense head. This yields the following picture:

(24)   [Tense [Perfect [Aspect [VP]]]]

Corroborating evidence for this structure comes from the fact that when the nodes are realized, they appear lined up in precisely this relationship with the perfect having scope over the progressive in English (e.g. *has been drinking*). We get the following two LFs for the present perfect (and parallel ones for the past perfect (*had been drinking*) – just exchange the tense node to Past).

(25) a. [Present   [Perfect   [Imp   [VP]]]]
         Present   have   be   drinking
      b. [Present   [Perfect   [Pfv   [VP]]]]
         Present   have   ∅   drunk

Let us figure out how the interpretation of this type of structure proceeds. First, the Perfect head takes as its input a set of times, namely those delivered by the aspect phrase (which, recall, converts the set of situations denoted by the VP into a set of times). The output of combining the aspect phrase with the Perfect is also a set of times, which in turn combines with the temporal pronoun at the top of the LF. That means that the Perfect takes a set of times and delivers another set of times. But what is the set of times that results after the application of the Perfect?

A current theory of the (English type of) perfect is known as the extended-now theory. We cannot say in general, as we have seen, that the perfect conveys ongoing events. But what does seem to be the case, is that either the event is explicitly said to go on at the utterance time, as in the continuative cases, or that at least it has some relationship to the utterance time. A simple but, for now, sufficient way of thinking about this is that the contribution of the perfect is to give us a time interval (the perfect time span). This time interval, also called extended now (XN), is an interval that extends backwards into the past, typically from the utterance time (or similarly from a relevant time in the past when the perfect is under the scope of a past tense). We define it as follows:

(26)   For any time t: $XN_C(t)$ is that t' such that $t' \in C$ and t' abuts t

   (where C is the set of time intervals t which are contextually relevant either by way of a relevant eventuality taking place during t, or by the result of such an eventuality holding during t).

Here is the rule that interprets the Perfect on this basis:

The perfect (PERF) If X = [PERF Y] and Y denotes a set of times, then $[\![X]\!] = \{t: XN_C(t) \in [\![Y]\!]\}$

Let's now calculate the truth conditions of the following sentence:

(27)   a. *Lisa has been working.*
   b. [Present$_i$ [Perfect [Imp [$_{VP}$ *Lisa work*]]]]

As usual, we first check that the presupposition is satisfied: the meaning of $[\![Present_i]\!]_{[tc/i]}{}^t$ and thereby of the entire sentence is only defined if the time t_c includes the utterance time t. If that's the case, then $[\![Present_i]\!]_{[tc/i]}{}^t = t_c$ and we have the following equivalences:

(28) $[\![[Pres_i [Perfect [Imp [_{VP} \textit{Lisa work}]]]]]\!]_{[tc/i]}{}^t = 1$ iff   (TENSEPRED)
   $t_c \in [\![Perfect\ Imp\ [_{VP} \textit{Lisa work}\ ]\ ]\!]$ iff   (PERFECT)
   $t_c \in \{z: XN_C(z) \in [\![Imp\ [_{VP} \textit{Lisa work}]\ ]\!]\}$ iff   (IMP)

282 Tense and aspect

$t_c \in \{z: XN_C(z) \in \{t: \text{there is a situation } s \in [\![\,Lisa\ work\,]\!] \text{ such that } t \subset ET(s) \}\}$ iff (INTENSION OF VP)

$t_c \in \{z: XN_C(z) \in \{t: \text{there is a situation } s \in \{s': [\![Lisa\ work]\!]^{s'} = 1\} \text{ such that } t \subset ET(s) \}\}$ iff (SUBJPRED, 3 x NONBR, 2 x LEX, SIMPL)

$t_c \in \{z: XN_C(z) \in \{t: \text{there is a situation } s \text{ of Lisa working such that } t \subset ET(s) \}\}$ iff (SIMPL)

$t_c \in \{z: \text{there is a situation } s \text{ of Lisa working such that } XN_C(z) \subset ET(s)\}$ iff (SIMPL)

there is a situation s of Lisa working such that $XN_C(t_c) \subset ET(s)$

That is, we obtain a so-called perfect time span which is the extended now of the contextually relevant time t_c (basically UT in this sentence); this extended now time span is included in the event time of a situation of Lisa working; the inclusion condition comes from the progressive. The time line can be informally depicted as in (28').

(28')

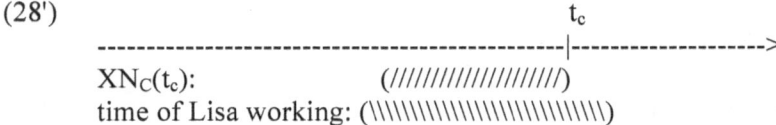

We see that the English Perfect appears to have a rather special interpretation. Next, we compare what we have found out about English tense and aspect to other languages.

4. Some tense and aspect contrasts crosslinguistically

4.1. On German tense and aspect

We compare English to German first. To be more precise, we compare English to our version of German, a variety spoken in the South (ff: Southern German). This variety has only one past tense, which looks like the English perfect: it is expressed with the auxiliary *haben* 'have' followed by a VP headed by the past participle form of a verb. (Some verbs use the auxiliary *sein*, 'be' instead, but we set that aside here.) The data below illustrate that the interpretation of this construction is not like the English Perfect. In particular, (29c,d) don't have continuative readings. The notion of extended now does not feature in the meaning of this German tense. Its meaning is better understood as a simple past tense.

(29) a. *Lisa hat Pride & Prejudice gelesen.*
Lisa has Pride & Prejudice read
'Lisa read Pride & Prejudice.'
b. *Lisa hat ein Papier geschrieben.*
Lisa has a paper written
'Lisa wrote a paper.'
c. *Lisa hat seit heute morgen ein Papier geschrieben.*
Lisa has since today morning a paper written
'Lisa wrote a paper since this morning.'
=> There is a paper that Lisa wrote (she's finished).
d. *Ich habe Marge 10 Jahre lang gekannt.*
I have Marge for 10 years known
'I knew Marge for 10 years.'
implicates: I no longer know Marge (maybe she died).

Here is an observation that points in the same direction: English has a restriction that bars the co-occurrence of a present perfect with a definite past tense adverbial like *yesterday*. This is known as the **present perfect puzzle**:

(30) **Josh has done his homework yesterday.*

Given the extended-now semantics of the perfect suggested here, we can observe that adverbs such as *yesterday, last year*, etc., which are barred in such contexts, refer to time intervals that are disjoint from UT. They are therefore presumably not good candidates for combining with the perfect. The XN is extending back from the present, i.e. under inclusion of UT.

The importance of this observation about English becomes clear when we look at other languages. The German version of (30) is perfectly acceptable.

284 *Tense and aspect*

(31) Josh hat gestern seine Hausaufgaben gemacht.
Josh has yesterday his.ACC homeworks.ACC done.
'Josh did his homework yesterday.'

The same form, consisting of the relevant auxiliary and the past participle, can be combined with past tense adverbials just fine. The same is true e.g. in French, but not in standard Spanish. Interestingly, even closely related languages can be different in this respect.

☕ **Exercise**. *More on the Perfect*. Within the Germanic languages, Swedish is an interesting case. First, it behaves like English with respect to past time adverbials and the tense formed by *have* + past participle:

(E3) *Sigurd har kommit igår.
Sigurd has come yesterday
'*Sigurd has come yesterday.'

However, the picture changes when an intensional adverb like *surely* is added. An example is given in (E4) (a so-called inferential perfect in traditional grammars); the sentence is acceptable. It seems that a type of perfect appears which is different from the one in English, unlike the 'normal perfect' in Swedish, which resembles English.

(E4) På försommaren 1814 har Stagnelius.
in early-summer-the 1814 has Stagnelius
säkerligen återvändt till hemmet i Kalmar
surely returned to home-the in Kalmar
'Stagnelius most likely returned to his home in Kalmar in the early summer of 1814.'

Try to find contexts in which the perfect in English also allows definite past tense adverbs and describe the interpretation you obtain. Can you reconcile your intuitions with the analysis of the perfect in section 3?
Hint: One way to do this is by taking inspiration from Swedish. But adverbs will not work – try to combine modals with auxiliary *have* and relevant adverbs in a different way. Does *have* still behave like a perfect then? Can you find another way (not related to modality) to suspend the restriction represented by the present perfect puzzle in English? ☐

For languages that pattern similarly to English, similar accounts would have to be sought. But what about languages like German? We suggest that those languages lack the English type of perfect. The simplest assumption is to analyze the German tense as a plain past tense.

Next, what about aspect? We have seen that English distinguishes two aspects by morphologically marking the imperfective/progressive aspect (what is not so marked, roughly, is perfective). Southern German does not mark aspect. To illustrate:

(32) a. *Bart hat seine Lieblingssendung angesehen.*
Bart has his favourite_show.ACC watched
'Bart watched/was watching his favourite show.'

b. *Bart hat seine Lieblingssendung angesehen,*
Bart has his favourite_show.ACC watched
als Marge ins Zimmer gekommen ist.
when Marge into.the room come is
'Bart was watching his favourite show when Marge entered the room.'

c. *Gestern Abend hat Bart seine Lieblingssendung angesehen.*
yesterday evening has Bart his favourite_show.ACC watched
Dann hat er eine warme Milch getrunken
then has he a warm milk drunk
und ist ins Bett gegangen.
and is in.the bed gone
'Last night, Bart watched (#was watching) his favourite show. Then he drank a warm milk and went to bed.'

(33) a. *Bart was watching his favorite show.*
b. *Bart watched his favourite show.*

The same perfect-like German construction (32a) is the appropriate form in contexts that ask for the imperfective aspect, (32b), and in contexts that ask for the perfective aspect, (32c), in English (33a,b). We conclude that the aspectual distinction is not overtly expressed in Southern German and that the construction can be interpreted as either perfective or imperfective.

Before we suggest a Logical Form for the German examples, there is an issue to discuss which closes the circle regarding our claims at the beginning (Chapter II-2) when we focused on syntax. What about the structural position of tense information in German? We have analyzed German as not having a designated Infl-like position. Infl is where we have located tenses in English. But tense is certainly encoded semantically and morphologically in German. We suggest that the auxiliary verb *haben* 'have' is of category V and projects its own VP, taking another VP as a complement. Its meaning is Past. The category label does not change anything in the way a tense is interpreted.

This leads us to the following LF representation:

(34) a. *Lisa   hat   Pride & Prejudice   gelesen.*
     Lisa   has   Pride & Prejudice   read
     'Lisa read Pride & Prejudice.'
  b. [$_{CP}$ _ [$_{C'}$ _ [$_{AspP}$ Pfv/Imp [$_{VP}$ [$_{V'}$ [$_{VP}$ *Lisa P&P gelesen*] Past$_i$]]]]

To sum up: Southern German has a much more restricted tense/aspect system than standard English. It lacks specialized forms for aspect proper (perfective/imperfective), and it does not have the English type of perfect. Besides Present tense, it has a Past tense expressed (for the most part) by the auxiliary verb *haben* 'have' plus past participle. It is interesting that there are such substantial differences between two languages as closely related as German and English.

⏲ **Exercise.** Translate the following sentences into your native language. That is, find a sentence in your native language that has truth conditions coming as close as possible to the truth conditions of each English sentence. What differences do you observe? What differences between the tense/aspect system of your language and English do they reveal?

(E5) a. *Peter is sleeping.*
  b. *Selina was climbing the east wall.*
  c. *Leo has grown immensely.*
  d. *Celine has been talking to them for an hour.*

What difficulties is a native speaker of your language likely to encounter when learning English? What difficulties is a native speaker of Southern German likely to encounter?   □

🕐 **Exercise.** Consider the verb form below (from Western varieties of German) and try to link it to a construction in the text. Give arguments for your choice and/or counterarguments. Give a complete analysis (LF and compositional interpretation) of (E6a).

(E6) a. *Ich bin am Kochen.*
    I   am at.the cooking
    'I am cooking.'
  b. *Als Marge in die Küche kam, war Bart*
    when Marge in the kitchen came was Bart
    am Kochen.
    at_the cooking
    'When Marge entered the kitchen, Bart was cooking.'
  c. #*Gestern Abend war Bart am Fernsehen.*
    Yesterday evening was Bart at.the tellywatching
    Dann hat er eine Milch getrunken und ist ins
    Then has he a milk drunk and is in.the
    Bett gegangen.
    bed gone
    'Last night, Bart watched TV. Then he had milk and went to bed.' □

4.2. The bigger picture

It is well-known that languages vary quite widely with regard to their tense/aspect sytems. We offer a glimpse of this variation in this subsection, with just a few illustrating examples.

We begin with a cautionary note: we have equivocated above between imperfective and progressive. Most likely, this is not accurate. The semantics given above is a standard semantics for the imperfective aspect. The English progressive probably has a stronger meaning which includes an intensional component. The example in (35) hints at that. An appropriate paraphrase is (36a), but not (36b): imagine the dog being run over in the middle of the road. The event of crossing the road would not be completed and (36b) (which paraphrases our simple imperfective aspect operator Imp) is false. But the sentence is true in such a situation. Hence (36a) captures its meaning better, where we consider eventualities other than what actually happened.

(35) The dog was crossing the road.

(36) a. 'There is an eventuality which, if everything goes as expected, extends into an event of the dog crossing the road whose run time includes the salient past time t_c.'
b. 'There is an event of the dog crossing the road whose run time includes the past time t_c.'

The English progressive is thus not a good candidate for an operator with the meaning of plain Imp, the imperfective aspect as we have defined it. Its meaning probably involves an intensional component. Imperfective verb forms in other languages (e.g. Slavic languages) may be better candidates, but the phenomena are not less complex – or interesting – there. This is another indication that the specific content of tense/aspect operators may vary across languages. The semantics we have seen can only be the beginning of a more serious investigation.

There are languages that have a richer repertoire of morphologically realized tense/aspect operators than English. An example are graded notions of temporal remoteness. Consider the following example from Gĩkũyũ (Kikuyu), a Bantu language of Kenya (from Cable 2013):

(37) a. 'Current Past':
Mwangi nĩekũinaga. 'Mwangi was dancing (within the day).'
b. 'Near Past':
Mwangi nĩarainaga. 'M. was dancing (within last few days).'
c. 'Remote Past':
Mwangi nĩānaga. 'M. was dancing (prior to 'Near Past').'

Some of the English auxiliaries (e.g. *be* and *do*) have developed particularly nuanced functions in African American English, as (38) and (39) illustrate (from Green 1998 and Terry 2006, respectively):

(38) The mirror BIN broke.   (remote past)
'The mirror has been broken for a long time.'
'The mirror broke a long time ago.'
(39) John done baked a cake.   (perfect)
'John has baked a cake.'

Paraphrasing as a remote past or a perfect leading far into the past in Mainstream English in the first case and a present perfect in the second are the closest renderings of the meanings of those sentences. But does the 'perfect present puzzle' observation hold for the perfect with *done* in African American English, too? That is: does the addition of an adverb like *yesterday/last month* etc. make the sentence in (39), the closest counterpart of the perfect, ungrammatical? This is an open question, especially if it is posed in this generality (there are usually different acceptability judgments to it by speakers in African American English communities, depending on a range of factors.) But if such adverbs are fronted, then they have been observed to be clearly ungrammatical:

(40)   *Yesterday, John done baked a cake.*

Why the semantic effect only holds under a particular syntactic confguration is a question worth pursuing.

⊕ **Exercise.** *Double Perfect.* Some varieties of German have a construction called the double perfect, which consist of three ingredients: a finite form of the verb *haben* 'have', a participle form of the same verb, and a participle of another verb, e.g. the translation of *forgotten* in (E7) below.

(E7)   Er hatte Wolfgang dann vergessen und vergessen,
        he had   Wolfgang then forgotten and forgotten
        daß er ihn **vergessen gehabt**   **hatte**.
        that he him forgotten had.PART   had.FINITE   (DWDS CORPUS)

Double perfects are considered non-standard if the finite form is in the present even though they are frequently used. But they are acceptable even in written registers when the finite form is in the past. (For instance, we retrieved the example above from the DWDS corpus; and it is originally from a novel by Martin Walser.) We have included glosses but no translation. If you speak German, offer a translation and discuss semantic issues that arise. If you do not, try to consult native speakers or the grammar indicated in the reference section. Then offer a semantic rule that interprets this form. *Hint*: Note that the past double perfect is neither a regular past nor a perfect in the past. You may consider the following two options: try to push it into the corner of a remote past, or try to connect it to iterated relevant times. The example gives some indication, consider more data if possible.   □

A lot more data could be discussed, and we have not offered an analysis even for the ones we have mentioned. In the next section, you will find some work on tense and aspect in formal syntax and semantics, which can guide you in pursuing the topic further.

☞ THE BASICS BOX: *Tense and aspect*
- ✓ Tenses can be interpreted as variables with presuppositions regarding time intervals (parallel to how pronouns are interpreted presupposing certain characteristics of individuals).
- ✓ For the Past, it is necessary to have a relevant interval preceding UT; the Present requires inclusion of UT in such an interval.
- ✓ Viewpoint aspect comes in two main guises: perfective and imperfective; the progressive instantiates the latter in English.
- ✓ The perfect needs to be distinguished from perfective aspect; a widely adopted analysis is that of an 'extended now'.
- ✓ Tense/Aspect systems vary considerably between languages, both in terms of how rich they are and in terms of the specific information conveyed.

---

5. Selected references

The pronominal theory of tense begins with the Partee problem (Partee 1973; cf. Kusumoto 2005 for recent discussion). Kratzer (1998) follows a similar line of reserach. Partee's problem can only be fully appreciated in view of older analyses of tenses as operators (cf. Prior 1967). The past in such earlier quantificational analyses says that there is a time in the past at which the sentence is true. There is a wealth of work in semantics pursuing different versions of theories of tense; cf. Ogihara (2011) for an overview in Maienborn, von Heusinger and Portner (2011).

Influential analyses of the English progressive include Dowty (1979) and Landman (1992). Example (35) is an instance of the progressive paradox discussed there. See also von Stechow (2002), Alexiadou, Rathert and von Stechow (2003) and Kratzer (1998) on LF architecture and the meanings of aspectual heads. Issues of the extended-now theory of the perfect are discussed e.g. in von Stechow (1999). The notions of eventualities and situations originate in different strands of research, but they can be used equivalently for our purposes – see Kratzer (2011) for an overview.

Something we have not made explicit in the semantic analysis is the background or reference time interval (for example in section 1.2. the time when Marge came into the room). This is also called topic time in the wake of Wolfgang Klein's work (cf. Klein 1998 and Kusumoto 2005 for discussion). Klein's work has also coined the term present perfect puzzle.

The Oxford Handbook of Tense and Aspect (Binnick 2012) contains contributions from a variety of sub-fields of linguistics including syntax, morphology and many rich aspects of crosslinguistic variation, but also on specialized problems such as embedded tenses (Ogihara and Sharvit 2012). Musan (1995) is an influential work discussing the temporal interpretation of NPs, also Kusumoto (1999).

An analysis that ascribes the semantics of Past tense to the auxiliary verb *haben* 'have' in German is sketched in Sternefeld (2006). Double perfects have made it into thorough descriptive grammars of German (Fabricius-Hansen et al. 2009). Krause (2002) argues for a progressive in German, though not in a fully grammaticalized form.

Influential contrastive descriptions of tense and aspect system under inclusion of Slavic system(s) can be found in the classical work of Comrie (1976, 1981). There are several examples of recent comparative work putting formal semantics into the picture; see e.g. Arregui et al. (2013) on Mĕbengokre, Cable (2013) on remote tense in Gĩkũyũan, and Deo (2012) on progressive/imperfectives in Indo-Aryan languages. Spanish data on the imperfective paradox can be found in Cipria and Roberts (2000). Issues related to the perfect constructions in African American English have been recently discussed by Green (1998), Terry (2006), and Gergel and Ferguson (2014). Bhatt and Pancheva's (2005) MIT lecture notes contain important observations on Slavic, Hindi, Greek and go beyond the issues of particular languages; they have had a significant influence on this chapter. Rothstein (2008) offers a detailed contrastive discussion of the perfect in English, Swedish, and German within a similar framework and the possibility of having different concepts of an extended now in different languages.

An important issue that we have not discussed here is the semantics of other "shifters" from the actual situation besides tense. Other intensional operators include in particular modals. See von Fintel and Heim (2011), Gamut (1991), Portner (2009), Dowty, Wall and Peters (1981), as well as the overview in Hacquard (2011) (including the interaction of modality with aspect). An area in which tense and modality seem to fall together is the future and Copley (2011) discusses this in detail.

Chapter II-8
Conclusions

This book was written using 100% recycled words.
(Terry Pratchett, *Wyrd Sisters*[1])

1. What we have done

This book has given you an introduction to the theory of grammar – its syntax and semantics components. For us, a grammar is a system of rules that models people's linguistic ability. The information contained in the rule system is the knowledge that native speakers must have in order to speak and understand their language.

Our goal has been to convince our readers that in order to describe and explain what people are able to do, certain concepts are central. We come back to three such concepts in this conclusion: (i) structure and constituency, (ii) meaning and inferences, and (iii) composition and scope.

Re (i) structure and constituency: The syntax trees you have been introduced to model the basic fact that sentences are not unstructured strings of words. In those strings, certain groups of words belong together more closely than others; and this matters for all sorts of phenomena. One obvious such phenomenon is V2 in German. Remember that the finite verb in a German matrix clause is preceded by one constituent. You would not be able to state this basic fact without the notion of a constituent.

Once you have syntax trees at your disposal, you can see that they help you to understand important properties of language. For example, we have investigated the possibility that there is a universal building plan for constituents – the X'schema. There is also variation between languages that can be identified clearly on the basis of syntactic structures. One example is headedness within the X' schema: differences between, say, English and Japanese are revealed as systematic, one language being head-first and the other head-final. (Notice how one simple sentence replaces what would be a long list of observations about sentence structure, verbs and objects,

---

[1] Taken from http://www.goodreads.com/work/quotes/1494222-wyrd-sisters.

prepositional phrases, and so on.) Another example is clause structure. A special feature of the English sentence structure - the Infl position - is the source of a bunch of observational differences to German concerning modal auxiliaries, questions, negation, and do-support.

Re (ii) meaning and inferences: You have been introduced to a semantic theory that builds on people's intuitions about the truth and falsity of sentences. Speakers know the meaning of a sentence if they know when it would be true and when it would be false. The meanings of the sentence parts are deduced from that. For example, a quantified determiner denotes a relation between two sets; given two input sets, the resulting sentence is true iff the determiner relation holds between them. This concept of linguistic meaning allows you to understand certain intuitions people have, e.g. intuitions about inferences. You now know why you may infer from *Every EU citizen is eligible for the grant* that *Every citizen of Italy is eligible for the grant*. Interestingly, the fact that you understand the validity of the inference – *every* is downward monotonic in its first argument – allows you to understand why *every* licenses NPIs like *any* and *ever* in its first argument (as in *Every student with any interest in the subject was hired*). Human languages have expressions that care about the inferential properties of their linguistic context: NPIs are only acceptable in downward monotonic environments. Once more you see that the linguistic concepts that you have worked towards are directly needed in order to describe simple facts about language.

Re (iii) composition and scope: It is very important that structure and meaning are considered together. Syntactic structures are mapped to truth conditional meaning by the interpretation component of the grammar. This means that they must be suited to generate the right meaning, and we have introduced you to the concept of Logical Form to make this possible. Movement operations like quantifier raising generate Logical Forms that may be different from Surface Structure. This analysis accounts for phenomena that link structure to interpretation: various kinds of scope ambiguity (now you know why *Karen read a book about every South Pole explorer* is ambiguous) and various kinds of ellipses. For example, Antecedent Contained Deletion ACD (*I stayed at the same hostel you did*) can be analyzed as a normal VP ellipsis once we know about Logical Form and quantifier raising.

Logical Form is linked to meaning via the rules of composition that interpret it. It is part of the syntax component by virtue of how it is generated: we get the Logical Form from the surface syntax via movement operations, and we have seen some very close connections between those movements and movements we already knew from our discussion of syntax. Differences between English and German related to scope and ambiguity, for instance, can be traced to the availability of scrambling and the connection between scrambling and quantifier raising. Throughout the book, we have concentrated on linguistic phenomena that allow us to see such connections between structure and meaning.

It has been our purpose in these chapters to show that one could not even begin to describe the phenomena we have looked at (ACD, pseudogapping, NPIs, scope ambiguity, contrast in ellipsis) without the concepts of syntactic structure, truth conditional meaning, and compositional interpretation. A grammar - i.e. a model of our linguistic knowledge - therefore needs to make reference to these notions. Any successful grammar book will need to do the same. With the Cambridge Grammar (Huddleston and Pullum 2002), we have a good example of a descriptive grammar incorporating the insights that linguistics has produced over the past 50 or so years. These insights are indispensible for anyone working with language, from the language teacher to the language pathologist as well as the computational linguist.

2. Where to go from here

2.1. For the linguist

We have sought to give you a relatively uncomplicated but still worked-out approach to a theory of the syntax-semantic interface, using a selection of crosslinguistic contrasts to highlight important features of the theory.

For those who are interested in pursuing syntactic theory further, there are many good introductions to formal syntax that will refine the theory we have worked with here. Haegeman and Guéron (1999) is written in the same syntactic framework as the present book, but it contains a richer inventory of syntactic constructions and analyses. Carnie (2013) offers a recent introduction to syntax. Detailed textbook-level analyses of the structure of German are offered, e.g., in von Stechow and Sternefeld (1988) and Sternefeld (2006). For syntactic analyses of a variety of languages, e.g. the *Cambridge Syntax Guides* series offers a wealth of material (cf. Fischer et al. 2000 on early English and É. Kiss on Hungarian, to only name two).

For those who want to understand semantics in more depth, Heim and Kratzer (1998) links up with our presentation most directly. Much of our discussion is strongly inspired by that work. The key difference in implementation is that we have used a simple set theoretic framework. Practically all current work in semantics uses a framework that replaces sets with functions, and is able to define a system of such functions, simplifying composition greatly (see Heim and Kratzer 1998, Chierchia and McConnell-Ginet 2000 and Büring 2005, a.m.o., for advanced introductions to semantics compatible with our general approach, but using such frameworks). You should be conceptually quite well-prepared to approach those more formal introductions now. We have pushed the naive framework as far as it will go. Indeed, perhaps we have pushed it a little too far: the observant reader will have noticed that our definitions get somewhat messy in places. This is remedied in the works mentioned.

Let's look beyond introductions to the field a little bit. We have discussed a basic semantic analysis of tense and aspect. Temporal semantics is one part of intensional semantics. Von Fintel and Heim (2011) give an introduction to intensional semantics, taking an extensional semantics as in Heim and Kratzer as their starting point. Gamut (1991) makes a connection to logic-based approaches; an older reference doing the same is Dowty, Wall and Peters (1981).

You have found more detailed and specific references to specific topics in semantics in the individual chapters. You should be in a position now to understand what such works on focus, ellipsis, quantifiers and so on are about, given your introduction here. Once you have taken the time to work through a more formal introduction to semantics, you will also understand the technical details.

If the contrasts between languages that we have observed have raised your interest in comparison between languages and in crosslinguistic variation, here are a couple of further sources: von Fintel and Matthewson (2008) discuss possible semantic universals. Interestingly, they observe rather more variation than they do plausible universal aspects of language. Newmeyer (2008) and Keenan and Stabler (2010) make partly similar points regarding variation and universals in syntax.

We mention papers on particular topics that contrast languages in the individual chapters.

Overall, it is important to realize that what you have seen is only a beginning.

2.2. Related fields

In this book, we have concentrated on the areas we know most about: the syntax and semantics components of the grammar. We are excited about those areas not only because they are fascinating in their own right, but also because understanding them is a prerequisite for understanding language in the numerous roles it plays for human beings.

Take language learning. You have seen that some properties of language are the same across all languages. Is a language learner going to have much difficulty in mastering those properties? Probably not. But you have also seen that language is highly variable in other respects. How about learning those properties? It is clear that there is a task here. How hard it is may depend on what you already know. So if you know one language and are learning a second language that differs from the first, the aspects that are different may give you trouble. This shows that a syntactic and semantic analysis is a prerequisite for identifying language acquisition tasks.

What we have described informally here is discussed e.g. in Snyder (1995, 2007) for first language acquisition. Interesting facets of second language acquisition are discussed in this light in Doughty and Long (2008), VanPatten (2004), Bryant (2012) and Yamane (2003).

But if the universal and the variable properties that are revealed by detailed linguistic analysis matter to the language learner, then they also matter to the language teacher. At the very least, the language teacher has to be able to offer to her/his students data that clearly reveal the differences of the target language compared to the students' native language. (For example, it would be important to offer to the English learning native speaker of German the continuative uses of the English Perfect, and specifically those, because they differentiate between the English Perfect on the one hand and the English Past and German 'Perfect' on the other). This means that the teacher has to have understood the underlying grammars of both languages in order to identify and provide such key data. (See once more Bryant (2012) for this kind of observation.)

The above discussion tells you in part our motivation for the use of contrastive data. We could go on now to stress the importance of syntactic and semantic analysis for other fields concerned with language, but we won't. Generally speaking, another purpose of our book, beyond interesting people in linguistics, is to open our field to readers who have a more applied motivation for studying syntax and semantics. We hope that it will prove helpful.

☞ THE BASICS BOX: *Grammar*
- ✓ Language has structure.
- ✓ Meaning is based on structure.
- ✓ A formal model of language is needed to understand its behavior, and the differences between languages.
- ✓ Everybody needs to know this.

References

Alexiadou, Artemis, Monika Rathert, and Arnim Stechow, von. 2003. Introduction: the modules of perfect constructions. In *Perfect Explorations*, edited by Artemis Alexiadou, Monika Rathert, and Arnim von Stechow, vii–xxxviii. Berlin/New York: Mouton de Gruyter.

Anderson, Catherine. 2004. The structure and real-time comprehension of quantifier scope ambiguity. Ph.D. dissertation, Northwestern University.

Aoun, Joseph, and Yen-hui Audrey Li. 1989. Scope and constituency. *Linguistic Inquiry* 20 (2): 141–172.

Aoun, Joseph, and Yen-hui Audrey Li.. 1993. *Syntax of Scope*. Cambridge, Massachusetts: MIT Press.

Bach, Emmon, Eloise Jelinek, Angelika Kratzer, and Barbara Partee, eds. 1995. *Quantification in Natural Languages*. Dordrecht: Kluwer Academic Publishers.

Baker, Mark. 1985. The mirror principle and morphosyntactic explanation. *Linguistic Inquiry* 16 (3): 373–415.

Barwise, Jon, and Robin Cooper. 1981. Generalized quantifiers and natural language. *Linguistics and Philosophy* 4 (2): 159–219.

Bauer, Markus, Matthias Bauer, Sigrid Beck, Carmen Dörge, Burkhard von Eckartsberg, Michaela Meder, Katja Riedel, Janina Zimmermann, and Angelika Zirker. 2010. The two coeval come: Emily Dickinson and ambiguity. *Zeitschrift Für Literaturwissenschaft und Linguistik* 40 (158): 98–124.

Bayer, Josef. 1984. COMP in Bavarian syntax. *The Linguistic Review* 3 (3): 209–274.

Bayer, Josef. 2007. Wh-in-situ. In *The Blackwell Companion to Syntax*, edited by Martin Everaert and Henk van Riemsdijk, 376–438. Malden, MA, USA: Blackwell Publishing.

Beaver, David, and Bart Geurts. 2012. Presupposition. In *Semantics: An International Handbook of Natural Language Meaning*, edited by Claudia Maienborn, Klaus Heusinger von, and Paul H. Portner, 2460–2486. Berlin/New York: Mouton de Gruyter.

Beck, Sigrid. 1996a. Quantified structures as barriers for LF-movement. *Natural Language Semantics*, 4: 1–54.

Beck, Sigrid. 1996b. Wh-constructions and transparent logical form. Ph.D. dissertation, Tübingen: Universität Tübingen (SfS-report).

Beck, Sigrid. 2000. The semantics of 'different': Comparison operator and telational adjective. *Linguistics and Philosophy*, 23: 101–139.

Beck, Sigrid. to appear. Focus sensitive operators. In *The Handbook of Information Structure,* edited by Caroline Féry and Shinichiro Ishihara. Oxford: Oxford University Press.

Beck, Sigrid, Sveta Krasikova, Daniel Fleischer, Remus Gergel, Stefan Hofstetter, Christiane Savelsberg, John Vanderelst, and Elisabeth Villalta. 2009. Crosslinguistic variation in comparison constructions. *Linguistic Variation Yearbook* 9 (1): 1–66.

Berko, Jean. 1958. The child's learning of English morphology. *Word* 14: 150–177.

Besten, Hans den. 1977. On the interaction of root transformations and lexical deletive rules. In *Studies in West Germanic Syntax*. Amsterdam: Rodopi.

Bhatt, Rajesh, and Roumyana Pancheva. 2005. The syntax and semantics of aspect. Lecture Notes – LSA Institute MIT. Cambridge, Massachusetts.

Binnick, Robert I. 2012. *The Oxford Handbook of Tense and Aspect*. Oxford: Oxford University Press.

Birner, Betty J., and Gregory Ward. 2009. Information Structure and Syntactic Structure. *Language and Linguistics Compass* 3 (4): 1167–1187.

Bobaljik, Jonathan David. 2002. Realizing Germanic inflection: Why morphology does not drive syntax. *The Journal of Comparative Germanic Linguistics* 6 (2): 129–167.

Bogal-Allbritten, Elizabeth. 2010. Distribution and function of comparative aspect in Athabaskan/Dene. In *Proceedings of the 2009 Dene/Athabaskan Languages Conference*, edited by Justin Spencer and Siri Tuttle. Fairbanks: Alaska Native Language Center.

Bott, Oliver, Sam Featherston, Janina Radó, and Britta Stolterfoht. 2011. The application of experimental methods in semantics. In *Semantics: An International Handbook of Natural Language Meaning*, edited by Claudia Maienborn, Klaus Heusinger von, and Paul H. Portner, 305–321. Berlin/New York: Mouton de Gruyter.

Bott, Oliver, and Janina Radó. 2009. How to provide exactly one interpretation for every sentence, or What eye movements reveal about quantifier scope. *The Fruits of Empirical Linguistics, vol. 1: Process*, edited by Sam Featherston & Susanne Winkler, 25–46. Berlin/New York: Mouton de Gruyter.

Bott, Oliver, and Fabian Schlotterbeck. 2012. Incremental truth value judgments. *Empirical Approaches to Linguistic Theory*, edited by Britta Stolterfoht and Sam Featherston, 3–28. Berlin/New York: Mouton de Gruyter.

Bryant, Doreen. 2012. *Lokalisierungsausdrücke Im Erst-Und Zweitspracherwerb: Typologische, Ontogenetische Und Kognitionspsychologische Überlegungen Zur Sprachförderung in DaZ*. Baltmannsweiler: Schneider Verl. Hohengehren.

Büring, Daniel. 1997. The great scope inversion conspiracy. *Linguistics and Philosophy*, 20: 175–194.

Büring, Daniel. 2005. *Binding Theory*. Cambridge: Cambridge University Press.

Büring, Daniel. 2012. Syntax, information structure and prosody. *The Cambridge Handbook of Generative Syntax*. Cambridge, Cambridge University Press.

Büring, Daniel, and K. Hartmann. 2001. The syntax and semantics of focus-sensitive particles in German. *Natural Language and Linguistics Theory*, 19: 229–281.

Bußmann, Hadumod. 2002. *Lexikon Der Sprachwissenschaft*. Stuttgart: Kröner.

Cable, Seth. 2013. Beyond the past, present, and future: Towards the semantics of 'graded tense' in Gĩkũyũ. *Natural Language Semantics* 21 (3): 219–276.

Carnap, Rudolf. 1947. *Meaning and Necessity*. Chicago: The University of Chicago Press.

Carnie, Andrew. 2013. *Syntax: A Generative Introduction*. 3rd edn. Oxford: Wiley-Blackwell.

Chierchia, Gennaro. 2013. *Logic in Grammar: Polarity, Free Choice, and Intervention*. Oxford: Oxford University Press.

Chierchia, Gennaro, and Sally McConnell-Ginet. 2000. *Meaning and Grammar: An Introduction to Semantics*. Cambridge, MA: MIT Press.

Chomsky, Noam. 1977. On Wh-movement. In *Formal Syntax*, edited by Peter Culicover, Thomas Wasow, and Adrian Akmajian, 71–132. New York: Academic Press.

Chomsky, Noam. 1981. *Lectures on Government and Binding*. Dordrecht: Foris Publ.

Chomsky, Noam. 1986. *Knowledge of Language: Its Nature, Origins, and Use*. Westport: Greenwood Publishing Group.

Chomsky, Noam. 1995. *The Minimalist Program*. Cambridge: Cambridge University Press.

Chomsky, Noam. 2002. *Syntactic Structures*. 2nd ed. Berlin/New York: Walter de Gruyter.

Cipria, Alicia, and Craige Roberts. 2000. Spanish imperfecto and pretérito: Truth conditions and aktionsart effects in a situation semantics. *Natural Language Semantics* 8 (4): 297–347.

Comrie, Bernard. 1976. *Aspect: An Introduction to the Study of Verbal Aspect and Related Problems*. Cambridge: Cambridge University Press.

Comrie, Bernard. 1985. *Tense*. Cambridge: Cambridge University Press.

Crain, Stephen, and Diane Carolyn Lillo-Martin. 1999. *An Introduction to Linguistic Theory and Language Acquisition*. Oxford: Blackwell.

Dayal, Veneeta. 2007. Multiple-wh-questions. In *The Blackwell Companion to Syntax*, edited by Martin Everaert and Henk van Riemsdijk, 275–326. Malden, MA, USA: Blackwell Publishing.

Dechaine, Rose-Marie, Strang Burton, and Eric Vatikiotis-Bateson. 2012. *Linguistics for Dummies*. Oxford: John Wiley & Sons.

Denison, David. 1993. *English Historical Syntax: Verbal Constructions*. London: Longman.

Deo, Ashwini. 2009. Unifying the imperfective and the progressive: Partitions as quantificational domains. *Linguistics and Philosophy* 32 (5): 475–521.

Diesing, Molly. 1990. Verb movement and the subject position in Yiddish. *Natural Language & Linguistic Theory* 8 (1): 41–79.
Diesing, Molly. 1992. Bare plural subjects and the derivation of logical representations. *Linguistic Inquiry* 3 (23): 353–380.
Doughty, Catherine J., and Michael H. Long. 2008. *The Handbook of Second Language Acquisition*. Oxford: John Wiley & Sons.
Dowty, David R. 1979. *Word Meaning and Montague Grammar: The Semantics of Verbs and Times in Generative Semantics and in Montague's PTQ*. New York: Springer.
Dowty, David, Robert Wall, and Stanley Peters. 1981. *Introduction to Montague Grammar*. Dordrecht: Reidel.
Drach, Erich. 1937. *Grundgedanken der Deutschen Satzlehre*. Frankfurt am Main: Diesterweg.
Eisenberg, Peter, and A. Klosa. 2009. DUDEN die Grammatik. *Der Duden in Zwölf Bänden* 4.
Elbourne, Paul D. 2005. *Situations and Individuals*. Cambridge, MA: MIT Press.
Emonds, Joseph. 1978. The verbal complex V'-V in French. *Linguistic Inquiry*, 151–175.
Fanselow, Gisbert. 2008. In need of mediation: The relation between syntax and information structure. *Acta Linguistica Hungarica* 55 (3): 397–413.
Fanselow, Gisbert, and Denisa Lenertová. 2011. Left peripheral focus: Mismatches between syntax and information structure. *Natural Language & Linguistic Theory* 29 (1): 169–209.
Featherston, Sam. 2009. Relax, lean back, and be a linguist. *Zeitschrift Für Sprachwissenschaft* 28 (1): 127–132.
Féry, Caroline, and Shinichiro Ishihara, ed. forthcoming. *The Oxford Handbook of Information Structure*. Oxford: Oxford University Press.
Fintel, von, Kai. 1999. NPI licensing, strawson entailment, and context dependency. *Journal of Semantics* 16 (2): 97–148.
Fintel, von, Kai, and Irene Heim. 2011. Intensional semantics. Lecture Notes. Cambridge, MA: Massachusetts Institute of Technology.
Fintel, von, Kai, and Lisa Matthewson. 2008. Universals in semantics. *The Linguistic Review* 25 (1-2): 139–201.
Fischer, Olga, Ans van Kemenade, Willem Koopman, and Wim van der Wurff. 2000. *The Syntax of Early English*. Cambridge: Cambridge University Press.
Fox, Danny. 1995. Economy and scope. *Natural Language Semantics* 3 (3): 283–341.
Fox, Danny. 1999. Focus, parallelism and accommodation. In *Proceedings of SALT*, 9:70–90.
Fox, Danny. 2003. On logical form. In *Minimalist Syntax*, edited by Randall Hendrick, 82–123. Oxford: Blackwell Publishing.
Frazier, Lyn, and Charles Clifton. 2005. The syntax-discourse divide: Processing ellipsis. *Syntax* 8 (2): 121–174.

Frege, Gottlob. 1906. Einleitung in die Logik. In *Sprachwissenschaft: Ein Reader*, edited by Ludger Hoffmann, 682–686. Berlin/New York: Walter de Gruyter.

Frege, Gottlob. 1980. Über Sinn und Bedeutung. *Zeitschrift für Philosophie und Philosophische Kritik*, 25–50.

Frey, Werner. 1993. *Syntaktische Bedingungen Für die Semantische Interpretation*. Berlin: Akademie Verlag.

Frey, Werner, and Thilo Tappe. 1991. Zur Interpretation der X-Bar-Theorie und zur Syntax des Mittelfeldes. *Grundlagen eines GB-Fragmentes*. SFB-340, Ms., Universität Stuttgart.

Fromkin, Victoria, Robert Rodman, and Nina Hyams. 2013. *An Introduction to Language*. 10th edn. Andover: Cengage Learning.

Gamut, L. T. F. 1991. *Logic, Language, and Meaning*. Vol. 1 & 2. Chicago: University of Chicago Press.

Gazdar, Gerald, Ewan Klein, Geoffrey K. Pullum, and Ivan Sag. 1985. *Generalized Phrase Structure Grammar*. Cambridge, MA: Harvard University Press.

Gergel, Remus. 2009. *Modality and Ellipsis: Diachronic and Synchronic Evidence*. Berlin/New York: Mouton de Gruyter.

Gergel, Remus and Daniel Ferguson. 2014. 'Done gone: On expressivity in the perfect in African American English. Ms. University of Graz.

Giannakidou, Anastasia. 2011. Negative and positive polarity items. In *Semantics: An International Handbook of Natural Language Meaning*, edited by Claudia Maienborn, Klaus Heusinger von, and Paul H. Portner, 2:1660–1712. Berlin/New York: Mouton de Gruyter.

Green, Lisa. 1998. Aspect and predicate phrases in African-American Vernacular English. *African American English: Structure, History, and Use*. London: Routledge.

Green, Lisa J. 2002. *African American English: A Linguistic Introduction*. Cambridge: Cambridge University Press.

Greenberg, Joseph. 1963. Some universals of grammar with particular reference to the order of meaningful elements. In *Universals of Language*, edited by Joseph Greenberg, 73–113. Cambridge, MA: MIT Press.

Grewendorf, Günther, Fritz Hamm, and Wolfgang Sternefeld. 1987. *Eine Einführung in Moderne Theorien Der Grammatischen Beschreibung*. Frankurt a. M.: Suhrkamp.

Grewendorf, Günther, and Wolfgang Sternefeld. 1990. *Scrambling and Barriers*. Amsterdam, Philadelphia: John Benjamins Publishing.

Hackl, Martin. 2009. On the grammar and processing of proportional quantifiers: Most versus more than half. *Natural Language Semantics* 17 (1): 63–98.

Hackl, Martin, Jorie Koster-Hale, and Jason Varvoutis. 2012. Quantification and ACD: Evidence from real-time sentence processing. *Journal of Semantics* 29 (2): 145–206.

Hacquard, Valentine. 2011. Modality. In *Semantics: An International Handbook of Natural Language Meaning*, edited by Claudia Maienborn, Klaus Heusinger von, and Paul H. Portner. Berlin/New York: Mouton de Gruyter.
Haegeman, Liliane. 1994. *Introduction to Government and Binding Theory*. Oxford: Blackwell.
Haegeman, Liliane, and J. Guéron. 1999. *English Grammar: A Generative Perspective*. Oxford: Blackwell.
Haider, Hubert. 1993. *Deutsche Syntax, Generativ - Vorstudien zur Theorie einer Projektiven Grammatik*. Tübingen: Narr.
Haider, Hubert, and Inger Rosengren. 2003. Scrambling: Nontriggered chain formation in OV languages. *Journal of Germanic Linguistics* 15 (03): 203–267.
Hamblin, Charles L. 1973. Questions in Montague English. *Foundations of Language* 10: 41–53.
Han, Chung-hye, Dennis Ryan Storoshenko, and Yasuko Sakurai. 2008. An experimental investigation into scope rigidity in Japanese. In *18th International Congress of Linguistics, Seoul, Korea*.
Hankamer, Jorge, and Ivan Sag. 1976. Deep and surface anaphora. *Linguistic Inquiry*, 391–428.
Hartmann, Katharina, and Malte Zimmermann. 2009. Morphological focus marking in Gùrùntùm (West Chadic). *Lingua* 119 (9): 1340–1365.
Hegarty, Michael. 2005. *A Feature-Based Syntax of Functional Categories: The Structure, Acquisition and Specific Impairment of Functional Systems*. Berlin: Mouton de Gruyter.
Heim, Irene. 1982. Definite and indefinite noun phrases. Ph.D. dissertation, Amherst: University of Massachusetts.
Heim, Irene. 1991. Artikel und Definitheit. *Semantik: Ein Internationales Handbuch Der Zeitgenössischen Forschung*, 487–535.
Heim, Irene. 2011. Definiteness and indefiniteness. *Semantics: An International Handbook of Natural Language Meaning*. Berlin: Mouton de Gruyter.
Heim, Irene, and Angelika Kratzer. 1998. *Semantics in Generative Grammar*. Malden, Oxford: Blackwell.
Heycock, Caroline, and Joel Wallenberg. 2013. How variational acquisition drives syntactic change. *The Journal of Comparative Germanic Linguistics*, 1–31.
Hinterwimmer, Stefan. 2011. Information structure and truth-conditional semantics. In *Semantics: An International Handbook of Natural Language Meaning*, edited by Claudia Maienborn, Klaus Heusinger von, and Paul H. Portner, 1908–1934. Berlin/New York: Mouton de Gruyter.
Höhle, Tilman. 1986. Der Begriff 'Mittelfeld', Anmerkungen über die Theorie der Topologischen Felder. *Akten Des Siebten Internationalen Germanistenkongresses 1985*, 329–340.
Höhle, Tilmann. 1991a. On reconstruction and coordination. In *Representation and Derivation in the Theory of Grammar*, edited by Hubert Haider and Klaus Netter, 139–198. Dordrecht: Kluwer.

Höhle, Tilmann. 1991b. Projektionsstufen Bei V-Projektionen: Bemerkungen zu F/T. Universität Tübingen.
Hoop, de, Helen. 2012. Type shifting. In *Semantics: An International Handbook of Natural Language Meaning*, edited by Claudia Maienborn, Klaus Heusinger von, and Paul H. Portner, 2271–2296. Berlin/New York: Mouton de Gruyter.
Horn, Laurence, and Gergory Ward. 2008. *Handbook of Pragmatics*. Oxford: Blackwell Publishing.
Huang, C.-T. James. 1995. Logical Form. In *Government and Binding Theory and the Minimalist Program*, edited by Gert Webelhuth, 127–175. Oxford: Blackwell Publishing.
Huddleston, R, and G Pullum. 2002. *The Cambridge Grammar of the English Language*. Cambridge: Cambridge University Press.
Iatridou, Sabine, and David Embick. 1995. Conditional inversion. In *Proceedings of NELS*, 24:189–203.
Iatridou, Sabine, and Hedde Zeijlstra. 2010. On the scopal interaction of negation and deontic modals. In *Logic, Language and Meaning*, 315–324. Springer.
Jackendoff, Ray. 1977. *X' Syntax*. Cambridge, Massachusetts: MIT Press.
Jacobs, Joachim. 1982. *Syntax und Semantik der Negation im Deutschen*. München: Fink.
Jacobs, Joachim. 1989. Skopus und Kohärenz. Universität Wuppertal.
Jacobson, Pauline. 1999. Towards a variable-free semantics. *Linguistics and Philosophy* 22 (2): 117–185.
Jespersen, Otto. 1937. *Analytic Syntax*. Copenhagen: Levin and Munksgaard.
Johnson, Kyle. 1996. In search of the middle field. University of Massachusetts.
Johnson, Kyle. 2000. How far will quantifiers go? In *Step by Step*, edited by Roger Martin, David Michaels, and Juan Uriagereka, 187–210. Cambridge, MA: MIT Press.
Johnson, Kyle. 2001. What VP ellipsis can do, what it can't, but not why. In *The Handbook of Contemporary Syntactic Theory*, edited by Mark Baltin and Chris Collins, 439–479. Oxford: Blackwell Publishers.
Johnson, Kyle. 2004. Introduction to Transformational Grammar. *Lecture Notes*. Ms. University of Massachusetts, Amherst.
Johnson, Kyle.2010. *Topics in Ellipsis*. Oxford: Oxford University Press.
Johnson, Kyle, and Satoshi Tomioka. 1997. Lowering and mid-size clauses. In *Reconstruction: Proceedings of the 1997 Tübingen Workshop*, Universität Stuttgart and Universität Tübingen, 185–206.
Kadmon, Nirit. 2000. *Formal Pragmatics*. Oxford: Blackwell Publishing.
Kamp, Hans. 1975. Two theories about adjectives. *Formal Semantics of Natural Language*, edited by Edward Keenan, 123–155.
Kamp, Hans. 1981. A theory of truth and semantic representation. In *Truth, Interpretation and Information: Selected Papers from the Third Amsterdam Colloquium*, edited by Jeroen Groenendijk. Dordrecht: Foris.

Kamp, Hans, and Barbara Partee. 1995. Prototype theory and compositionality. *Cognition* 57 (2): 129–191.
Kaplan, Ronald M., and Joan Bresnan. 1982. Lexical-functional grammar: a formal system for grammatical representation. *Formal Issues in Lexical-Functional Grammar*, 29–130.
Karttunen, Lauri. 1977. Syntax and semantics of questions. *Linguistics and Philosophy*, 1: 3–44.
Kayne, Richard S. 1994. *The Antisymmetry of Syntax*. Cambridge, MA: MIT Press.
Keenan, Edward L. 2011. Quantifiers. In *Semantics: An International Handbook of contemporSemantics: An International Handbook of Natural Language Meaning.*, edited by Klaus Heusinger von, Claudia Maienborn, and Paul Portner, 2:1058–1087. Berlin/New York: Mouton deGruyter.
Keenan, Edward L., and Edward P. Stabler. 2010. language variation and linguistic invariants. *Lingua* 120 (12): 2680–2685.
Keenan, Edward L., and Jonathan Stavi. 1986. A semantic characterization of natural language determiners. *Linguistics and Philosophy* 9 (3): 253–326.
Kennedy, Chris. 2010. Argument contained ellipsis. In *Topics in Ellipsis*, edited by Kyle Johnson, 95–131. Oxford: Oxford University Press.
Kim, Jong-Bok, and Peter Sells. 2008. *English Syntax: An Introduction*. Stanford: CSLI Publications.
Kiss, Katalin É. 2002. *The Syntax of Hungarian*. Cambrdige: Cambridge University Press.
Koopman, Hilda, and Dominique Sportiche. 1991. The position of subjects. *Lingua* 85 (2): 211–258.
Kratzer, Angelika. 1989. An investigation of the lumps of thought. *Linguistics and Philosophy* 12 (5): 607–653.
Kratzer, Angelika. 1991. The representation of focus. In *Handbuch Semantik/Handbook Semantics*, edited by Arnim von Stechow and Dieter Wunderlich, 825–834. Berlin/New York: de Gruyter.
Kratzer, Angelika. 1998. More structural analogies between pronouns and tenses. In *Proceedings of SALT*, 8:92–110.
Kratzer, Angelika. 2011. Situations in natural language semantics. *Stanford Encyclopedia of Philosophy*. http://www.science.uva.nl/~seop/entries/situations-semantics/.
Krifka, Manfred. 1991. A compositional semantics for multiple focus constructions. *Cornell Working Papers in Linguistics* 10: 127–158.
Krifka, Manfred. 1995. The semantics and pragmatics of polarity items. *Linguistic Analysis* 25 (3-4): 209–257.
Krifka, Manfred. 2007. Semantik. Lecture notes. Humboldt University, Berlin.
Krifka, Manfred. 2008. Basic notions of information structure. *Acta Linguistica Hungarica* 55 (3): 243–276.

Krifka, Manfred. Questions. In *Semantics: An International Handbook of Natural Language Meaning*, edited by Claudia Maienborn, Klaus Heusinger von, and Paul H. Portner, 1742–1785. Berlin/New York: Mouton de Gruyter.

Kroch, Anthony. 1989. Reflexes of grammar in patterns of language change. *Language Variation and Change* 1 (3): 199–244.

Kroch, Anthony, Anne Taylor, and Donald Ringe. 2000. The Middle English verb-second constraint. In *Textual Parameters in Older Languages*, edited by Susan C. Herring, Pieter Th. van Reenen, and Lene Schøsler, 195:353–391. Amsterdam/Philadelphia: John Benjamins.

Kusumoto, Kiyomi. 1999. Tense in embedded contexts, Department of Linguistics, University of Massachusetts at Amherst. Ph. D. Dissertation, Amherst: University of Massachusetts.

Kusumoto, Kiyomi. 2005. On the quantification over times in natural language. *Natural Language Semantics* 13 (4): 317–357.

Ladusaw, William. 1978. Polarity sensitivity as inherent scope relation. Ph.D. Dissertation, University of Texas, Austin.

Ladusaw, William. 1996. Negation and polarity items. In *The Handbook of Contemporary Semantic Theory.*, edited by Shalom Lappin, 321–341. Oxford: Blackwell.

Lechner, Winfried. 2006. An interpretive effect of head movement. In *Phases of Interpretation*, edited by Mara Frascarelli, 45–71. Berlin: Mouton de Gruyter

Lenerz, Jürgen. 1977. *Zur Abfolge nominaler Satzglieder im Deutschen.* Tübingen: TBL-Verlag Narr.

Lewis, David. 1970. General semantics. *Synthese* 22 (1): 18–67.

Lewis, David K. 1986. *On the Plurality of Worlds.* Cambridge: Cambridge Univ Press.

Liberman, Mark. 2009. No detail too small. *Language Log.* http://languagelog.ldc.upenn.edu/nll/?p=1924.

Lopez, Luis, and Susanne Winkler. 2000. Focus and topic in VP-anaphora constructions. *Linguistics* 38 (4): 623–664.

Los, Bettelou, and Erwin R. Komen. 2012. Clefts as resolution strategies after the loss of a multifunctional first position. In *The Oxford Handbook of the History of English*, edited by Terttu Nevalainen and Elizabeth Closs Traugott, 884–898. Oxford: Oxford University Press.

Lutz, Uli, Gereon Müller, and Arnim von Stechow (eds.). 2000. *Wh-Scope Marking.* Amsterdam/Philadelphia: John Benjamins Publishing.

Matthewson, Lisa. 2001. Quantification and the nature of crosslinguistic variation. *Natural Language Semantics* 9 (2): 145–189.

May, Robert. 1985. *Logical Form: Its Structure and Derivation.* Cambridge MA: MIT Press.

May, Robert, and Alan Bale. 2005. Inverse linking. *The Blackwell Companion to Syntax* 2: 639–667.

McCloskey, James. 1991. Clause structure, ellipsis and proper government in Irish. *Lingua* 85 (2): 259–302.
McCloskey, James. 2000. Quantifier float and Wh-movement in an Irish English. *Linguistic Inquiry* 31 (1): 57–84.
McCloskey, James, and Kenneth Hale. 1984. On the syntax of person-number inflection in Modern Irish. *Natural Language & Linguistic Theory* 1 (4): 487–533.
Merchant, Jason. to appear. Ellipsis. In *Syntax – Theory and Analysis. An International Handbook*, edited by Artemis Alexiadou and Tibor Kiss. Berlin/New York: Mouton de Gruyter.
Merchant, Jason. 2013. Voice and ellipsis. *Linguistic Inquiry* 44 (1): 77–108.
Montague, Richard. 1970. Pragmatics and intensional logic. *Synthese* 22 (1-2): 68–94.
Montague, Richard. 1973. The proper treatment of quantification in ordinary English. In *Approaches to Natural Language*, 221–242. Springer.
Müller, Stefan. 2013. *Grammatiktheorie*. 2nd ed. Tübingen: Stauffenburg.
Musan, Renate. 1995. Temporal interpretation of NPs. Ph. D. Dissertation, Cambridge, MA: Massachusetts Institute of Technology.
Napoli, Donna J., and Joel Nevis. 1987. Inflected prepositions in Italian. *Phonology Yearbook* 4: 195–209.
Newmeyer, Frederick J. 2008. Universals in syntax. *The Linguistic Review* 25 (1-2): 35–82.
Ngonyani, Deo. 1996. VP Ellipsis in Ndendeule and Swahili applicatives. *Syntax at Sunset: UCLA Working Papers in Syntax and Semantics* 1: 109–128.
O'Grady, William, Michael Dobrovolsky, and Francis Katamba. 1997. *Contemporary Linguistics: An Introduction*. Harlow: Longman.
Pafel, Jurgen. 2009. Zur linearen Syntax des deutschen Satzes. *Linguistische Berichte* 2009 (217): 37–79.
Pafel, Jürgen. 1991. Zum relativen Quantorenskopus im Deutschen. *Arbeitspapiere Des Sonderforschungsbereiches*, no. 340: Bericht Nr. 5.
Pafel, Jürgen. 2005. *Quantifier Scope in German*. Amsterdam: John Benjamins.
Parsons, Terence. 1970. Some problems concerning the logic of grammatical modifiers. *Synthese* 21 (3-4): 320–334.
Partee, Barbara. 1987. Noun phrase interpretation and type-shifting principles. In *Studies in Discourse Representation Theory and the Theory of Generalized Quantifiers*, edited by J. Groenendijk, D. de Jongh, and M. Stokhof, 115–143. Dordrecht: Foris.
Partee, Barbara. 2007. Compositionality and coercion in semantics: the dynamics of adjective meaning. *Cognitive Foundations of Interpretation*, 145–161.
Partee, Barbara Hall. 1973. Some structural analogies between tenses and pronouns in English. *The Journal of Philosophy*, 601–609.
Partee, Barbara, and Mats Rooth. 1983. Generalized conjunction and type ambiguity. In *Meaning, Use and Interpretation of Language*, edited by Rainer Bäuerle,

Christoph Schwarze, and Arnim von Stechow, 361–383. Berlin: Walter de Gruyter.
Partee, Barbara, Alice Ter Meulen, and Robert Wall. 1990. *Mathematical Methods in Linguistics*. Dordrecht: Kluwer.
Penka, Doris. 2011. *Negative Indefinites*. Oxford: Oxford University Press.
Pesetsky, D. M. 1982. Paths and categories. Ph.D. Dissertation, Cambridge, MA: Massachusetts Institute of Technology.
Pesetsky, David. 1989. Language-particular processes and the earliness principle. Manuscript. Massachusetts Institute of Technology.
Pinker, Steven. 1994. *The Language Instinct: How the Mind Creates Language*. New York: William Morrow.
Pollard, Carl, and Ivan A. Sag. 1994. *Head-Driven Phrase Structure Grammar*. Chicago: University of Chicago Press.
Pollock, Jean-Yves. 1989. Verb movement, UG and the structure of IP. *Linguistic Inquiry* 20: 365–424.
Popper, Karl R. 1959. *The Logic of Scientific Discovery*. London: Hutchinson.
Portner, Paul. 2005. *What Is Meaning?: Fundamentals of Formal Semantics*. Oxford: Blackwell Publishers.
Portner, Paul. 2009. *Modality*. Oxford: Oxford University Press.
Portner, Paul. 2011. Verbal mood. In *Semantics: An International Handbook of Natural Language Meaning*, edited by Claudia Maienborn, Klaus von Heusinger, and Paul Portner, 1262–1291. Berlin/Boston: Walter de Gruyter.
Portner, Paul H., Claudia Maienborn, and Klaus Heusinger von, ed. 2011. *Semantics: An International Handbook of Natural Language Meaning*. Berlin/New York: Walter de Gruyter.
Portner, Paul H., and Barbara H. Partee. 2002. *Formal Semantics: The Essential Readings*. Oxford: Blackwell Publishing.
Quine, Willard V. 1960. *Word and Object*. Cambridge, MA: MIT Press.
Radford, Andrew. 1988. *Transformational Grammar*. Cambridge: Cambridge University Press.
Radford, Andrew. 1997. *Syntactic Theory and the Structure of English*. Cambridge: Cambridge University Press.
Radford, Andrew. 2004. *Minimalist Syntax: Exploring the Structure of English*. Cambridge: Cambridge University Press.
Reich, Ingo. 2011. Ellipsis. In *Semantics: An International Handbook of Natural Language Meaning*, edited by Klaus Heusinger von, Claudia Maienborn, and Paul H. Portner, 1849–1874. Berlin/New York: Mouton de Gruyter.
Reinhart, Tanya. 1997. Quantifier scope: how labor is divided between QR and choice functions. *Linguistics and Philosophy* 20 (4): 335–397.
Reis, Marga. 1977. *Präsuppositionen und Syntax*. Tübingen: Niemeyer.
Reis, Marga. 1980. On justifying topological frames: ‚positional field' and the order of nonverbal constituents in German. *DRLAV. Revue de Linguistique* 22/23: 59–85.

Reis, Marga. 2001. Modalität und Modalverben im Deutschen. In *Bilden Modalverben Im Deutschen Eine Syntaktische Klasse*, edited by Reimar Müller and Marga Reis, 287–318. Hamburg: Buske.

Reis, Marga. 2013. „Weil-V2-Sätze und (k)ein Ende? Anmerkungen zur Analyse von Antomo & Steinbach (2010)". *Zeitschrift Für Sprachwissenschaft* 32 (2): 221–262.

Roberts, Ian G. 1993. *Verbs and Diachronic Syntax: A Comparative History of English and French*. Dordrecht: Kluwer.

Roberts, Ian, and Anna Roussou. 2003. *Syntactic Change: A Minimalist Approach to Grammaticalization*. Cambridge: Cambridge University Press.

Rooth, Mats. 1985. Association with focus. Ph.D. Dissertation, Amherst: University of Massachusetts.

Rooth, Mats. 1992. A theory of focus interpretation. *Natural Language Semantics*, 1: 75–116.

Ross, John. 1969. Auxiliaries as main verbs. *Studies in Philosophical Linguistics*, 77–102.

Rothstein, Björn. 2008. *The Perfect Time Span: On the Present Perfect in German, Swedish and English*. Amsterdam: John Benjamins Publishing.

Russell, Bertrand. 1905. On denoting. *Mind*, 479–493.

Sag, Ivan A. 1980. *Deletion and Logical Form*. New York: Garland.

Santorini, Beatrice. 1992. Variation and change in Yiddish subordinate clause word order. *Natural Language & Linguistic Theory* 10 (4): 595–640.

Santorini, Beatrice, and Anthony Kroch. 2006. The syntax of natural language: An online introduction using the trees program. http://www.ling.upenn.edu/~beatrice/syntax-textbook/.

Sauerland, Uli. 1999. Erasability and interpretation. *Syntax* 2 (3): 161–188.

Sauerland, Uli. 2005. DP is not a scope island. *Linguistic Inquiry* 36 (2): 303–314.

Sauerland, Uli. 2012. The computation of scalar implicatures: pragmatic, lexical or grammatical? *Language and Linguistics Compass* 6 (1): 36–49.

Sauerland, Uli, and Oliver Bott. 2002. Prosody and scope in German inverse linking constructions. In *Speech Prosody 2002, International Conference*.

Sauerland, Uli, and Fabian Heck. 2003. LF-intervention effects in pied-piping. *Proceedings of the North East Linguistic Society* 33: 347–366.

Schütze, Carson T. 1996. *The Empirical Base of Linguistics: Grammaticality Judgments and Linguistic Methodology*. Chicago: University of Chicago Press.

Schwarz, Florian. 2013. Two kinds of definites cross-linguistically. *Language and Linguistics Compass* 7 (10): 534–559.

Siegel, Laura. 2009. Mood selection in Romance and Balkan. *Lingua* 119 (12): 1859–1882.

Snyder, William. 2007. *Child Language: The Parametric Approach*. Oxford: Oxford University Press.

Snyder, William Brandon. 1995. Language acquisition and language variation: The role of morphology. PhD dissertation, Massachusetts Institute of Technology.

Speyer, Augustin. 2010. *Topicalization and Stress Clash Avoidance in the History of English*. Berlin/New York: Walter de Gruyter.
Stalnaker, Robert. 1973. Presuppositions. *The Journal of Philosophical Logic* 2: 447–457.
Stechow, von, Arnim. 1990. Current issues in the theory of focus. In *Semantics: An International Handbook of Contemporary Research/ Semantik – Ein Internationales Handbuch Zeitgenössischer Forschung.*, edited by Arnim Stechow, von and Dieter Wunderlich, 804–825. Berlin: de Gruyter.
Stechow, von, Arnim. 2002. German seit 'since' and the ambiguity of the German perfect. *More than Words: A Festschrift for Dieter Wunderlich*, 393–432.
Stechow, von, Arnim, and Wolfgang Sternefeld. 1988. *Bausteine syntaktischen Wissens. Ein Lehrbuch der generativen Grammatik*. Opladen: Westdeutscher Verlag.
Sternefeld, Wolfgang. 2006. *Syntax: eine morphologisch motivierte Beschreibung des Deutschen*. Tübingen: Stauffenburg.
Stowell, Timothy A. 1981. Origins of phrase structure. Ph.D. Dissertation, Cambridge, Massachusetts: Massachusetts Institute of Technology.
Strawson, Peter Frederick. 1950. On referring. *Mind* 59 (235): 320–344.
Szabó, Zoltán G. 2013. Compositionality. Stanford Encyclopedia of Philosophy. URL: Http://plato. Stanford. Edu/entries/compositionality.
Szabolcsi, Anna. 2010. *Quantification*. Cambridge: Cambridge University Press.
Tarski, Alfred. 1935. Der Wahrheitsbegriff in den formalisierten Sprachen. *Studia Philosophica* 1: 261–405.
Terry, J. Michael. 2006. A present perfect Puzzle for African-American English. In *Proceedings of NELS*, 36:599.
Thornton, Rosalind Jean. 1990. Adventures in long-distance moving: the acquisition of complex Wh-questions. Doctoral Dissertation, Storrs: University of Connecticut.
Tomioka, S. 1997. Focussing effects in VP ellipsis and NP interpretation. Ph.D. Dissertation, Amherst: University of Massachusetts.
Travis, Lisa Demena. 1984. *Parameters and Effects of Word Order Variation*. Cambridge, Massachusetts: MIT Press.
Truckenbrodt, Hubert. 2006. On the semantic motivation of syntactic verb movement to C in German. *Theoretical Linguistics* 32 (3): 257–306.
VanPatten, Bill. 2004. Input processing in second language acquisition. *Processing Instruction: Theory, Research, and Commentary*, 5–31.
Vikner, Sten. 1995. *Verb Movement and Expletive Subjects in the Germanic Languages*. Oxford: Oxford University Press.
Villalta, Elisabeth. 2008. Mood and gradability: an investigation of the subjunctive mood in Spanish. *Linguistics and Philosophy* 31 (4): 467–522.
Wagner, Michael. 2012. Contrastive topics decomposed. *Semantics and Pragmatics* 5 (8): 1–54.

Ward, Gregory, and Betty J. Birner. Discourse effects of word order variation. In *Semantics. An International Handbook of Natural Language Meaning*, edited by Klaus Heusinger von, Claudia Maienborn, and Paul H. Portner, 1934–1963. Berlin/New York: Mouton de Gruyter.

Warner, Anthony. 1993. *English Auxiliaries: Structure and History*. Cambridge: Cambridge University Press.

Wason, Peter C., and Shuli S. Reich. 1979. A verbal illusion. *The Quarterly Journal of Experimental Psychology* 31 (4): 591–597.

Weiß, Helmut. 2005. Inflected complementizers in continental West Germanic dialects. *Zeitschrift für Dialektologie und Linguistik*, 148–166.

Whitman, John. 2008. The classification of constituent order ceneralizations and diachronic explanation. In *Language Universals and Language Change*, edited by Jeff Good, 233–252. Oxford: Oxford University Press.

Winkler, Susanne. 2005. *Ellipsis and Focus in Generative Grammar*. Berlin/New York: de Gruyter.

Yamane, Maki. 2003. On interaction of first-language transfer and Universal Grammar in adult second language acquisition: WH-movement in L1-Japanese/L2-English interlanguage. Ph.D. Dissertation, Storrs: University of Connecticut.

Yang, Charles. 2006. *The Infinite Gift: How Children Learn and Unlearn the Languages of the World*. Simon and Schuster.

Young, Robert W., and William Morgan. 1987. *The Navajo Language: A Grammar and Colloquial Dictionary*. Albuquerque: University of New Mexico Press.

Zagona, Karen T. 1982. Government and Proper Government of Verbal Projections. University of Washington.

Zimmermann, Malte, and Caroline Féry. 2009. *Information Structure: Theoretical, Typological, and Experimental Perspectives*. Oxford: Oxford University Press.

Zimmermann, Malte, and Edgar Onea. 2011. Focus marking and focus interpretation. *Lingua* 121 (11): 1651–1670.

Zimmermann, Thomas Ede, and Wolfgang Sternefeld. 2013. *Introduction to Semantics: An Essential Guide to the Composition of Meaning*. Berlin/Boston: Walter de Gruyter.

Zwicky, Arnold M., and Geoffrey K. Pullum. 1983. Cliticization vs. inflection: English n't. *Language* 59: 503–512.

Index

adjective 19–26, 29, 49–55, 117, 118, 122
adjunction 20, 41–58, 115–117, 181, 205, 212, 262
adverb 20, 41, 48, 179, 182, 221, 224, 237–238, 243, 247, 251, 261, 283–284, 289
Affix Hopping 69–75, 86, 145, 156, 163–164, 156
African American English (AAE) 288, 289, 291, 109, 110, 156
alternatives 155, 156, 177, 238–251
Antecedent Contained Deletion (ACD) 156, 253, 262–267, 293
aspect 157–158, 205, 251, 269–296
Austrian (German) 21-22
auxiliary (s. modals, *have* and *be*) 7, 20, 67–95, 112–114, 145, 162–175, 279, 282–286

Balkan languages 65, 88
bare-argument ellipsis 238, 257-67
Basque 57, 238
Bavarian (German) 21, 57, 238
be 67-73
Burmese 1, 57

cleft construction 25, 78
competence 7, 78
complement 36, 41–67, 78–98, 136, 140, 160–182, 257, 280, 286
complementizer (C) 63–73, 86, 88, 161–165, 178–182

constituent 30–64, 80, 111, 123–129, 156, 167, 175–199
contrast condition 253, 259–168, 247
contrasting phrases 245, 247
coordination 25–30, 40, 44–51, 64, 103, 136
counterfactual(ity) 88

daughter node 32, 78, 111-114
Deep Structure (D-Structure) 75–87, 168–169, 178, 194
denotation 105, 107-109, 111, 119-125, 130-136, 272, 281
descriptive linguistics 6, 182, 234
disjoint 98, 187, 283
disjunction 40, 104, 110
do so substitution 28, 31, 47, 48, 84, 95, 99, 253, 257
do-support 70, 72, 75, 80, 86, 145, 163, 164, 171, 253, 293
downward entailment 227, 233

elements of sets (s. members) 95, 96, 98, 99,
ellipsis 28, 36, 40, 95, 151–171, 204, 237–238, 253–268, 295
even 156, 222, 228, 237
eventualities 275, 287, 290
extension 274, 278, 102–110
extraction 174

Index 313

factive verbs 128
focus 151–158, 233, 235–267, 295
focus-semantic value 241–247, 267, 273
former 41, 46, 117–118, 122, 146, 278
French 47, 66,74, 87, 108, 117, 128, 133 , 202, 172

gapping 241, 257, 258, 261, 294
German 5–6, 21, 55, 58, 82, 84, 152–184, 209–241, 248–251, 265, 282–296
Gĩkũyũ (Kikuyu) 288
Greek 222, 291

have 67–69, 74–76, 86
head 40–42, 56–58, 161, 165–168, 170, 174, 181
head movement 67–87, 159, 165, 167, 168, 182, 219, 220
Head Movement Constraint (HMC) 73, 75, 87
headedness parameter 58, 59, 174
Hungarian 84, 109, 248, 294

Ignore Traces (rule) 133
immediate scope (s. also PPIs) 229, 233
imperfective 158, 271, 276, 280
implicature 101, 246, 247
index 80, 167, 194, 196, 199–201
individual 105 -124, 132–135
Inflection (I) 137, 152, 160, 163, 169
intension 102–104, 110, 122, 239, 274, 277–282, 287, 295
intermediate projection (bar level) 40, 46–49, 51, 58
interpretability 121

intersection 98, 103–104, 116-117, 131, 134, 140, 186, 190
inverse linking, scope 207–209, 217–219
Irish 36, 262, 268
Irish English (s. Ulster English) 86
Italian 21, 36
I-to-C movement 71, 73–78, 81–82, 87–88, 145, 165–170

Japanese 57, 177, 182, 216, 220, 292

Korean 57, 288

label 20, 23, 31, 50, 88, 172, 286
lexicon 20, 30–31, 38, 55, 76, 112, 241
Logical Form (LF) 204, 207, 214, 215, 218, 227, 254, 267, 286, 293

maximal projection (full phrase) 40, 49, 51
middle field 179, 181, 209, 211, 213, 214, 218
modal 20, 62–70, 137, 152–154, 160
mood 57, 65–67
mother node 32, 50–53

Navajo 22
negation 67–74, 125–130, 135–142, 154–162
negation phrase 71
negative polarity item (NPI) 155, 221–233, 293, 294
Non branching trees 113, 122, 146,
noun 10, 19, 22, 29, 44, 49, 95, 117, 153, 183

objects of relations 119, 120, 146
Old English 71, 88, 234
one substitution
only 167, 168, 174, 202, 230, 237
ordinary semantic value 241–243

perfect 158, 271, 276, 279–297
perfective 158, 269, 271, 275–6
performance 7
Phonetic Form (PF) 276
phrase (cf. phrase structure)
phrase structure (PS) 15–29, 31–42, 53–75, 159–161
polarity 151–158, 221–234
Polish 122
Portuguese 65–66, 262
positive polarity item (PPI) 221–233, 257–267, 294
pragmatic meaning 95, 101, 181
pragmatics 101, 142
Predicate Modification 116, 117, 122, 146, 190
prefield 175, 176, 181, 182, 209, 213–219, 248–252
preposing 23, 167
preposition 20, 49, 51, 57, 120, 122, 293
prescriptive (rules) 6
presupposition 123–129, 272, 281, 290
processing 7, 268
proposition 142, 239, 243, 244, 274
projection 39–47, 49–58, 76, 129, 152
pseudogapping 261, 267–268, 294

quantified NPs (rule)131-135, 142, 147, 183, 186–170
quantifier 20, 86, 130–188, 190-235
quantifier raising (QR) 204–230, 258, 261 - 268

quantified NP 131–153, 183, 186–187, 198, 208–212, 218, 264
question-answer congruence 240, 245–247

raising (of verbs) 69–75, 145, 163
reconstruction 195, 214, 219
reference 16, 21, 36, 59, 87, 100, 110, 122, 142, 181, 218–235, 251, 268, 289, 290–295
relation between individuals (transitive verb) 111, 118–121
relation between sets (quantifier) 86, 98, 99
relative clause 82, 173, 190, 196, 200, 225, 263
Romanian 66

scalar implicature 101, 246–247
scales 247
scope 135–152, 183–256
semantic meaning 101, 110
semantically vacuous elements 113–116, 146
sense 7, 8, 110, 137, 140, 168, 200, 208, 212, 215
sets 19, 90, 98, 99, 104–118, 122, 123, 130–134, 142, 164, 167, 184–190, 218–219, 226, 269, 293
situations 90–120, 134, 158, 189, 193, 227, 239, 269, 270, 275, 276, 280
Slavic 262, 288, 291
sluicing 257
specifier 52, 53, 57, 65, 82, 86, 137, 145, 161, 166, 168, 169, 173
Stray Affix filter 70, 72, 76
stripping (s. bare argument ellipsis) 238, 257, 258, 260, 267

subject 7, 19, 27, 30, 57, 62–65, 71–81, 107, 119, 131
Subject-Auxiliary Inversion (SAI) 164, 165, 167, 170
Subject-Predicate rule 108, 132, 138, 146, 185, 187
subjunctive 65–67
Surface Structure 75–78, 82, 86, 87, 141, 166, 194, 203–218, 262, 267, 293
Swedish 284, 291

tense 20, 62, 88, 109, 112, 122, 151, 157, 160, 269–290
Tense-Predicate rule 275
three-place relations 120–121
to (infinitival marker) 160
topicalization 23–36, 45, 75, 210, 248, 258
traces 84, 86, 113, 146, 167, 196, 199, 219, 220
transformations 61, 69, 75–77, 87, 145, 161, 166, 169, 181, 204
transitive verb 111, 118–121, 189

truth conditions 11–13, 95, 100, 107–111, 121, 130–133, 189–195, 197–198, 206, 237, 243, 247, 275 truth value 102–108, 136, 147, 178, 185, 196, 204, 274, 278

union 98, 99 , 135
Ulster English (cf. Irish English)

verb 7, 19, 22, 46–88
verb phrase ellipsis (VPE) 263
verb second (V2) 175–183, 213, 292
Viennese (German) 22
VP internal subject hypothesis 88, 137, 142, 168, 173, 274

wh-movement 77–87, 145, 166, 176
wh-phrase 78–87, 155, 166, 240
wh-pronoun 80
wug test 16

X' schema 38, 49–75, 145, 159, 160, 169, 181, 292

www.ingramcontent.com/pod-product-compliance
Lightning Source LLC
Chambersburg PA
CBHW030522230426
43665CB00010B/728